"In this timely and insightful volume, Robin Br[...] reintroduce spirituality into psychoanalytic theo[...] the artificial divide left by the falling out betwe[...]. [...] eruditely argues for the important recognition of the transpersonal aspects of the unconscious that underpin insight-oriented psychotherapies. *Groundwork for a Transpersonal Psychoanalysis* is an important text for all psychotherapists committed to a deeper understanding of the human struggle."

Marilyn Charles, PhD, Austen Riggs Center and
University of Monterrey

"If you are already interested in the relationship of spirituality and psychoanalysis (in particular, Jungian and relational psychoanalysis), you will want not only to read this book, but also to study it carefully. You will want to keep it ready to hand. And if you are someone for whom psychoanalysis and spirituality don't usually mix, consider giving this book your serious attention, anyway. It is strong, thoughtful, and original. It is lucid about difficult matters, and its scholarship is deep and thorough. Brown doesn't settle for well-worn paths. He thinks through every issue for himself, and that makes it well worth going with him."

Donnel Stern, PhD, William Alanson White Institute

"Brown's *Groundwork for a Transpersonal Psychoanalysis* explains how developments in contemporary psychoanalysis might be extended beyond current limits if re-examined from a spiritual perspective. Brown identifies ideas from Jung's work that can add spiritual meaning to recent themes in relational psychoanalysis. He also suggests how both relational psychoanalysis and Jungian psychology might be brought into focus by transpersonal theory, especially participatory thinking, which stresses the co-created and irreducibly pluralistic character of spirituality. This important book brings contemporary psychoanalysis, Jungian psychology, and transpersonal theory into mutually beneficial engagement."

Michael Washburn, PhD, Indiana University South Bend (emeritus)

"Robin Brown's *Groundwork for a Transpersonal Psychoanalysis* masterfully lays out the need for a transpersonal dimension in relational psychoanalysis, while at the same time building a bridge between contemporary psychoanalysis and analytical psychology. Written in an articulate, well-referenced, and insightful manner, Brown's text has far-reaching implications for relational thinking. His argument is also carefully grounded in clinical examples. The volume is a cutting-edge, thought-provoking 'must' read for psychoanalytic scholars and psychoanalytic practitioners of all theoretical orientations."

Mark Winborn, PhD, NCPsyA, author of *Interpretation in Jungian Analysis: Art and Technique*

Groundwork for a Transpersonal Psychoanalysis

This book explores how a deeper engagement with the theme of spirituality can challenge and stimulate contemporary psychoanalytic discourse.

Bringing relational psychoanalysis into conversation with Jungian and transpersonal debates, the text demonstrates the importance of questioning an implicit reliance on secular norms in the field. With reference to recognition theory and shifting conceptions of enactment, Brown shows that the continued evolution of relational thinking necessitates an embrace of the transpersonal and a move away from the secular viewpoint in analytic theory and practice.

With an outlook at the intersection of intrapsychic and intersubjective perspectives, *Groundwork for a Transpersonal Psychoanalysis* will be a valuable resource to analysts looking to incorporate a more pluralistic approach to clinical work.

Robin S. Brown, PhD, LP, NCPsyA, is a psychoanalyst in private practice and a member of adjunct faculty for the Counseling and Clinical Psychology Department at Teachers College, Columbia University. He is the author of *Psychoanalysis Beyond the End of Metaphysics: Thinking Towards the Post-Relational* and the editor of *Re-Encountering Jung: Analytical Psychology and Contemporary Psychoanalysis*.

Psyche and Soul: Psychoanalysis, Spirituality and
Religion in Dialogue Book Series
Series Editors: Jill Salberg, Melanie Suchet & Marie Hoffman

The *Psyche and Soul: Psychoanalysis, Spirituality and Religion in Dialogue* series explores the intersection of psychoanalysis, spirituality and religion. By promoting dialogue, this series provides a platform for the vast and expanding interconnections, mutual influences and points of divergence amongst these disciplines. Extending beyond Western religions of Judaism, Christianity and Islam, the series includes Eastern religions, contemplative studies, mysticism and philosophy. By bridging gaps, opening the vistas and responding to increasing societal yearnings for more spirituality in psychoanalysis, *Psyche and Soul* aims to cross these disciplines, fostering a more fluid interpenetration of ideas.

For a full list of titles in this series, please visit the Routledge website: www.routledge.com/Psyche-and-Soul/book-series/PSYSOUL

Groundwork for a Transpersonal Psychoanalysis

Spirituality, Relationship, and Participation

Robin S. Brown

Routledge
Taylor & Francis Group

LONDON AND NEW YORK

First published 2020
by Routledge
2 Park Square, Milton Park, Abingdon, Oxon OX14 4RN

and by Routledge
52 Vanderbilt Avenue, New York, NY 10017

Routledge is an imprint of the Taylor & Francis Group, an informa business

© 2020 Robin S. Brown

The right of Robin S. Brown to be identified as author of this
work has been asserted by him in accordance with sections 77
and 78 of the Copyright, Designs and Patents Act 1988.

British Library Cataloguing-in-Publication Data
A catalogue record for this book is available from the British Library

Library of Congress Cataloging-in-Publication Data
A catalog record has been requested for this book

ISBN: 978-1-138-57188-4 (hbk)
ISBN: 978-1-138-57189-1 (pbk)
ISBN: 978-0-429-46731-8 (ebk)

Typeset in Times
by Apex CoVantage, LLC

Contents

Preface

My formation as a clinician has reflected an undertaking to synthesize relational ideas with my interest in Jungian and transpersonal thinking. In my first book, *Psychoanalysis Beyond the End of Metaphysics: Thinking Towards the Post-Relational*, I offered an initial outline of what I consider to be a necessary shift in relational psychoanalysis. The focus of my concern was a sense that relational thinking has often tended to insufficiently address its own foundational commitments, and that this failure may subtly promote a reductively secular outlook on treatment. In service of both clinical and theoretical diversity, I argued for the need of a "post-relational" perspective which would entail a reconciliation with analytical psychology and transpersonal theory. Subsequent to the publication of this text, I edited a volume of papers entitled *Re-Encountering Jung: Analytical Psychology and Contemporary Psychoanalysis*. This collection sought to draw lines of communication between Jungian psychology and the psychoanalytic mainstream. Building on this work, the present text situates my approach more categorically in terms of spirituality. An inevitable shortcoming of this endeavor is that I have often been forced to paint with broad brushstrokes. For example, in blithely speaking of "relationalists" or "Jungians" it may very well be objected that these schools are far too diverse as to be addressed in such generic terms. While I have considerable sympathy for such objections, it is unfortunately the case that any interdisciplinary undertaking that aspires to more than mere comparison must risk throwing caution to the wind in order that the reader not be bogged down in endless qualification. Another challenge is reflected in the question of the reader's assumed exposure to the literature. This book is not intended as an introduction to Jungian or transpersonal theory for a mainstream psychoanalytic audience, nor is it intended as an introduction to contemporary relational analysis aimed at a Jungian or transpersonal audience. Therefore, the uninitiated reader may at times find themselves needing to refer to the relevant literature. The "groundwork" that the title of the present work so grandly announces is not, in a final analysis, my own. Rather, my intention is to show how a cross-pollination of ideas between the relational, Jungian, and transpersonal fields might challenge received ideas and perhaps stimulate further conversation.

An earlier version of Chapter 2 was published in my book *Re-Encountering Jung: Analytical Psychology and Contemporary Psychoanalysis* (Brown, 2018b). Chapter 3 includes excerpts from an earlier paper "On the Significance of Psychodynamic Discourse for Consciousness Studies," which was published in *CONSCIOUSNESS: Ideas and Research for the Twenty-First Century* (Brown, 2015). Chapter 4 features a few brief passages that originally appeared in my paper "Evolving Attitudes," which was published in the *International Journal of Jungian Studies* (Brown, 2014). Chapters 5 and 8 were first published in the *Journal of Analytical Psychology* as "Imaginal Action: Towards a Jungian Conception of Enactment, and an Extraverted Counterpart to Active Imagination" (Brown, 2018a) and "Bridging Worlds: Participatory Thinking in Jungian Context" (Brown, 2017). Both papers have been lightly revised and expanded for republication. Thanks go to Allan Combs, Lucy Huskinson, and William Meredith-Owen for editorial guidance and copyright permissions. In bringing the present text to publication, special thanks go to Melanie Suchet, Kate Hawes, and Marie.

References

Brown, R. S. (2014). Evolving attitudes. *International Journal of Jungian Studies*, *6*(3), 243–253.

Brown, R. S. (2015). On the significance of psychodynamic discourse for the field of consciousness studies. *Consciousness*, *1*.

Brown, R. S. (2017). Bridging worlds: Participatory thinking in Jungian context. *Journal of Analytical Psychology*, *62*(2), 284–304.

Brown, R. S. (2018a). Imaginal action: Towards a Jungian conception of enactment, and an extraverted counterpart to active imagination. *Journal of Analytical Psychology*, *63*(2), 186–206.

Brown, R. S. (2018b). Where do minds meet? Intersubjectivity in light of Jung. In R. S. Brown (Ed.), *Re-encountering Jung: Analytical psychology and contemporary psychoanalysis* (pp. 160–179). Abingdon, UK & New York: Routledge.

Part I

Foundations

Chapter 1

The spiritual ground of psychoanalysis

Establishing a basic sense of theoretical orientation, this introductory chapter focuses on conceptualizations of the unconscious in relationship to the notion of a transpersonal psychoanalysis. I argue that a spiritually receptive approach to psychoanalysis entails that "the unconscious" be considered transpersonal and in some degree accessible to conscious experience. To address this theme invites a rapprochement between Jungian psychology and contemporary psychoanalysis. Identifying the insufficiency of efforts to promote spirituality merely by endorsing the creative value of fantasy, I begin to articulate how the fear of paranoia has limited the field's development.

Seeking to define what makes a therapeutic approach "psychoanalytic" has become a surprisingly complex task. Historically, efforts to circumscribe the field have often been undertaken for political reasons and in order to preserve professional advantage – a tendency that can be traced at least as far back as Freud's Secret Committee.[1] Wherever the task of defining the field has been undertaken by a self-identified "psychoanalyst," the results of this inquiry are liable to be reflective of the standards to which the clinician has been made subject over the course of their own professional development. Disputes concerning training and technique have tended to be central, and it is along such lines that one's entitlement to identify as a practicing psychoanalyst has often been claimed to rest. Emphasis has thus been placed on debating such variables as use of the couch; the frequency with which patients attend treatment; and the pedigree of a clinician's training analyst, supervisors, and teachers.

With the changing nature of the clinical, intellectual, and economic landscape, however, psychoanalysis has shifted from a profession of prestige to one that has been significantly marginalized. The psychoanalytic community has thus been forced circumstantially to take a more relaxed attitude towards the question of professional membership. As the field has slowly become less preoccupied with defining a limiting stance on what psychoanalysis *ought* to be, it becomes apparent that the task of definition is aided in seeking to establish commonalties rather than defining a basis for exclusion. Antonino Ferro offers a minimally dogmatic definition of the field as follows:

> In my view, in order for the term "psychoanalysis" to be used legitimately, three invariants are indispensable: first, the conviction that an unconscious exists (even if it may assume a variety of forms); second, respect for the unvarying elements of the setting; and, third and last, an asymmetry, with the analyst taking full responsibility for what happens in the consulting room.
>
> (Ferro, 2009, p. 210)

Of the three points identified, the latter two are concerned with the technicalities of clinical practice. If we are to inquire, more simply, what makes a particular approach to the mind psychoanalytic, then the one pertinent feature Ferro identifies is *the conviction that an unconscious exists*. It is with this foundational idea of an unconscious mind that any psychoanalytic practice ultimately organizes its claims. Attending to the origins of this idea offers the possibility of a fundamental reconfiguration in our understanding of psychoanalysis, for while the technical prescriptions Ferro eludes to might cogently be traced to the specific nature of Freud's intellectual contribution, the idea of the unconscious is by no means a Freudian invention. Freud himself states: "The poets and philosophers before me discovered the unconscious; what I discovered was the scientific method by which the unconscious can be studied" (quoted in Trilling, 2008, p. 34). This statement makes clear that Freud's own claim to importance hangs upon the development of a "scientific method" that furnishes us with the proof of an idea that was already widespread.[2] The practice of psychoanalysis is itself grounded in a theoretical notion not of Freud's making.

The philosophical unconscious

In considering how "the unconscious" [*das Unbewusste*] came to emerge as an idea, we might first turn to René Descartes (1596–1650). It is in the work of Descartes that we recognize a shift in Western consciousness that would later be expressed in the emergence of "psychology" as a distinct discipline. Descartes is known for theorizing that the mind is an entity that should be conceptualized in distinction from the physical body. His famous statement *cogito ergo sum* – "I think therefore I am" – identifies selfhood with the conscious mind. Any question of an unconscious would thus appear to destabilize the basis upon which Descartes's philosophical enterprise rests. Nevertheless, a forerunner to the idea of the unconscious is still discernible in Descartes's thinking. In order to preserve the self-transparency of the mind, this conception is associated with the domain of matter. As Eshelman (2007) states:

> Descartes's account of unconscious psychic life centers upon the claim that mental transparency does not hold for material causes of our emotional lives. Since the subject has no awareness of these causes, there will be cases where it cannot tell that its thoughts are by secret impressions implanted in the brain (due to a traumatizing experience), but not from current sensory perceptions (someone who resembles the offender).
>
> (p. 299)

For Descartes, the unconscious is conceptualized in terms of an environmental event resulting in a physical trauma registered upon the brain. However, despite Descartes's willingness to recognize the possibility of the past impacting our perceptions of the present, the main thrust of his philosophy hinges upon establishing the self-transparency of consciousness. This is why it is necessary for Descartes's outlook that he consign unconscious processes to the material domain of the body. Yet in separating the mind from the body and emphasizing the role of thought in his definition of selfhood, Descartes's philosophy inadvertently casts doubt upon the soul's constant activity. This is most evident with respect to the phenomenon of sleep. If the soul is to go on existing, Descartes's approach requires that we always be thinking. How, then, are we to explain the state of dreamless sleep? Descartes is required to offer a rather convoluted justification:

You say you want to stop and ask whether I think the soul always thinks. But why should it not always think, since it is a thinking substance? It is no surprise that we do not remember the thoughts that the soul had when in the womb or in a deep sleep, since there are many other thoughts that we equally do not remember, although we know we had them when grown up, healthy and wide-awake. So long as the mind is joined to the body, then in order for it to remember thoughts which it had in the past, it is necessary for some traces of them to be imprinted on the brain; it is by turning to these, or applying itself to them, that the mind remembers. So is it really surprising if the brain of an infant, or a man in a deep sleep, is unsuited to receive these traces?

(Descartes, 1984, pp. 246–247)

The questionable nature of this justification led Gottfried Wilhelm Leibniz (1646–1716) to argue that a neurological understanding of the unconscious is insufficient. Owing to the hardline separation Descartes establishes between mind and matter, the unconscious is associated with the material world while the conscious mind is associated only with thinking. Like Descartes, Leibniz wishes to preserve a notion of the soul's constant activity, but unlike Descartes, he suggests that supporting this notion requires a more nuanced conception of consciousness – one that acknowledges different degrees of intensity, thus establishing a spectrum of mental experience ranging from relatively conscious states to relatively unconscious states. Thus, for Leibniz, not all thought is conscious, and the notion of the unconscious is framed as something mental. The self-transparency of the Cartesian mind can thus be contrasted with the Leibnizian mind's multifaceted complexity.

It was Descartes's philosophy that was to exert a more powerful influence on the development of the Western intellectual tradition. While Descartes's adoption of a skeptical method in order to combat skepticism fell short, his dualist separation of mind from body emphasized a mechanistic conception of the material world that helped clear a path for the development of Western science. Although Descartes's project was explicitly concerned with establishing the thinking subject as the ground upon which to refute skepticism, the more lasting impact of his philosophy came to be reflected in the implication that if there is to be a basis for certainty then it is to be found in a material world that could now be thought of as though existing in distinction from the thinking subject; a thinking subject that Descartes wished to establish as primary, but which seemed only less certain as a consequence of his emphasis on the *cogito*. It might be argued that Descartes's rationalism only fostered the subsequent rise of empiricism.

David Hume (1711–1776) would come to criticize the *cogito* from an empirical standpoint, arguing that the mind is nothing but a bundle of sense perceptions. The empirical refusal of rationalism had a powerful basis in the politics of the time, for empiricism was considered a revolutionary movement standing for independence of thought and a resistance to religious dogma. The work of Immanuel Kant (1724–1804) can be understood as an attempt to establish a balance between the extremes of rationalist dogmatism and empirical skepticism. His concern is to protect the autonomy of reason – he wishes to deny that reason is merely contingent on habits of belief. Kant's critical philosophy seeks to argue for an a priori knowledge upon which our experience of the world can be shown to unavoidably rest. In approaching this undertaking, Kant establishes a different form of dualism from the one endorsed by Descartes. While Descartes's philosophy hinges upon the separation of mind from matter, Kant establishes a distinction between the *phenomenal* world (our experience of things) and the *noumenal* world (the things in themselves).

Although Kant's philosophy sought to protect the autonomy of reason, it did so without adequately addressing the relationship between self and world. In Kant's view, the law of cause and effect only applies as a function of subjective experience. If this is so, however, it becomes impossible to say how objects in the world (*noumena*) could give rise to our experiences (*phenomena*). The German philosophical tradition coming after Kant sought to offer a more comprehensive (and for this reason speculative) philosophy of consciousness. It was out of this endeavor that the philosophical idea of the unconscious proper arose. The term was coined in its German original by Friedrich Schelling (1775–1854) who, under the influence of Jakob Böhme's (1575–1624) Christian theosophy, built on Leibniz's *petits perceptions* (perceptions that are not apperceived) and Kant's *dunkele Vorstellungen* (obscure presentations) to formulate an evolving philosophy of the unconscious. For Schelling, reflecting the idea that reason can never gain mastery of its own conditions, an unconscious ground is asserted such as to express the original unity out of which self and other emerge. Spiritualized nature – the world soul – is conceptualized as the unconscious other in relationship to which self-consciousness comes into existence.

The notion of the unconscious articulated by Schelling was subsequently expanded upon by Carl Gustav Carus (1789–1869), and reframed in the work of Arthur Schopenhauer (1788–1860) as the Will. In 1869, Eduard von Hartmann (1842–1906) published his compendious *Philosophy of the Unconscious* – a work of more than 1,000 pages surveying the various permutations of "the unconscious" to have arisen in the recent history of Germanic philosophy. Such was the popularity of this idea in the mid-nineteenth-century German-speaking world that by the time Freud and Breuer's 'Preliminary Communication' was published some 24 years later, von Hartmann's book had already made its way through nine editions (Dufresne, 2000).

Broadly speaking, the notion of the philosophical unconscious can be understood as a unificatory principle that reflects a response to the dualisms of both Descartes and Kant. It offers itself as a speculative basis upon which to conceptualize the unity of self-consciousness, the unity of self and world,[3] and the unity of mind and body. Reflective of its speculative and inherently murky status, it should be noted that the unificatory function of the philosophical unconscious is enlisted not to annul difference but to *preserve* it. This is worth underscoring, for it suggests the extent to which the idea upon which psychoanalytic practice is founded might serve to support diversity – this has perhaps been clouded by the extent to which our conceptions of what it means to invoke "the unconscious" have been shaped by Freudian dogmatism, and a consequent concern that orienting practice to this idea is liable to result in abuses of clinical authority. As Kugler (2005) writes:

> The realization that our clinical grounds are not as absolute as we once thought does not lead to a radical relativism, nor to a nihilism. It leads, instead, to a psychological realism based upon the awareness that all systems of clinical interpretation gain their authority through a grounding in a god-term, a transcendental "ultimate." But this "ultimate" is no longer so absolute, so ultimate. In therapeutic analysis we must still, on one level, believe in our god-term, and use it as if it were the ultimate explanatory principle. But on a deeper level, we also know it is not. And it is precisely this deeper level of awareness that prevents our psychological theories from becoming secular religions

and differentiates professional debates from religious idolatry. *The ultimate ground of depth psychology is not a known god-term, but the ultimately unknowable, the unconscious itself. And this is the absolute ground which gives authority to all schools of depth psychology.*

(pp. 37–38, italics in original)

In the extent that the reformative thrust of much recent psychoanalytic thinking has tended to emphasize the need of incorporating a recognition of the sociocultural (see Brown, in press), this movement is perhaps fueled on the limited fashion in which a Freudian reading of the unconscious had previously come to reflect a culture of essentialism. This essentialism is quite inconsistent with the ethos of the idea of the philosophical unconscious as it was originally formulated, and is very much contingent on Freud's belief that he had discovered a "scientific method" by which the unconscious might be studied as an empirical fact.

Spirituality and the psychoanalytic unconscious

Given the idealist and romantic philosophy out of which the idea of the philosophical unconscious came to be given shape, it is a curious state of affairs that Freud – a professed atheist and materialist – would come to offer a "scientific approach" by means of which the unconscious's existence might be confirmed. Furthermore, it is Freud's assertion that he is offering an empirical basis for a philosophical idea that is itself seemingly concerned with the limits of knowledge. If this unknowable ground is to become accessible to experience, then it remains to be asked in what manner. Should the unconscious be understood in the fashion of Descartes, as a quality of matter, then there would seem to be two clear possibilities for discerning this unconscious at work: the first is in terms of neurobiology, and the second is as an *inference* from experience and/or observed behavior. If, however, the unconscious is understood in relationship to a spectrum of different intensities of consciousness (as was suggested by Leibnitz, and later William James),[4] then the possibility emerges that the unconscious might in some respect be experienced directly.

Psychoanalysis has historically been concerned with demonstrating the existence of the unconscious via clinical observation. The forerunner to this tendency is reflected in the practice of hypnotism, wherein striking effects could be achieved by the hypnotist (and verified by an audience) without the hypnotized subject's conscious recall. Freud was to forego a reliance on this technique. This contributed to his developing a psychological approach to the mind that circumvented some of the challenges posed to "good science" by the inherent messiness of hypnosis. The practice of hypnosis had given rise to something of an epistemic crisis within the still new field of psychology, for the hypnotic subject's suggestibility had broader implications for the study of the mind (Kline, 1972; Makari, 2008). What were the limits of this phenomenon? Was everyone suggestible? If not, why? If so, how could any approach to the mind not orienting itself to the purportedly material facts of neuroanatomy expect to stabilize its truth claims? The idea of transference enabled a rational way of conceptualizing this phenomenon and limiting its purview. Freud's technique and the subsequent notion of a training analysis would come to offer the basis upon which a clinician's claims to scientific objectivity might henceforth be founded.

The reception to Freud's work is best appreciated with a recognition of the manner in which the intellectual climate was informed by the philosophical idea of the unconscious and the clinical use of hypnosis, yet Freud is careful to distance himself from both. The three domains he initially turns to as the basis from which to demonstrate unconscious processes are the subject of his first three major works: dreams, jokes, and parapraxes. But while Freud seeks to establish his scientific credentials by positioning himself as the disinterested observer of his patients' unconscious minds, in subtle ways Freud's three domains of inquiry nevertheless cause us to notice the ways in which we might directly apprehend the workings of the unconscious in our own lives – not simply as something implied, but as an experience of a mildly altered state of consciousness. The possibility of being able to gain direct experiential access to the unconscious seems also to be suggested in Freud's self-analysis. This intensely subjective undertaking is posited by Freud to offer the basis upon which the central truth about the unconscious came to be realized. Yet in order to protect his authority, Freud would come to assert that his own primary experience could not be repeated by others – that an initiation at the hands of himself or one of his disciples was the only valid means to acquire knowledge of one's own unconscious. The decisive factor in the training analysis was not framed in terms of a direct experience of the unconscious, but as the analysand's capacity to accept the training analyst's interpretation of their free associations.

While Freud clears the table of the speculative – i.e. scientifically problematic – notions of the philosophical unconscious and hypnotic suggestion, in subtle ways his work nevertheless invites a certain measure of introspective validation. In teaching psychoanalysis to skeptically minded graduate students, I have found that the notion of the unconscious is often difficult to grasp until it is situated as a way of understanding one's own experience. Before students are asked to apply psychoanalytic ideas clinically, it is helpful to first have them recall the otherworldly experience of being wakened from a powerful dream. Alternatively, their attention might profitably be turned to the felt experience of meditation, of being in love, of ingesting mind altering substances, of attending a large and energized gathering (such as a music concert, sports event, or political rally), or the experience of being very unwell. These personally verifiable experiences are invariably more compelling as an initial starting point than attempting to demonstrate psychoanalytic ideas on the basis of case material.

Drawing from personal experience has not tended to be a feature of psychoanalytic teachings on the unconscious. Emphasis has usually been placed on the *inference* of an unconscious mind, not on direct experience. Yet it is upon this experiential question that the relevance of psychoanalysis as a spiritually receptive practice ultimately rests. If by "spirituality" we intend relationship to a sense of meaning that is felt to exist beyond ourselves then, psychologically speaking, this implies some question of relationship with the unconscious – assuming that by "unconscious" we intend that which is fundamental to who we are and yet *other* to our everyday sense of ourselves. But if psychoanalysts wish to adopt a non-reductive attitude towards spirituality then we must assume that in some extent the unconscious can itself be considered transpersonal – or, as Jung would have it, *collective*.

With the extent to which psychoanalysis can trace its intellectual roots to Germanic romanticism, it should come as no surprise that Jung was able to find in the tropes of depth psychology a resonance with his own more explicitly spiritual sensibility. Yet the personal split between Freud and Jung was carried forward by their supporters and, even now, more than a hundred years subsequent to the collapse of their relationship, reflects a significant and still inadequately addressed rift in intellectual discourse (see Brown, 2018). If a single theoretical theme were to be identified as the lasting cause of contention between these two schools, then the broadly "spiritual" orientation of Jung's work would perhaps be most obvious.

Jung's emphasis on the importance of establishing a personal relationship with a spiritual meaning amounts to a claim that psychological health is ultimately dependent upon being able to establish meaningful experiential contact with the unconscious. This was a huge challenge to Freud's authority. Direct experiential access to the unconscious had to be denied by Freud as inevitably regressive, for to allow for this possibility posed a fundamental threat to the finality of his own system. The idea of experiential access was historically minimized by Freudian psychoanalysis for the same reason that religious authority is liable to categorize mystical experience as heretical – to protect the authority of established scripture.

Freud seeks to posit his self-analysis as the foundational act upon which all of psychoanalysis would subsequently be based. This act is not to be repeated by others. Instead, Freud wishes to translate his own experience into theory so that the feat need not be repeated. This is evidenced most clearly in Freud's relationship to Jung. It was as a protection against the threat posed by Jung that Freud (1913) was compelled to imagine a myth such as to protect the finality of his claims against gnostic heresy. Hogenson (1994) writes:

> Freud presents to Jung the image of a complete world of meaning in his acting out of the primal killing. Jung, however, rejects this image as the only one suitable for the interpretation of the numinous. This necessitates that he relinquish the immediate possibility of secure interpretation, provided by Freud's system, and step into the void, acting out the mythology of self-sacrifice.
>
> (p. 147)

Jung's self-sacrifice was reflected in the outbreak of his own "creative illness" – a term that historian of psychiatry Henri Ellenberger adopts to signify a period of mental distress and creative preoccupation which optimally results in a lasting transformation of the personality. Ellenberger (1968) cites Fechner, Nietzsche, Freud, and Jung as all having undergone such an experience:

> Freud's biographers have termed Freud's self-analysis an heroic achievement, and they are right. But is it necessary to agree with them, when they assert, like Jones, that it is something unique in the history

of humanity, that is, constitutes an event which had no precedent, and will never be paralleled?

(p. 453)

Jung's "confrontation with the unconscious" (Jung, 1963, p. 170) offered itself as a basis from which the Freudian mainstream could further discredit Jung's work with cursory accusations of his having suffered a psychotic break. Henceforth, experiential contact with the unconscious would be deemed all the more suspect; this being reflected both in a pathologizing of the interior life and in an aggressive commitment to the Cartesian subject in a bid to claim scientific credibility (Freud, 1914). Mental health would be defined in terms of one's capacity to engage with and correctly discern *material* reality; that is, without evading this reality by way of subjective fantasy or having one's perception of this reality clouded by paranoid delusion. By arguing that his own psychology was in alinement with the scientifically accepted worldview of his day, Freud could make the claim that his outlook was somehow free from philosophical supposition and hence not subject to accusations of paranoia. As Kofman (1985) states:

It is indeed against the potential suspicion of paranoia that Freud seeks in particular to defend himself whenever he distinguishes, like a typical positivist, between (philosophical) speculation and (scientific) observation, or whenever he denies having any sort of gift for philosophy. It is always his opponents – Jung, for example – who are speculative. Thus what is fundamentally at stake in 'On Narcissism: An Introduction' is the demonstration that narcissism, particularly with regard to paranoia, lends itself to sterile and insane speculations. The text is a polemical denunciation of Jung's philosophical monism. [. . .] By way of contrast, Freud's distinctions, his persistent dualism, result from elaborations based on close observation.

(pp. 16–17)

Jung was quite aware of the difficulty that he faced in rendering his psychospiritual outlook acceptable to the scientific community of his day. Thus the implications of his philosophical monism – reflected in the idea that psyche and matter are two aspects of the same underlying "psychoid" reality – only becomes apparent in his later, more explicitly speculative work, and is not central to the way his ideas are presented and employed clinically.

Jung's dual-aspect monism echoes Schelling; both consider that the unconscious ground is fundamentally non-dual but that the conditions for self-consciousness require a dualism such that the original unity might come to know itself.[5] Jung arrives at this approach ostensibly owing to his interest in synchronicity – the notion that there exists a non-casual relationship of meaningful coincidence between our inner life and events in the external world. Such an outlook is of course "paranoid" through and through, and is reflective of the ensoulment of matter posited in Schelling's nature philosophy. Jung surely realized that explicitly pursuing this outlook would have made his work all the more discreditable. Thus his efforts to argue for the importance of establishing an experiential relationship with the unconscious tend to focus on a defense of the inner life. For this reason, Jung can sometimes seem to be offering a conception of the unconscious as a domain of reference existing exclusively "inside" the person. The extent to which Jung sought to protect his audience from the paranoid implications of the synchronistic paradigm is reflected in the emphasis his clinical approach often places on the retraction of projections. For example, Jung (1959) states:

> The effect of projection is to isolate the subject from his environment, since instead of a real relation to it there is now only an illusory one. Projections change the world into the replica of one's own unknown face. In the last analysis, therefore, they lead to an autoerotic or autistic condition in which one dreams a world whose reality remains forever unattainable.
>
> (para. 17)

And yet, elsewhere we read:

> The word "projection" is not really appropriate, for nothing has been cast out of the psyche; rather, the psyche has attained its present complexity by a series of acts of introjection. Its complexity has increased in proportion to the despiritualization of nature.
>
> (Jung, 1954, para. 54)[6]

It is as a consequence of the extent to which the *practice* of Jungian psychology has tended to emphasize the role of projection that Jung can be misread as a one-person psychologist very much in keeping with the classical Freudian mold. Hence, Goldenberg (1993) goes so far as to suggest that Jung's approach culminates in "a psychology which downplays the significance of human relationships" (p. 98). Severe though this misreading is (see Jung, 1946), it nevertheless underscores Jung's efforts to minimize the transpersonal aspects of his thinking to a notion of the inner life. Reading Jung, one might often suppose that his view of the unconscious is only "collective" insofar as he is willing to posit the archetypes as Platonic a priori givens. Some interpreters of Jung have even sought to restrict the collectivity of his conception of the unconscious to a notion of the archetypes limited to the logic of evolutionary biology.[7]

In an effort to maintain some modicum of professional credibility, Jungians have been fairly conservative in seeking to deepen the question of direct engagement with the unconscious as it manifests in the external world or to expand upon the clinical implications of Jung's late work. The officially sanctioned means of preserving the question of engagement with the unconscious has been limited to the practice of active imagination – a meditation technique developed by Jung wherein unconscious imagery is allowed to enter conscious awareness via the free play of fantasy, and is subsequently elaborated via the expressive arts (Hannah, 1981).[8] It has largely been left to the field of transpersonal psychology to explore some of Jung's more esoteric interests, such as the occult, astrology, shamanism, and the spiritual dimensions of psychotic experience. Stanislav Grof encapsulates many of the criticisms that are often leveled against Jung on the basis of Jung's apparent emphasis on interiority:

> There seems to be no genuine recognition of transpersonal experiences that mediate connection with various aspects of the material world. Here belong, for example, authentic identification with other people, animals, plants, or inorganic processes, and experiences of historical, phylogenetic, geophysical, or astronomical events that can mediate access to new information about various aspects of "objective reality."
>
> (Grof, 1985, p. 192)

A careful reading of Jung's late work should fundamentally challenge this claim, yet a confusion of this kind is altogether understandable given the ways in which Jung's ideas were perhaps curbed in an effort to keep them from seeming any more "insane" (from the perspective of secular science) than they were already liable to. One of Jung's main strategies to avoid betraying a paranoid outlook was to emphasize his aversion to metaphysics, even as a great deal of his work clearly enters this territory. With respect to questions of religion and spirituality, he consistently claims that he is dealing in "psychological facts" – i.e. restricting himself to a phenomenological approach. He seeks to argue that while numinous or religious experiences are an undeniable fact of psychological life, these experiences cannot be taken as proof of the metaphysical reality of God. This attempt to curb the truth claims of his psychology serves to try to make his work more scientifically acceptable – a strategy that was largely unsuccessful and that additionally earned him the ire of theologists who read him as seeking to psychologize religion. One of Jung's most prominent critics on this score was Martin Buber:

> For if religion is a relation to psychic events, which cannot mean anything other than to events of one's own soul, then it is implied by this that it is not a relation to a Being or Reality which, no matter how fully it may from time to time descend to the human soul, always remains transcendent to it. More precisely, it is not the relation of an I to a Thou. This is, however, the way in which the unmistakably religious of all ages have understood their religion even if they longed most intensely to let their I be mystically absorbed into that Thou.
>
> (Buber, 1977, p. 67)

Jung's work has often seemed too psychological for theologists, and too theological for psychologists. In his efforts to avoid a paranoid outlook, Jung's attempts to support the importance of spiritual values were largely constrained to an emphasis on fantasy and the inner world (even as his more speculative late work points beyond this). This led to his being accused of upholding a reductive attitude towards religion.

Interestingly, a very similar state-of-affairs is evident in the extent to which mainstream psychoanalysis has itself come to take up the theme of spirituality with a more sympathetic attitude. The emergence of this tendency can be broadly understood in terms of Klein's claim that consciousness is founded in phantasy, and the influence that this idea would have on Winnicott and Bion.[9] As with Jung, ostensibly receptive approaches to religious experience offered on the basis of this theoretical trajectory have often emphasized the value of imagination, yet doing so without sufficiently acknowledging that religious experience makes claims that go beyond this. Furthermore, emphasizing the inner life has led to a psychoanalytic focus on spiritual experience as a fundamentally private concern, with this being to the neglect of more relational, communal, ecological, or cosmic forms of spirituality.

In an effort to address this kind of one-sidedness, recent developments in the field of transpersonal psychology have been centrally concerned with articulating an approach to spirituality that is less confined to individuals. In this connection, Jorge Ferrer's (2002) participatory "revisioning" of the field has been particularly influential. Ferrer argues that understanding spirituality in terms of individual experience is fundamentally incompatible with the nature of spiritual insights, and that this emphasis further reinforces the state of disenchantment that has come to characterize Western consciousness. Ferrer's approach is complementary to the ecopsychology movement (Adams, 2010; Fisher, 2012; Hillman, 1995; Kahn & Hasbach, 2012; Merritt, 2012; Metzner, 1995; Roszak, 1992; Tacey, 2010), which has likewise sought to draw attention to the ways in which excessively private conceptions of the psyche and spirituality reinforce a disconnect between the individual and the wider environment. These claims are often linked to indigenous forms of spirituality that are more closely associated with the wider world than tends to be evidenced in the monotheistic religions. As cultural ecologist David Abram (1996) writes:

It is only as a result of her continual engagement with the animate powers that dwell beyond the human community that the traditional magician is able to alleviate many individual illnesses that are *within* the community. The sorcerer derives her ability to cure ailments from her more continuous practice of "healing" or balancing the community's relation to the surrounding land. [. . .] Only those persons who, by their everyday practice, are involved in monitoring and maintaining relations *between* the human village and the animate landscape are able to appropriately diagnose, treat, and ultimately relieve personal ailments and illnesses arising *within* the village. Any healer who was not simultaneously attending to the intertwined relation between the human community and the larger, more-than-human field, would likely dispel an illness from one person only to have the same problem arise (perhaps in a new guise) somewhere else in the community. Hence, the traditional magician or medicine person functions primarily as an intermediary between human and nonhuman worlds, and only secondarily as a healer.

(pp. 7–8)

An outline for the following chapters

I have suggested that the notion of a psychologically receptive approach to spirituality implies relationship with "the unconscious," and that this can be understood both in terms of inner experience *and* the external world. Psychoanalytic attempts to support spiritual concerns have tended to focus on valuing the inner life by considering fantasy/imagination to be enlivening rather than merely evasive. But while this claim is noteworthy, the consequence of taking this step without also addressing the external world is that attributions of personal meaning that extend beyond the individual are liable to be treated reductively in terms of projection. Jung's notion of synchronicity offers a significant and inadequately explored basis from which we might start to challenge this tendency. In the present text, I build on this notion while also seeking to show that the field's fear of paranoia is, in subtle ways, already being challenged by contemporary analysts.

The extent to which the unconscious might now be understood to register directly in terms of the external world has come about as a consequence of changing views concerning countertransference and the therapeutic relationship. However, interpreted in these challenging terms this aspect of recent theoretical developments is only implicit and has not been clearly identified or articulated. The relational[10] movement in psychoanalysis has tended to align itself much more centrally with a rhetoric of the social rather than the spiritual. Consequently, rather than opening psychoanalysis to an explicitly transpersonal conception of the psyche, the field's social emphasis has often been expressed in the adoption of epistemologies that seek to establish the personally circumscribed limits of knowing. While relational psychoanalysis greatly values pluralism – thus reflecting, *in principle*, a more open attitude towards spirituality – relationalists have often supported diversity by emphasizing social context and by asserting that the experience of meaning is always bound to language. Thus, the very endeavor to support pluralism is frequently shot through with secular values that implicitly delegitimize spirituality. Rather than broadening our conceptions of the spiritual to supplement and/or challenge an emphasis on fantasy and the individual, what often happens is quite the reverse: the inner life comes to be understood as nothing more than a product of the social environment, while *the unconscious* ceases to be a signifier for the cosmic mystery and stands merely for the ways in which we have been shaped by social forces.

Nevertheless, it might be noted that the movement from a one-person to a two-person psychology appears to in itself be an inherently transpersonal gesture. Although this gesture has not been carried out with much emphasis on broader questions of spiritualty, it is certainly evident that in a notion such as "mutual recognition" (Benjamin, 2004) we are dealing with a subject that has significant implications for a transpersonal psychoanalysis. In Chapter 2, I offer a comparative approach to intersubjectivity and seek to demonstrate the necessity of what might loosely be termed a "spiritual outlook" in grounding recognition. I argue that for this notion to appear meaningful, intersubjective recognition must be founded in a transpersonal conception of the psyche. Building on this claim, in Chapter 3, I explore what it means to uphold a "psychological" position, and the implications if we are to reemphasize the centrality of the unconscious as a means to professional orientation while maintaining an essentially relational outlook. In Part II, I turn to the literature on enactment and draw attention to the importance that this idea has for the question of re-enchantment. In Chapter 4, with reference to the interplay between private experience and the external environment, I examine the ways in which a teleological perspective on enactment may challenge our approach to clinical work. Exploring how a more explicitly panpsychic outlook on treatment might function in practice, I begin to articulate some therapeutic gains. Chapter 5 reflects an examination of the idea of enactment in relationship to Jungian thinking. I outline a notion of relational synchronicity wherein the intrapsychic is conceptualized as emerging directly (i.e. non-projectively) within the interpersonal field. Chapter 6 approaches enactment in relationship to the question of therapeutic change. I relate shifting conceptions of therapeutic action to the Taoist notion of *wu-wei*. Drawing from the work of Harold Searles, I adopt a transpersonal perspective to explore the role played in clinical practice by the analyst being able to grow through his or her work. In Part III, I explore the relevance of "participatory" thinking for contemporary psychoanalysis. Chapter 7 considers recent approaches to the question of truth in the clinical setting.

I argue for an emerging participatory orientation in relational psychoanalysis which I consider offers a more clinically receptive attitude towards spiritual and religious concerns. Finally, in Chapter 8, drawing further parallels between analytical psychology and relational psychoanalysis, I offer a participatory reading of Jungian archetypes. I propose that this reading suggests a nuanced basis upon which relational thinking may yet reconcile with drive theory.

Notes

1 The Secret Committee – initially consisting of Ernest Jones (whose idea the committee was), Sándor Ferenczi, Otto Rank, Hanns Sachs, and Karl Abraham – was a circle of Freud's most trusted allies who, in response to the "defection" of Adler and Jung, tasked themselves with protecting the definition and future of psychoanalysis.

2 This claim is also profoundly questionable – figures such as Herbart, Fechner, von Helmholtz, Wundt, and Janet had all made significant contributions prior to Freud. As Gardner (2003) observes: "Unconscious mental entities and processes were explicitly postulated many times over in the context of nascent empirical psychology" (p. 108).

3 Schopenhauer invokes the notion of *will* as a basis from which to overcome the Kantian dualism between appearance and actuality as follows:

> The kernel and chief point of my doctrine, its Metaphysic proper, is this, that what Kant opposed as *thing-in-itself* to mere appearance (called more decidedly by me "representation") and what he held to be absolutely unknowable, that this *thing-in-itself*, I say, this substratum of all appearances, and therefore of the whole of Nature, is nothing but what we know directly and intimately and find within ourselves as *will*; that accordingly, this *will*, far from being inseparable from, and even a mere result of, knowledge, differs radically and entirely from, and is quite independent of, knowledge, which is secondary and of later origin; and can consequently subsist and manifest itself without knowledge: that this will, being the one and only *thing-in-itself*, the sole truly real, primary, metaphysical thing in a world in which everything else is only appearance, i.e., mere representation, gives all things, whatever they may be, the power to exist and to act; . . . is absolutely identical with the will we find within us and know as intimately as we can know any thing.
>
> (Schopenhauer, 1907, p. 216)

4 For a refutation of the often encountered notion that James denied the existence of unconscious processes outright, see Weinberger (2000).

5 The alchemical Axiom of Maria states: "Out of the One comes Two, out of Two comes Three, and from the Third comes the One as the Fourth" (quoted in von Franz, 1974, p. 65).

6 Freud adapted the idea of projection from the neurologist Theodor Meynert, who used this notion both in explaining how a unified subject of perception arises as a consequence of the body projecting itself onto the brain, and in terms of how the brain projects its reception of sensory experience back onto the body. As Hogenson (1994) observes, Freud's adaptation of this notion neglects the question of reciprocity (p. 120).

7 The work of Anthony Stevens, in his effort to provide an evolutionary account of the archetypes, is perhaps the best known of these endeavors. Concerning synchronicity, Stevens does not reject the phenomenon outright (1982, pp. 259–260), yet an evolutionary account of the archetypes would seem to clash significantly with the synchronistic paradigm.

8 Shamdasani (2015) goes so far as to posit active imagination as the one truly distinctive feature of Jungian clinical technique.

9 Black (2006) suggests that most psychoanalytic writing on religion has stemmed from these two figures.

10 Throughout the present text, I adopt this term in its broad sense to reflect a range of clinical approaches that emphasizes "the experiential and relational aspects of human development, of psychopathology, and of the therapeutic efforts at relieving psychopathology" (Ghent, 1989, p. 177). While there is considerable theoretical breadth evident across the relational tradition (Harris, 2011), I consider that it is possible to usefully speak to this tradition in general terms. The various schools of relational thinking do share a basic sensibility. As Katz (2017) puts it: "This common core includes emphases on human development and language, as well as the analytic goal of freeing the analysand from ossified experiential structures" (p. 19).

References

Abram, D. (1996). *The spell of the sensuous: Perception and language in a more-than-human world*. New York: Pantheon Books.

Adams, W. W. (2010). Nature's participatory psyche: A study of conscousness in the shared earth community. *The Humanisitic Psychologist, 38*, 15–39.

Benjamin, J. (2004). Beyond doer and done to: An intersubjective view of third-ness. *Psychoanalytic Quarterly, 73*, 5–46.

Black, D. M. (2006). Introduction. In D. M. Black (Ed.), *Psychoanalysis and religion in the 21st century: Competitors or collaborators?* (pp. 1–20). London & New York: Routledge.

Brown, R. S. (2018). *Re-encountering Jung: Analytical psychology and contemporary psychoanalysis*. London & New York: Routledge.

Brown, R. S. (in press). Relational normativity in the politics of North American psychoanalysis: Some clinical reflections on the notion of privilege. *Psycho-analytic Dialogues.*

Buber, M. (1977). *Eclipse of God: Studies in the relation between religion and philosophy.* Westport, CT: Greenwood Press.

Descartes, R. (1984). Authors replies to the fifth set of objections (J. Cottingham, R. Stoothoff, & D. Murdoch, Trans.). In *The philosophical writings of descartes* (Vol. 2, pp. 241–267). Cambridge, UK: Cambridge University Press.

Dufresne, T. (2000). *Tales from the Freudian crypt: The death drive in text and context.* Stanford: Stanford University Press.

Ellenberger, H. F. (1968). The concept of creative illness. *The Psychoanalytic Review, 55*(3), 442–456.

Eshelman, M. C. (2007). The Cartesian unconscious. *History of Philosophy Quarterly, 24*(3), 297–315.

Ferrer, J. N. (2002). *Revisioning transpersonal theory: A participatory vision of human spirituality.* Albany, NY: State University of New York Press.

Ferro, A. (2009). Transformations in dreaming and characters in the psychoanalytic field. *International Journal of Psychoanalysis, 90*(2), 209–230.

Fisher, A. (2012). *Radical ecopsychology: Psychology in the service of life.* Albany, NY: State University of New York Press.

Freud, S. (1913). Totem and Taboo: Some points of agreement between the mental lives of savages and neurotics (1913 [1912–13]). In *The standard edition of the complete psychological works of Sigmund Freud* (Vol. 13, pp. vii–162). London: The Hogarth Press.

Freud, S. (1914). On narcissism: An introduction. In J. Strachey (Ed.), *The standard edition of the complete psychological works of Sigmund Freud* (Vol. 14, pp. 67–102). London: The Hogarth Press.

Gardner, S. (2003). The unconscious mind. In T. Baldwin (Ed.), *The Cambridge history of philosophy 1870–1945* (pp. 107–115). Cambridge, UK: Cambridge University Press.

Ghent, E. (1989). Credo: The dialectics of one-person and two-person psychologies. *Contemporary Psychoanalsis, 25,* 169–211.

Goldenberg, N. R. (1993). *Resurrecting the body: Feminism, religion, and psychotherapy.* New York: Crossroad.

Grof, S. (1985). *Beyond the brain.* Albany, NY: State University of New York Press.

Hannah, B. (1981). *Encounters with the soul: Active imagination as developed by C.G. Jung.* New York: Sigo Press.

Harris, A. (2011). The relational tradition: Landscape and canon. *Journal of the American Psychoanalytic Association, 59*(4), 701–736.

Hillman, J. (1995). A psyche the size of the earth. In T. Roszak, M. E. Gomes, & A. D. Kanner (Eds.), *Ecopsychology: Restoring the earth, healing the mind* (pp. xvii–xxiii). San Francisco: Sierra Club Books.

Hogenson, G. B. (1994). *Jung's struggle with Freud* (revised ed.). Wilmette, IL: Chiron Publications.

Jung, C. G. (1946). The psychology of the transference. In *Collected works* (Vol. 16, pp. 353–537). Princeton, NJ: Princeton University Press.

Jung, C. G. (1954). Archetypes of the collective unconscious. In *Collected works* (Vol. 9i, pp. 3–41). Princeton, NJ: Princeton University Press.

Jung, C. G. (1959). Aion: Researches into the phenomenology of the self. In G. Adler, R. F. C. Hull, & H. Read (Eds.), *Collected works* (Vol. 9ii). Princeton, NJ: Princeton University Press.

Jung, C. G. (1963). *Memories, dreams, reflections* (R. Winston & C. Winston, Trans. A. Jaffe, Ed.). New York: Pantheon Books.

Kahn, P. H., & Hasbach, P. H. (Eds.). (2012). *Ecopsychology: Science, totems, and the technological species*. Cambridge, MA: MIT Press.

Katz, S. M. (2017). *Contemporary psychoanalytic field theory: Stories, dreams, and metaphor*. London & New York: Routledge.

Kline, M. V. (1972). Freud and hypnosis: A reevaluation. *International Journal of Clinical and Experimental Hypnosis, 20*(4), 252–263.

Kofman, S. (1985). *The enigma of woman: Woman in Freud's writings* (C. Porter, Trans.). Ithaca & London: Cornell University Press.

Kugler, P. (2005). *Raids on the unthinkable: Freudian and Jungian psychoanalysis*. New Orleans, LA: Spring Journal Books.

Makari, G. (2008). *Revolution in mind: The creation of psychoanalysis*. New York: Harper Perennial.

Merritt, D. L. (2012). *Jung and ecopsychology: The dairy farmer's guide to the universe* (Vol. 1). Carmel, CA: Fisher King Press.

Metzner, R. (1995). The psychopathology of the human-nature relationship. In T. Roszak, M. E. Gomes, & A. Kanner, D. (Eds.), *Ecopsychology: Restoring the earth, healing the mind* (pp. 55–67). San Francisco: Sierra Club Books.

Roszak, T. (1992). *The voice of the earth: An exploration of ecopsychology*. New York: Simon & Schuster.

Schopenhauer, A. (1907). *On the fourfold root of the principle of sufficient reason and on the will in nature* (K. Hillebrand, Trans.). London: George Bell and Sons.

Shamdasani, S. (2015). Jung's practice of the image. *Journal of Sandplay Therapy, 24*(1), 7–21.

Stevens, A. (1982). Archetypal theory: The evolutionary dimension. In R. Withers (Ed.), *Controversies in analytical psychology* (pp. 252–264). New York, NY: Brunner & Routledge.

Tacey, D. (2010). Ecopsychology and the sacred: The psychological basis of the environmental crisis. *Spring: A Journal of Archetype and Culture, 83*, 329–352.

Trilling, L. (2008). *The liberal imagination: Essays on literature and society*. New York: The New York Review of Books.

von Franz, M.-L. (1974). *Number and time: Reflections leading towards a unification of psychology and physics*. London: Rider & Company.

Weinberger, J. (2000). William James and the unconscious: Redressing a century-old misunderstanding. *Psychological Science, 11*(6), 439–445.

Chapter 2

Where do minds meet?[1]

Contemporary psychoanalytic theorizing has been centrally concerned with the theme of intersubjectivity – a term that has been employed broadly within the field to reflect a number of theoretical approaches. This chapter suggests that despite their ostensible intent, relational conceptions of intersubjectivity may subtly belie an underlying tendency towards objectifying people. While classical approaches have conceptualized relationship in terms of the subject experiencing the other as an object of their own needs, in seeking to question this notion, contemporary relational perspectives have minimized the self as a construct and implicitly grounded their thinking in the body considered as a material object. Jung's transpersonal approach to the psyche has sometimes been understood to reinforce classical notions of the self as fundamentally alienated from others – this is reflected in the notion of the other as an image bearer for archetypal influences. Readings of this kind fail to acknowledge that Jung's thinking about the objective psyche extends beyond conceptions of spiritual a prioris and expresses a radically communal approach to psychic life rooted in Western esotericism. The author shows how post-Jungian conceptions of intersubjectivity might challenge and supplement mainstream psychoanalytic ideas about relationship.

TALK TO YOUR BABY   THEIR BRAIN DEPENDS ON IT

Thus ran the slogan for a recent New York City public health campaign (nyc.gov, 2015). Alarming though it is that parents might require encouragement to communicate with their newborn children, a more insidious danger is perhaps reflected in the justification given – that the lived experience of the child (or parent) would be deemed a less persuasive basis for argument than the health of a bodily organ is, I feel, a less readily acknowledged concern than might be warranted. For people to be valued first and foremost as material objects has alarming implications. In the extent to which the human subject is interpreted on the assumption of an objective recognition of his or her physical nature (whether in terms of neuroanatomy or, more simply, physical appearance), a gesture is made such as to disempower the individual. For this reason, it may be considered significant that the relational turn in psychoanalysis has placed considerable emphasis on the role of subjectivity. But in what extent have contemporary analysts succeeded in challenging the fundamentally totalitarian assumption of the subject's one-sided dependence on the object?

The question is complicated, for while relational analysts have emphasized the clinician's irreducible subjectivity (Renik, 1993), the thrust of contemporary discourse has concerned itself not with championing subjectivity *per se*, but more in recognizing the role played by the *analyst's* subjectivity in terms of clinical technique. In fact, the constructivist leanings of some relational thinkers have sometimes threatened to reduce subjectivity itself to a depthless and purely social phenomenon (Brown, 2017b). But while relational conceptions of the individual are thus sometimes prone to inadvertently legitimize systemic power, this tendency is seemingly counterbalanced by the fashion in which relationalists have sought to destabilize clinical authority. Correspondingly, the notion of subjectivity has tended to be raised in context of a different kind of conversation concerning *inter*subjectivity, with shifting assumptions concerning the former only becoming more apparent through careful engagement with the latter. Thinking again of our brainy babies, we might ask in what extent psychoanalytic conceptions of intersubjectivity offer a less reductive means of interpreting the encounter with another person.

This chapter will argue that, despite appearances, relational conceptions of intersubjectivity often imply a fundamentally isolated model of mind resulting in lingering implications of biological and/or linguistic reductionism. In seeking to challenge this tendency it will be suggested that Jungian thinking has much to offer. Jung's transpersonal approach to the psyche has sometimes been understood to reinforce classical conceptions of the self as fundamentally alienated from others – this being reflected in the implication of the other as a "screen" for archetypal projections. I will suggest that readings of this kind fail to acknowledge that Jung's notion of the collective unconscious moves beyond reductive conceptions of spiritual a prioris to express a radically communal approach to the psyche. How might post-Jungian notions of intersubjectivity challenge and supplement mainstream psychoanalytic ideas about relationship? With particular attention to the work of Jessica Benjamin and Thomas Ogden, I argue that a transpersonal conception of the third is theoretically essential if the notion of mutual recognition is to be considered meaningful in its own right.

An equivalent center of being

As is often acknowledged, the term "intersubjectivity" has been adopted by analysts to encompass a range of theoretical perspectives so diverse as to render casual use of the term problematic. Nevertheless, that the term itself has been adopted so broadly suggests that it exhibits a connotative appeal which appears to express something of the recent psychoanalytic zeitgeist. In the present context, I am concerned to emphasize the fashion in which this notion has come to suggest the possibility of what Lewis Aron (1996), following Loewald (1980), refers to as a "meeting of minds." It should be noted that this use of the word is at odds with the intersubjectivist thinking associated with Robert Stolorow and his colleagues. While Stolorow, Atwood, and Ross (1978) are widely regarded as having introduced the term "intersubjectivity" to American psychoanalysis, they adopt it to signify "any psychological field formed by interacting worlds of experience" (Stolorow & Atwood, 1992, p. 3). This definition has been criticized by Jessica Benjamin for failing to differentiate the intersubjective from the interpersonal. Benjamin (1999a) suggests that the term should be reserved for "the specific matter of recognizing the other as an equivalent center of being" (p. 201). For Benjamin, intersubjectivity thus expresses a relationship of "mutual recognition" such that each participant acknowledges the other as an equivalent yet distinct center of consciousness.

Benjamin conceptualizes mutual recognition in terms of the emergence of *thirdness*. The third is a notion that has frequently been invoked to signify a point of reference existing outside of the relational dyad, such as to enable the creation of triangular space and the possibility of bi-directionality. This notion is given early expression by Lacan, for whom the third is considered necessary so as to prevent relationship from becoming a fight to the death. Benjamin objects to the emphasis common both to

Lacanians and Kleinians on perceiving the Oedipal father as emblematic of the third. Drawing from infant attachment studies, she argues that a latent form of nonverbal thirdness is established from the outset within the maternal situation. In this connection, Benjamin's conceptualization of intersubjectivity is significantly influenced by Daniel Stern, who in turn draws his own definition from Trevarthen and Hubley (1978): "a deliberately sought sharing of experiences about events and things" (p. 213). Trevarthen (1979) elsewhere posits a condition of "primary intersubjectivity." Similarly, while Stern contends that intersubjectivity proper does not emerge until 9 to 12 months, he nevertheless asserts that "beginning at birth the infant enters into an intersubjective matrix" (2004, p. 90). Benjamin (1988) wishes to supplement this line of thought by drawing attention to the role played by conflict. While emphasizing the notion of primary intersubjectivity, Benjamin also seeks to accommodate Margaret Mahler's notion of separation-individuation. Drawing from Winnicott's (1971) ideas concerning the destruction of an object, Benjamin argues that the object's negation and subsequent survival is what enables mutual recognition – a developmental accomplishment that she links to Winnicott's potential space. Although a basic condition of intersubjectivity is given to the infant from the outset, the other person only comes to exist for them in their own right having been able to withstand the infant's omnipotent attacks. In coming to recognize the existence of other people, we thus come to realize that our own existence is contingent upon their recognition of us. The stark contrast experienced between the needs of self-assertion and those of recognition results in a conflict of interests that is, in Benjamin's view, best resolved by maintaining a constant tension between object-relational and intersubjective positions.

The paradoxical nature of recognition expresses the extent to which Benjamin's reading of Winnicott is informed by Hegel's master-slave dialectic. Yet for Benjamin, intersubjectivity is about more than the clash of wills and the mirroring function of the other. Essential to her approach is what she postulates as our inherent need for recognition of others *as* others. This need is considered additional to the needs of object relating, and is posited to operate alongside of them. Aron (2000) emphasizes that both patient and analyst are pulled back and forth between intersubjective and intrapsychic modes of relating, and that the triangular space of recognition must inevitably make way for perceiving the other as an object of needs and wishes. As Benjamin (2004) states: "This collapse can take the form of merger (oneness), eliminating difference, or of a two-ness that splits the differences – the polarized opposition of the power struggle" (p. 12). These dynamics can be seen at play in the clinical situation, in which context the recognition of the analyst as a distinct subject plays a central role in enabling the emergence of reflective space in the patient.

The notion of mutual recognition clearly suggests a major challenge to earlier psychoanalytic conceptions of relationship. While in classical terms the concept of cathexis has given expression to the idea that individuals are not directly invested in other people but merely in their representations of them, Benjamin (1990) boldly states: "Where objects were, subjects must be" (p. 34). The nature of this intersubjective recognition, however, remains somewhat enigmatic. While the notion of "the real relationship" has historically served as a means to signify the interaction between individuals in the absence of the distorting influence of transference, the relational shift has indicated a rather complicated challenge to this – recognition of the other person has been empowered as a basis for change, yet the notion that we might speak of any relationship on essentially objective terms has been thrown into doubt. Benjamin surely doesn't intend mutual recognition in such light. Intersubjectivity is essentially described as the capacity to *imagine* the possibility of difference – this does not seem equivalent to a concern for directly encountering it. Benjamin's lack of engagement with what we might term the "substance" of intersubjective experience is reflected in her approach to thirdness – for Benjamin (2004), the third is defined as "anything one holds in mind that creates another point of reference outside the dyad" (p. 7). As such, thirdness is posited as a mental space that creates room for the other person thus enabling surrender of the need to coerce or control. Benjamin therefore professes not to be concerned with the different kinds of third that might be postulated (examples of which would include the Oedipal father, speech/language, the analyst's theory, or the professional community), but rather with the emergence of the mental space that seemingly allows for such a notion to be held in the first place.

While Benjamin explicitly acknowledges the interdependence of the intrapsychic and intersubjective domains, she nevertheless conceptualizes them in relative independence. An alternative approach might seek to locate intersubjectivity more directly within the framework of object relations. Doing so, however, clearly jeopardizes the explicit conscious recognition of the other which Benjamin posits as the essential feature of an intersubjective position. Following Freud's claim that the analyst should "turn his own unconscious like a receptive organ towards the transmitting unconscious of the patient" (1912, p. 115), and reflecting his contention that "the *Ucs.* of one human being can react upon that of another, without passing through the *Cs.*" (1915, p. 194), such an approach has been particularly associated with the Kleinian lineage, and has been exemplified in North America by the work of Thomas Ogden. It is this strand of thinking that also bears most direct comparison to Jung.

Projective identification and *participation mystique*

In distinction to Benjamin's emphasis on mutual recognition, Ogden's approach to intersubjectivity focuses on the communication of unconscious affect. His notion of thirdness is fundamentally informed by the clinical experience of projective identification. Benjamin (2004) differentiates her understanding of the third from Ogden's (1994) "subjugating third" by pointing out that Ogden's approach doesn't have to do with the creation of space but rather with the consumption of it – she thus suggests we would be more correct to speak of Ogden's third as "the negative third" (p. 10). While for Benjamin the third is conscious and enables relief from the merger vs kill-or-be-killed dynamics of the dyad, for Ogden the third is largely unconscious and is experienced as imposing on freedom. Ogden (1994) describes the third as follows:

> The analytic process reflects the interplay of three subjectivities: the subjectivity of the analyst, of the analysand, and of the analytic third. The analytic third is the creation of the analyst and analysand, and at the same time the analyst and analysand (qua analyst and analysand) are created by the analytic third. (There is no analyst, no analysand, no analysis in the absence of the third.)
>
> (p. 93)

Drawing from the work of Bion, Ogden emphasizes the use of reverie as a means of accessing a third area that is co-constructed by both partners in the relationship. Entering into a mild hypnogogic state, the analyst is encouraged to attend to their fleeting thoughts and somatic experiences so as to intuitively recover unconscious elements of the patient's experience.

Expanding on the work of Klein and Bion, Ogden (1986) argues that projective identification shouldn't be understood simply in terms of the caregiver metabolizing experiences for the infant, since a definition of this nature fails to explain how the infant's capacity to process experience is itself transformed in the process. Ogden therefore argues that only by recognizing the caregiver-infant relationship as an entity does the possibility emerge for new forms of experience. This would appear to move projective identification beyond the kind of symbolic exchange potentially implied in weaker readings of this idea. In fact, Ogden goes so far as to state that projective identification "bridges the intrapsychic and the interpersonal" (p. 39).

Ogden's conclusions find extensive support in the Jungian literature. Drawing attention to shifting conceptions of countertransference during the mid-twentieth century, Gordon (1965) provides an early recognition of the importance that Jung's thinking may have in terms of understanding projective identification as a transpersonal phenomenon:

> It is probably a process which, if it is sufficiently primitive and elemental, may really break down the boundaries between persons and lead to truly shared experiences. Admittedly, some of the emotional sharing may be the result of conscious or pre-conscious and subliminal perceptions. But some of these so-called perceptions, when they are described, seem almost more truly *post hoc* than *propter hoc*. [. . .] However, in order to account for projective identification as a fact rather than as merely a phantasy, we must have recourse to Jung's own concepts, such as *participation mystique*, the collective unconscious, and his conception of the psychoid.
>
> (p. 145)

Some 50 years ago, Gordon had already recognized that Jung's psychology might provide a suitable vocabulary to give voice to emerging psychoanalytic concerns pertaining to the nature of relationship. Nevertheless, Jung's own thinking in this respect remains inconclusive and at times contradictory. The fashion in which he deploys the notion of *participation mystique*[2] demonstrates the ways in which his approach might appear to align with conventional psychoanalytic assumptions concerning disenchantment. In *Psychological Types* he defines "identity" as an unconscious phenomenon:

It is a characteristic of the primitive mentality, and is the actual basis of *participation mystique*, which in reality is merely a relic of the original psychological non-differentiation of subject and object, and hence of the primordial unconscious state. It is also a characteristic of the mental state of early infancy, and, finally, of the unconscious of the civilized adult, which, in so far as it has not become a content of consciousness, remains in a permanent state of identity with objects.

(Jung, 1921, p. 441)

Ironically, from a contemporary vantage it seems that Jung's approach to *participation mystique* might suffer from its own lack of differentiation – the experience of the newborn child, "the primitive," the neurotic, and the mob are all interpreted in terms of the same underlying phenomenon, and in a fashion that is liable to seem reductive. Segal (2007) has claimed that Jung's approach to this notion in fact reflects a misreading: "By *participation mystique* Lévy-Bruhl means the ascription to others of what we recognize, not what we deny, in ourselves. He means the assumption of outright identity between us and others" (p. 645). With the emphasis that Jung's understanding of *participation mystique* places on projection, a sense emerges that the process of individuation entails an increasing awareness of fundamental alienation – a sense that seems to be reinforced by the nature of the term itself. Objecting to this tendency in Jung, Schwartz-Salant (1988) draws attention to the way in which Jung emphasizes the negative aspects of projective identification as reflected in his explicit emphasis on psychotherapy being concerned with the dissolution of *participation mystique* (Jung, 1929, p. 45).

Nevertheless, in "The Psychology of the Transference" Jung (1946) is at pains to emphasize the shared nature of the analytic relationship. This is reflected both in his well-known analogy of transformation in chemical substances and his claim that the analyst must take on the sufferings of the patient. Jung's illustrative use of the alchemical woodcuts of the *Rosarium Philosophorum* further underscores the theme of intimacy. As Stevens (1986) observes:

The image of the king and queen meeting, uniting, and being mutually transformed in the process, is a double image of the essential nature of any therapeutic relationship that works. On the one hand, it is an image of the individual patient's intrapsychic experience in which his

conscious self meets and unites with some portion of his unconscious
self, releasing a fresh current of energy for life. On the other hand, it
is an image of the patient's union with the analyst, a highly charged
emotional experience within which the patient is transformed.

(p. 188)

According to this reading, Jung is effectively suggesting that the desire to
be whole is the flipside of the desire to merge with the other. As Jung
(1946) himself puts it: "Wholeness is the product of an intrapsychic process which depends essentially on the relationship of one individual to
another" (p. 245). Stevens emphasizes that where the transference has
been fully constellated the central therapeutic factor is, in Jung's view, the
analyst's willingness to enter as far as possible into the experience. This
fundamentally relational model of clinical action appears to suggest that,
by virtue of the shared experience of the archetypal material activated in
the transference, the analyst is able to access something of the patient's
subjective world. Yet in what extent this line of thinking can be thought to
reflect a direct apprehension of the other remains open to question; the
shared quality of the analytic encounter is seemingly given by virtue of
a relationship to the archetype as a third entity. Whether this shared state
of participation constitutes a direct relationship between partners may
seem unclear. In fact, Jung conceptualizes the potential for an enduring
quality of the relationship that remains subsequent to the retraction of
projections – the development of "kinship libido" (p. 233), which expresses
a communal feeling that has its original basis in *participation mystique*.[3]
Confusingly, however, this notion is defined as the "instinct" underlying
the transference. While for Jung, self and other are ultimately to be understood as parts of a transcendent unity (p. 245), it isn't clear in what extent
the development of kinship libido constitutes a direct apprehension
of this.

Change in the third

For Jung, the central therapeutic factor in the archetypal transference is
expressed by the analyst's capacity to immerse in the analytic encounter
while abstaining from acting out. This approach thus recalls the problem
raised by Ogden in seeking to account for the fashion in which the analyst's
role as a container enables structural change in the patient – a problem that

Ogden seeks to resolve by considering the analytic couple as an entity formed of the subjugating dynamics of the third. As has already been touched upon, however, this approach is far removed from Benjamin's notion of mutual recognition defined as the *conscious* acknowledgement of the other person as an equivalent center of being. Yet if mutual recognition is to be considered most fundamentally reflective of a shift in the relationship itself (and not merely a solipsistic achievement of the respective partners), then it seems necessary to ground this position in a collective dimension of the psyche; one that would presumably be considered otherwise inaccessible by virtue of its being unconscious. If such a notion is to be linked with mutual recognition, however, then the unconscious as third must be considered in some respect accessible to consciousness. Thus, while Jung and Ogden both have significant recourse to defining the third as unconscious, it should be noted that without some question of challenging one's relationship to this third the analyst would presumably be barred from upholding therapeutic agency. That the patient must in Jung's (1946) view become "a problem" for the analyst clearly indicates a question of conscious engagement. This is equally apparent in Ogden's use of reverie, for in lowering the threshold of consciousness Ogden is suggesting that the analytic third can be made in some respect more accessible to the conscious mind. The concept of reverie clearly bears comparison with Jung's technique of active imagination where, in the notion of a "confrontation with the unconscious" the meaning of "unconscious" has likewise seemingly been stretched beyond its natural capacity. But where the technique of active imagination was developed by Jung as a means to self-analysis and stresses direct engagement with one's own imagery (by establishing an internal dialogue), the notion of reverie is essentially passive and was developed in the clinical setting as a means to working with projective identification. It is perhaps owing to these fundamental differences that while reverie has come to occupy a central role in post-Kleinian technique, the clinical uses of active imagination have been less centrally emphasized. Von Franz (1980) reports that Jung usually warned against doing active imagination with images of living persons, since "The borderline between active imagination and magic is sometimes very subtle" (p. 132). Such a statement indicates that Jung went so far as to assert that the patient can be directly influenced by means of a conscious engagement with the imagery of the unconscious. Clearly, however, the specifically *active* quality of this practice raises ethical questions.

Reflecting the conceptual difficulties that arise in speaking of "the unconscious," James Hillman (1972) suggests that this term obscures Jung's emphasis on image. In seeking to challenge the conscious/unconscious dichotomy, Hillman draws from the French philosopher and theologian Henry Corbin who refers to an order of reality that he terms the *mundus imaginalis*. Corbin (1977) observes that Islamic mysticism makes a distinction between three metaphysical worlds: the intellectual world (*Jabarut*), the imaginal world (*Malakut*), and the sensible world (*molk*). In emphasizing the notion of the psyche as a third term serving to connect body and mind, Hillman's approach to Jung underscores the notion that therapy is fundamentally concerned with developing the capacity to imagine. The imaginal thus bears comparison with Winnicott's notion of transitional space, yet with the notable difference that the former is postulated to correspond with a preexistent dimension of reality.[4] Similar implications attend Ogden's work – Cwik (2006, 2011) observes that Ogden's outlook is in keeping with an imaginal approach to the clinical situation, but that it lacks an underlying theoretical basis. While Ogden (2004) speaks of the "subjugating third" and thus acknowledges how the intersubjective field can subsume the personalities of analyst and analysand, he nevertheless posits that this field is a joint creation of the two individuals. While acknowledging the need of a directly shared experience if reverie is to bring about a change in the other person, Ogden abstains from further exploring this. Samuels (1985) states that Corbin's notion of the *mundus imaginalis* offers a basis from which to understand the functioning of projective identification. In this frame of reference, projective identificatory processes corresponds with a particular dimension of reality – one that preexists the participation of analyst and patient.

Corbin's notion of the *mundus imaginalis* provides an ontological grounding for Jung's archetypes. Significantly, the conception of the collective unconscious thus offered potentially disrupts the assumption that archetypes should be considered as though existing in distinction from human participation. Among Jungians, clinical interest in imaginal insight has therefore led to an increasing emphasis on mutual understanding in preference to self-understanding (Reed, 1996). Schwartz-Salant (1988) suggests:

> Projective identification has the goal of transforming the structure and
> dynamics of processes in the third area, and, with this, one's perception

of these processes. One may often refer to this area as 'in between' two people, for it can be experienced in this way, especially as an interactive field that is structured by images that have a strong effect upon the conscious personalities. But the more deeply it is entered, the more spatial metaphors vanish.

(p. 43)

This position leads Schwartz-Salant to emphasize that it is not things that are transformed in context of this kind of therapeutic work, so much as the relationship between them.[5] He recommends thinking of the analytic situation as an interactive field, the dynamics of which are best understood by conceptualizing projective identification in terms of the aspects of an unconscious couple that structure the third – "For then one moves out of a sphere of omnipotence [. . .] and into a domain in which both people can discover how they have, so to speak, been acting out a mutual dream, or how they have been being dreamed" (p. 50). Such an approach is fostered by refraining from interpreting in terms of projection and instead focusing on the quality of the field itself.

Although this approach seems to clearly complement recent psychoanalytic conceptions of intersubjectivity, the more explicitly metaphysical nature of the claims thus made are liable to be challenging. Yet it might be argued that the Jungian approach is merely drawing attention to theoretical problems that others have alluded to without directly addressing them. Reflecting this claim, Gerson (2004) objects to speaking of a "third" precisely because he feels that this language tends to foster what he perceives to be a mistaken sense of the intersubjective process as a "force beyond the dyad" (p. 80). Alongside the work of Ogden, Gerson cites Green's (1975) notion of intersubjective processes as an *analytic object*, the Baranger's (1993) *analytic field*, Bollas's (1987) *third intermediate object*, and Orange's (1995) *intersubjective triad*. Similarly, in outlining her conceptualization for a general psychoanalytic field theory, Katz (2013) objects to the fashion in which many theorists appear to endorse notions of the third as a distinct entity. She states: "A third, independent nonhuman entity with its own unconscious process is not necessary for general psychoanalytic field theory" (p. 285). It is precisely as a consequence of having taken this position, however, that Katz subsequently asserts an extreme dualism in stating that "just as there is no direct contact with the unconscious, neither is there with humans, couches, or other items purported to be in the world" (p. 286). Should such a position be allowed to stand then the notion of mutual recognition would appear fundamentally deluded and, in keeping with a Lacanian perspective, perhaps even unjustifiably coercive.[6]

Mutual recognition revisited

If the notion of recognition described by Benjamin is to be considered as more than an adaptive illusion, then a medium has to be posited through which this process takes place. Insofar as adopting an intersubjective position in the sense Benjamin intends is to be regarded as a capacity of the imagination, then a conception of the imagination is required such as to enable a meeting of minds. Yet pursuing this question in earnest readily invites accusations of woolly thinking. Responding to the notion of recognition, Orange (2010a) writes:

> Is there really any such thing as being "out of the fly-bottle"? Is there really enlightenment, Buddhist-style? Is there really, as in the politics and psychoanalysis of recognition, an almost magical mutual process that creates the other in subject – subject relating? I think not, and do not believe Wittgenstein did either. But, allusions in the psychoanalytic literature to the incompletely analyzed patient, and descriptions of putatively recognition-creating enactments, suggest that we still seek a path to Nirvana.
>
> (p. 241)

Although Orange (2010b) subsequently expresses regret for what she would retrospectively perceive to be her unnecessarily harsh wording, perhaps she is getting at something here – surely there *is* something altogether fantastical about the existence of other people. It is a testament to Benjamin's careful scholarship that she has been able to introduce this notion of mutual recognition in such a way as to retain intellectual respectability. Yet this accomplishment has required some deft juggling and a sense that the crux of the matter may have been left unaddressed.

It has been observed that Hegel's master slave dialectic does not in and of itself constitute a refutation of solipsism (R. Stern, 2012). In keeping with this observation, Reis (1999) argues that grounding a relational approach to intersubjectivity in Hegel can only be expected to result in a restrictive definition of subjectivity considered merely as an operation of thinking. In Benjamin's Winnicottian take on Hegel, it may seem that the existence of the other person is essentially an intellectual inference gained through the other's capacity to survive omnipotent attacks. As Varga (2011) observes, however, Winnicott's notion that the infant's recognition of the other is dependent on an initial frustration caused by the disjunction between what they want and what they get appears to require that the child is already aware of the distinction between self and other – in sum, frustration could never arise without prior acknowledgement of a reason to become frustrated.

Both Reis (1999) and Varga (2011) turn to the work of Merleau-Ponty in search of an alternative position. Recognizing that any question of comparing oneself to the other already seems to entail an intersubjective relationship, Merleau-Ponty argues that recognition of self and other should be considered ontologically co-primordial. If there is to be any question of comparison between self and other such as indicated in a clash of wills, then intersubjectivity must already have been achieved (Welsh, 2007). Intersubjectivity is thus considered an originary given rather than posited to evolve out of solipsism. Merleau-Ponty grounds this claim in the notion of a body-subject. As Reis explains:

> Bodily perception is our primordial experience of or in the world, and so the world first appears to us by way of perception. Primordial perception is not conscious reflection (i.e., thinking) but the immediacy of prereflective experience mediated by the relation of the body to the world.
>
> (p. 384)

Reis claims that this perspective is uniquely reflected in the work of Ogden, suggesting that Ogden's adoption of reverie is best understood not along the lines of Bionian containment but rather in terms of Merleau-Ponty's notion of *milieu* – "as a medium for the appearance of the world from which he is not separated" (p. 390). He positively compares this outlook to Benjamin's claim that "all fantasy is the negation of the real other"; a statement that suggests the extent to which Benjamin's theorizing can seem to have divorced her conception of the intersubjective from the intrapsychic.

In response to Reis, Benjamin (1999b) underscores that her thinking embraces both Winnicottian omnipotence and the primary intersubjectivity of Trevarthen and Stern – a fundamental contradiction that she
readily acknowledges. While indicating the possibility that this seeming tension may itself be worth preserving (the path effectively taken
by Merleau-Ponty in establishing both self and other as given from the
outset), Benjamin nevertheless suggests an approach to resolution – she
seeks to define two different intersubjective phases, the first emphasizing the notion of a gradual differentiation out of primary intersubjectivity,
and the second reflecting the developmental emergence of omnipotence
and (simultaneously) confrontation with the independent other. Elsewhere
Benjamin (1999a) posits the notion of a nascent third in order to emphasize her belief that intersubjectivity originates in nonverbal experiences of
shared interaction. Benjamin (2004) explicitly connects this notion with
infancy research. She states:

> I consider this early exchange to be a form of thirdness, and suggest
> that we call the principle of affective resonance or union that underlies
> it the *one in the third* – literally, the part of the third that is constituted
> by oneness.
>
> (p. 17)[7]

Benjamin seemingly requires this notion so as to [1] prevent her theory of
intersubjectivity from becoming excessively rational, and [2] to provide a
foundational awareness of the other such as to enable reflective recognition. It might be noted, however, that this is a strange ask to make of
infancy research thinking. The notion of an originary form of intersubjectivity points to a foundational claim about the nature of reality itself, yet
Trevarthen (1998) is content to portray primary intersubjectivity as a form
of "protoconversation." This notion is also reflected in Stern, for whom
the infant is able to discern a mental state in the other on the basis of the
intensity, timing, and shape of the partner's behavior (Beebe, Knoblauch,
Rustin, & Sorter, 2003). It should be noted that this is *not* equivalent to
intersubjectivity considered as an originary principle. If primary intersubjectivity is merely a form of protoconversation, this doesn't address how
the conversation comes to be established in the first place. At this point,
there seems to be a temptation to fall back on biology. Trevarthen (1998)
and Stern (2007) both explicitly link their ideas about intersubjectivity

with the nature of the brain, and Benjamin (2004) herself states that mirror-neurons may offer the "basis for appreciating this *intention* to align and to accommodate" (p. 19). However, if primary intersubjectivity is postulated to emerge from brain activity, surely we conflate subjective and objective ontologies and only reinforce the very disjunction between mind and body out of which the problem of other minds arises. Furthermore, in the notion of primary intersubjectivity as a form of protoconversation considered developmentally prior to thought *per se*, it seems that the charge of excessive rationality must still stand.

Because Benjamin enlists infancy research as a basis from which to theorize early forms of subjectivity, this approach is handicapped by the limitations attending engagement with what Daniel Stern (1985) has termed *the observed infant*.[8] Trevarthen and Stern both rely on the microanalysis of baby-mother interactions. When the basis for talking about early forms of intersubjectivity is behavioral observation, however, it goes without saying that the nature of the interaction will be interpreted in terms of protolanguage – this is merely to conclude what was already assumed in the design of the study. Since subjective experience is being inferred by means of observed behavior, the mother's and child's subjectivities are in fact excluded from direct consideration altogether. Such studies seek to achieve the false impression of having eliminated subjectivity from the conditions of the experiment, so as to then claim to have discovered it again in observed behavior. The danger thus arises of confusing Merleau-Ponty's body-subject with the body considered as a material object. In this light, intersubjectivity comes to be grounded in an objective ontology and conceptualized merely in terms of brain functioning. Such an approach therefore misses the notion of subjectivity altogether. The activity of the body comes to be interpreted as the function of a biological organism instinctually expressing an early form of language. Subsequently, an awkward transition is negotiated in seeking to explain intersubjectivity first as a product of the relationship between objects in space, and later as an operation of linguistic reflection. But neither of these positions offers a basis from which mutual recognition might be understood in such a way that the experience of intimacy can be considered more than illusion.

In emphasizing that the body-mind should be treated as fundamentally paradoxical, Dimen (2000) observes that psychoanalytic thinking tends more towards "indecision and contradiction" (p. 15). The transition between the two moments of subjectivity Benjamin outlines is perhaps indicative of Dimen's point, and does a disservice to Benjamin's own commitment to paradox (Benjamin, 2005). Starr (2008) argues that "the analytic relationship is embedded in and potentiates a transcendent Third" (p. 217). She suggests this claim is what Benjamin (2004) is angling for in her conceptualization of thirdness as "a deeper law of reality" (p. 18). This certainly seems to be reflected where Benjamin (1988) speaks of the mother attributing to the newborn child "a knowledge beyond ordinary knowing" (p. 13). But while Benjamin breaks new ground in seeking to draw attention to the role of the mother's subjectivity, the perspective she takes in negotiating this theme continues to emphasize the infant – that is, the relevance for psychoanalytic theorizing of the mother's subjectivity is explored in terms of the mother differing from her child and the impact that this difference has on the child's development. While this particular avenue of inquiry has borne much fruit, what of those elements of the mother's experience not associated with this question of divergence? Might we not also seek to learn from the mother's participatory experiences of belonging and merger?

In support of her opposition to the notion that mother and child ever exist in a state of unity, Benjamin (2004) invokes Lacan's objection to Balint's "primary love" – that if a recognition of difference wasn't present in the nursing mother from the outset then there would be nothing to prevent her, upon becoming hungry, from turning the tables and eating the baby. Amusing though this line of thinking might be, it also seems a little hastily dismissive. In failing to more fully explore mothers' experiences of union with their newborns, a danger emerges that we are liable to recapitulate Winnicott's (1956) potentially reductive portrayal of primary maternal preoccupation as a state of identification engendered in the mother purely to serve the baby's needs. In this light, the mother's subjectivity comes to be implicitly defined in terms of the extent she succeeds in breaking free of the state of maternal preoccupation. We thus come to value the mother's subjectivity as a marking phenomenon indicating the question of difference such as to enable mutual recognition, but fail to attend more seriously to experiences of unity and merger. While Benjamin (1995) acknowledges the significance of the mother's subjectivity in terms of the pleasure that she feels in contacting her child's mind and in being recognized by her baby to have her own "rights" and "feelings" (p. 32), she appears (2000) to dismiss the experience of primary maternal preoccupation as merely a product of Winnicott's romantic idealization of motherhood. It seems conceivable, however, that seeking to eliminate such a notion from the conceptualization of maternal subjectivity could be subtly linked with the societal pressure placed on women to pursue career alongside of motherhood, and the widespread idea that this state of affairs is by definition reflective of female empowerment. Motherhood thus increasingly comes to be perceived as a "sacrifice" (the broader psychodynamics of which needn't concern us here) preventing women from serving their "own needs" – i.e. taking up a position in the working world. Though for many women there may be a great deal of legitimacy in this narrative, we might note the extent to which this position has come to be assumed true by definition and at the expense of a more direct valuation of motherhood itself. It is this state of affairs that leads Fraser (2013) to argue that women have become the "handmaidens" of neoliberal capitalism, and it may also be this line of thinking that has significantly informed relational ideas about maternal subjectivity such as to shore up secular assumptions.

If primary maternal preoccupation is to be taken seriously as a phenomenon without reducing this experience to one concerned only with serving the needs of the infant, then the sense thus emerging raises questions of self-transcendence and spirituality[9] – something that Winnicott himself may quietly have been alluding to in speaking of a tendency in mothers to subsequently repress their memories of this experience. Owing to the ways in which the field of psychology has historically sought to retain a rigid adherence to secular values, attending to the prevalence of this theme in the experiences of mothers is perhaps only now emerging as a possibility.[10] In this light, we might consider Winnicott's claim that, in the absence of a child, the state of primary maternal preoccupation would qualify as a form of illness. If such a claim is allowed to stand, then we might recall Ellenberger's (1970) notion of "creative illness" (see Chapter 1).

Concluding thoughts

While objects in the material world are conventionally understood to relate to each other owing to their respective positions in space, relationships between subjects are less clearly defined. Loewald (1979) writes:

> There are kinds of relatedness between what conventionally we call self and object, that call into question the universal validity of these very terms. We have come to see that there are levels of mental functioning and experience where these distinctions are not made, or made only fleetingly and in rudimentary form. These are deep unconscious

layers showing modes of interpsychic relatedness, of emotional ties that are active under the surface in both analysand and analyst, and thus in their relatedness, forming ingredients of therapeutic potential. [. . .] These layers of experience, too, coexist with the more advanced levels of mental functioning and organization of mental content, and continue to exert their influence throughout life.

(p. 376)

In the present chapter I have sought to demonstrate that should the notion of mutual recognition be accepted in the spirit that it is seemingly intended, then Benjamin's (1999a) claim that "the third appears only in the relationship of recognition" (p. 204) is in need of revision. Benjamin (2016) has recently stated that mutual recognition should not be confused with empathy – that it goes beyond this to reflect an acknowledgement that something is "real." For an achievement of the imagination to be concerned with the recognition of "reality" surely registers Benjamin's thinking as more compatible with Jung than may have been supposed. The experience described by Benjamin in terms of "mutual recognition" appears to reflect the operation of what Jung terms *the transcendent function*. But where Benjamin limits her definition of recognition to the perception of the other as an equivalent center of being, Jung's notion of the transcendent function is concerned with the creation of meaning more broadly:

> It is an account of the meaning-making function of the psyche that suggests meaning to be the outcome of a process of opposition between two or more opposing elements that are somehow transcended in the creation of a third with a new level of complexity.
>
> (Colman, 2007)

For Jung, the transference relationship constitutes a struggle to effectuate a change in the collective, the byproduct of which is a feeling of participation not only between individuals, but in life itself. This feeling of correspondence between microcosm and macrocosm is the crux of his notion of synchronicity – a concept Jung developed in an apparent effort to reconcile the relationship between inner and outer (see Brown, 2014), thus potentially challenging his earlier emphasis on retracting projections in an effort to overcome *participation mystique*.

In her earlier work, Benjamin was already expressing an interest in how intersubjective and intrapsychic approaches might be synthesized: "The problem is that each focuses on different aspects of psychic experience which are too interdependent to be simply severed from one another" (Benjamin, 1988, p. 21n). For Jung (1946), both positions are interpreted as aspects of individuation:

> In the first place it is an internal and subjective process of integration, and in the second it is an equally indispensable process of objective relationship. Neither can exist without the other, although sometimes the one and sometimes the other predominates. This double aspect has two corresponding dangers. The first is the danger of the patient's using the opportunities for spiritual development arising out of the analysis of the unconscious as a pretext for evading the deeper human responsibilities, and for affecting a certain "spirituality" which cannot stand up to moral criticism: the second is the danger that atavistic tendencies may gain the ascendency and drag the relationship down to a primitive level.
>
> (p. 234)

Jung was surely speaking from experience: his questionable relationship to the rise of Nazism perhaps suggested in the former danger, and his sexual indiscretions with female patients in case of the latter.[11]

Just as Jung draws attention to the shifting emphasis between integration and what he terms "objective relationship," we might recall Aron's (2000) claim that the analytic couple is necessarily pulled between intrapsychic and intersubjective positions. In a related sense, Edinger (1985) makes a distinction between what he terms the "lesser" and "greater" aspects of the *coniunctio*[12] – in the extent to which the lesser aspect predominates, the union consists of substances that have yet to be fully discriminated. This lesser dimension of the *coniunctio* occurs as a consequence of the individual coming to identify with material emerging from the unconscious, thus signifying the need for dissolution and further discrimination. Both the lesser and greater aspects of the *coniunctio* are reflected in all experiences of union, with the task of individuation being conceived as an interminable refinement of relations between the ego and the unconscious. While moments of recognition are always colored by elements of the lesser *coniunctio*, this in no way undermines those elements of the *coniunctio* reflecting a less confused condition of union. Ulanov (2004)

thus emphasizes that a relatively fused state is nevertheless an achievement of trust:

> Heretofore this partner had remained mute, filled with a noxious sus-
> picion. To assume, now, that the other follows along with one implic-
> itly is an achievement. Some bit of ego trusts that it is held in attention
> by an unconscious inner matrix and by the receptive listening of the
> other person.
>
> (p. 134)

Clinical challenges are associated not only with entering this state but also
in leaving it. It might be suggested, therefore, that the analyst's role is to
mediate between the needs of immersing in the subjugating third versus
creating psychic space via the careful use of self-disclosure.

Notes

1 An earlier version of this chapter was published in *Re-Encountering Jung:
  Analytical Psychology and Contemporary Analysis* (Routledge). See Brown
  (2018).
2 A term adopted by Lévy-Bruhl (1926) to signify a state of non-differentiation
  from the wider world that is postulated to reflect the psychology of indigenous peoples. For a recent examination of this subject, see Winborn (2014).
3 The Barangers suggest that the validity of a moment of therapeutic insight
  is reflected in an experience of the analytic field that they describe as
  follows:

> The bond between analyst and analysand relies no longer on comple-
> mentarity but on sharing the same experience – of discovery and
> enrichment, of free communication, of non-eroticized affection, and,
> without denying the aggressive tensions that have been produced and
> will be produced again, the possibility of a future in the field and in
> life, since the latter depends on the former. It is to experience the
> shared analytic work as something positive and worthwhile. This
> appreciation has nothing to do, qualitatively, with the "blissful"
> moments in any analysis that reproduce the happy moments of union
> with the breast, with the mother, with the idealized object. This is not
> contemplation, but life, with a projection into the future. The moment
> of insight, thus defined, amounts to the essential, specific, authentic
> gratification the analyst may derive from his work, apart from others
> that are not so fundamental.
>
> (Baranger & Baranger, 1964, p. 13)

4 In calling for a paradigm shift in our notions of intersubjectivity, Suchet (2016) writes: "This field is not simply the co-construction arising out of the relationship between two people, but the result of both or either party resonating with the unified field to generate a new interpersonal experience. This is the generative, creative, emergent field that gives rise to superconscious states" (p. 755).

5 "In the deepest sense we all dream not out of ourselves but out of what lies between us and the other" (Jung, 1973, p. 172).

6 Furthermore, having assumed such a position, any question of uncanny or telepathic relatedness can only be dismissed out of hand. It has been widely observed that countertransferential reactions can sometimes elicit feelings so discrepant with the patient's presentation that it is difficult to credit the idea that nonverbal cues would be sufficient to trigger the experience. Field (1991) offers the example of a patient who is relating a dramatic story in animated fashion while the analyst experiences deep sleepiness. Without a conception of a transpersonal third, such clinical experiences can only be accounted for dismissively – Renik (1993) complains that the notion of unconscious communication tends to assume an unwarranted cast of mysticism, and argues that when the analyst is unaware of the basis for their responses it is merely because the analyst is motivated to keep them unconscious. For some clinicians, however, such a position remains unconvincing (e.g. Bass, 2001; de Peyer, 2016; Mayer, 2001; Suchet, 2004; Tennes, 2007). While the notion of the imaginal may readily be dismissed as farfetched, to some this idea may seem no less fanciful than a claim that the full range of projective identificatory experiences can be explained purely in terms of implicit communication and the analyst's defensively motivated unconsciousness.

7 The idea of positing two different kinds of intersubjectivity corresponding to different phases of early development is also forwarded by Beebe et al. (2003).

8 See the conclusion of Brown (2017b) for further discussion.

9 In an article drawing attention to the paucity of literature addressing motherhood as an opportunity for spiritual awakening, Athan and Miller (2013) identify six interrelated themes in the reports of new mothers: the emergence of unconditional love and interdependence, a sense of transcending ego or self-centeredness, the awakening of compassion and empathy, experiences associated with an attitude of mindfulness and heightened awareness, a heightened sense of meaning and purpose, and a tendency towards examining questions of faith and the existence of a higher power.

10 See Brown (2015, 2016, 2017a, 2017b) for reflections on the clinical challenges of cultural diversity, and the increasingly apparent need of a more extensive engagement among clinicians with the theme of spirituality. For an examination of the influence of Christian theology on Benjamin's work, see Hoffman (2010).

11 Needless to say, in the early history of psychoanalysis (and, to some extent, perhaps even still), Jung's susceptibility to these all-too human dangers has been exploited in seeking to discredit his work.

12 The alchemical operation by which two elements are combined to make a third, and which is reflective in Jung's work of the reconciliation of conscious and unconscious positions.

References

Aron, L. (1996). *A meeting of minds: Mutuality in psychoanalysis*. Hillsdale, NJ: Analytic Press.

Aron, L. (2000). Self-reflexivity and the therapeutic action of psychoanalysis. *Psychoanalytic Psychology, 17*(4), 667–689.

Athan, A. M., & Miller, L. (2013). Motherhood as opportunity to learn spiritual values: Experiences and insights of new mothers. *Journal of Prenatal and Perinatal Psychology and Health, 27*(4), 220–253.

Baranger, M. (1993). The mind of the analyst: From listening to interpretation. *International Journal of Psychoanalysis, 74*, 15–24.

Baranger, M., & Baranger, W. (1964). "Insight" in the analytic situation. In L. G. Fiorini (Ed.), *The work of confluence: Listening and interpreting in the psychoanalytic field*. London: Karnac Books.

Bass, A. (2001). It takes one to know one: Or, whose unconscious is it anyway? *Psychoanalytic Dialogues, 11*(5), 683–702.

Beebe, B., Knoblauch, S., Rustin, J., & Sorter, D. (2003). A comparison of Meltzoff, Trevarthen, and Stern. *Psychoanalytic Dialogues, 13*, 809–836.

Benjamin, J. (1988). *The bonds of love: Psychoanalysis, feminism, & the problem of domination*. New York: Pantheon Books.

Benjamin, J. (1990). An outline of intersubjectivity: The development of recognition. *Psychoanalytic Psychology, 7*, 33–46.

Benjamin, J. (1995). *Like subjects, love objects: Essays on recognition and sexual difference*. New Haven, CT: Yale University Press.

Benjamin, J. (1999a). Afterword. In S. A. Mitchell & L. Aron (Eds.), *Relational psychoanalysis: The emergence of a tradition* (pp. 201–210). New York: Routledge.

Benjamin, J. (1999b). A note on the dialectic: Commentary on paper by Bruce E. Reis. *Psychoanalytic Dialogues, 9*(3), 395–399.

Benjamin, J. (2000). Response to commentaries by Mitchell and by Butler. *Studies in Gender and Sexuality, 1*, 291–308.

Benjamin, J. (2004). Beyond doer and done to: An intersubjective view of thirdness. *Psychoanalytic Quarterly, 73*, 5–46.

Benjamin, J. (2005). From many into one: Attention, energy, and the containing of multitudes. *Psychoanalytic Dialogues, 15*(2), 185–201.

Benjamin, J. (2016). *Panel discussion*. Paper presented at the Celebrating Two New Developments from Beatrice Beebe's Lab: Book Release and Film Screening, Ferenczi Center, New School, NYC.

Bollas, C. (1987). *The shadow of the object*. New York: Columbia University.

Brown, R. S. (2014). Evolving attitudes. *International Journal of Jungian Studies, 6*(3), 243–253.

Brown, R. S. (2015). An opening: Trauma and transcendence. *Psychosis: Psychological, Social and Integrative Approaches, 7*(1), 72–80.

Brown, R. S. (2016). Spirituality and the challenge of clinical pluralism: Participatory thinking in psychotherapeutic context. *Spirituality in Clinical Practice, 3*(3), 187–195.

Brown, R. S. (2017a). Bridging worlds: Participatory thinking in Jungian context. *Journal of Analytical Psychology, 62*(2), 284–304.

Brown, R. S. (2017b). *Psychoanalysis beyond the end of metaphysics: Thinking towards the post-relational*. Abingdon, UK & New York: Routledge.

Brown, R. S. (2018). Where do minds meet? Intersubjectivity in light of Jung. In R. S. Brown (Ed.), *Re-encountering Jung: Analytical psychology and contemporary psychoanalysis* (pp. 160–179). Abingdon, UK & New York: Routledge.

Colman, W. (2007). Symbolic conceptions: The idea of the third. *Journal of Analytical Psychology, 52*, 565–583.

Corbin, H. (1977). *Spiritual body and celestial earth: From mazdean Iran to Shi'ite Iran* (N. Pearson, Trans., 2nd ed.). Princeton, NJ: Princeton University Press.

Cwik, A. J. (2006). The art of the tincture: Analytical supervision. *Journal of Analytical Psychology, 51*, 209–225.

Cwik, A. J. (2011). Associative dreaming: Reverie and active imagination. *Journal of Analytical Psychology, 56*, 14–36.

de Peyer, J. (2016). Uncanny communication and the porous mind. *Psychoanalytic Dialogues, 26*(2), 156–174.

Dimen, M. (2000). The body as rorschach. *Studies in Gender and Sexuality, 1*, 9–39.

Edinger, E. F. (1985). *Anatomy of the psyche: Alchemical symbolism in psychotherapy*. Peru, IL: Open Court Publishing Company.

Ellenberger, H. F. (1970). *The discovery of the unconscious: The history and evolution of dynamic psychiatry*. New York: Basic Books.

Field, N. (1991). Projective identification: Mechanism or mystery? *Journal of Analytical Psychology, 36*, 93–109.

Fraser, N. (2013, October, 14). How feminism became capitalism's handmaiden: And how to reclaim it. *The Guardian*. Retrieved from www.theguardian.com/commentisfree/2013/oct/14/feminism-capitalist-handmaiden-neoliberal

Freud, S. (1912). Recommendations to physicians practising psycho-analysis. In *The standard edition of the complete psychological works of Sigmund Freud* (Vol. 12, pp. 109–120). London: The Hogarth Press.

Freud, S. (1915). The unconscious. In J. Strachey (Ed.), *The standard edition of the complete psychological works of Sigmund Freud* (Vol. 14, pp. 159–215). London: The Hogarth Press.

Gerson, S. (2004). The relational unconscious: A core element of intersubjectivity, thirdness, and clinical process. *The Psychoanalytic Quarterly, 73*, 63–98.

Gordon, R. (1965). The concept of projective identification: An evaluation. *Journal of Analytical Psychology, 10*(2), 127–149.

Green, A. (1975). The analyst, symbolization and absence in the analytic setting. *International Journal of Psychoanalysis, 56*, 1–21.

Hillman, J. (1972). *The myth of analysis: Three essays in archetypal psychology.* Evanston: North Western University Press.

Hoffman, M. T. (2010). *Toward mutual recognition: Relational psychoanalysis and the Christian narrative.* New York & Hove, UK: Routledge.

Jung, C. G. (1921). Psychological types. In *Collected works* (Vol. 6). Princeton, NJ: Princeton University Press.

Jung, C. G. (1929). Commentary on "the secret of the golden flower". In *Collected works* (Vol. 13, pp. 1–56). Princeton, NJ: Princeton University Press.

Jung, C. G. (1946). The psychology of the transference. In *Collected works* (Vol. 16, pp. 353–537). Princeton, NJ: Princeton University Press.

Jung, C. G. (1973). *Letters* (R. F. C. Hull, Trans., Vol. 1). Princeton, NJ: Princeton University Press.

Katz, S. M. (2013). General psychoanalytic field theory: Its structure and applications to psychoanalytic perspectives. *Psychoanalytic Inquiry, 33*(3), 277–292.

Lévy-Bruhl, L. (1926). *How natives think* (L. A. Clare, Trans.). London: G. Allen & Unwin Ltd.

Loewald, H. W. (1979). Reflections on the psychoanalytic process and its therapeutic potential. In *The essential loewald: Collected papers and monographs* (pp. 372–383). Hagerstown, MD: University Publishing Group.

Loewald, H. W. (1980). *Papers on psychoanalysis.* New Haven, CT: Yale University Press.

Mayer, E. L. (2001). On "telepathic dreams?": An unpublished paper by Robert J. Stoller. *Journal of the American Psychoanalytic Association, 49*, 629–657.

nyc.gov. (2015). *Talk to your baby.* Retrieved from www1.nyc.gov/site/talktoyourbaby/index.page

Ogden, T. H. (1986). *The matrix of the mind: Object relations and the psychoanalytic dialogue.* Northvale, NJ: Jason Aronson.

Ogden, T. H. (1994). *Subjects of analysis.* Northvale, NJ & London: Jason Aronson.

Ogden, T. H. (2004). The analytic third: Implications foe psychoanalytic theory and technique. *The Psychoanalytic Quarterly, 73*, 167–195.

Orange, D. M. (1995). *Emotional understanding.* New York: Guilford.

Orange, D. M. (2010a). Recognition as: Intersubjective vulnerability in the psychoanalytic dialogue. *International Journal of Psychoanalytic Self Psychology, 3*, 227–243.

Orange, D. M. (2010b). Revisiting mutual recognition: Responding to Ringstrom, Benjamin, and Slavin. *International Journal of Psychoanalytic Self Psychology*, *5*(3), 293–306.

Reed, H. (1996). Close encounters in the liminial zone: Experiments in imaginal communication part I. *Journal of Analytical Psychology*, *41*, 81–116.

Reis, B. (1999). Thomas Ogden's phenomenological turn. *Psychoanalytic Dialogues*, *9*(3), 371–393.

Renik, O. (1993). Analytic interaction: Conceptualizing technique in light of the analyst's irreducible subjectivity. *The Psychoanalytic Quarterly*, *62*, 553–571.

Samuels, A. (1985). Countertransference, the "mundus imaginalis" and a research project. *Journal of Analytical Psychology*, *30*, 47–71.

Schwartz-Salant, N. (1988). Archetypal foundations of projective identification. *Journal of Analytical Psychology*, *33*, 39–64.

Segal, R. A. (2007). Jung and Levy-Bruhl. *Journal of Analytical Psychology*, *52*, 635–658.

Starr, K. E. (2008). Faith as the fulcrum of psychic change: Metaphors of transformation in Jewish mysticism and psychoanalysis. *Psychoanalytic Dialogues*, *18*, 203–229.

Stern, D. N. (1985). *The interpersonal world of the infant: A view from psychoanalysis and developmental psychology*. New York: Basic Books.

Stern, D. N. (2004). *The present moment in psychotherapy and everyday life*. New York: Norton.

Stern, D. N. (2007). Applying developmental and neuroscience findings on other-centred participation to the process of change in psychotherapy. In S. Bråten (Ed.), *On being moved: From mirror neurons to empathy* (pp. 35–47). Amsterdam: John Benjamins Publishing Company.

Stern, R. (2012). Is Hegel's master: Slave dialectic a refutation of solipsism? *British Journal for the History of Philosophy*, *20*(2), 333–361.

Stevens, B. (1986). A Jungian perspective on transference and countertransference. *Contemporary Psychoanalysis*, *22*, 185–200.

Stolorow, R. D., & Atwood, G. E. (1992). *Contexts of being: The intersubjective foundations of psychological life*. New York: Routledge.

Stolorow, R. D., Atwood, G. E., & Ross, J. M. (1978). The representational world in psychoanalytic therapy. *The International Review of Psycho-Analysis*, *5*, 247–256.

Suchet, M. (2004). Whose mind is it anyway? *Studies in Gender and Sexuality*, *5*, 259–287.

Suchet, M. (2016). Surrender, transformation, and transcendence. *Psychoanalytic Dialogues*, *26*(6), 747–760.

Tennes, M. (2007). Beyond intersubjectivity. *Contemporary Psychoanalysis*, *43*, 505–525.

Trevarthen, C. (1979). Communication and cooperation in early infancy: A description of primary intersubjectivity. In M. Bullowa (Ed.), *Before speech*. Cambridge, UK: Cambridge University Press.

Trevarthen, C. (1998). The concept and foundations of infant intersubjectivity. In S. Braten (Ed.), *Intersubjective communication and emotion in early ontogeny* (pp. 15–46). Cambridge, UK: Cambridge University Press.

Trevarthen, C., & Hubley, P. (1978). Secondary intersubjectivity: Confidence, confiders and acts of meaning in the first year. In A. Lock (Ed.), *Action, gesture and symbol*. New York: Academic Press.

Ulanov, A. B. (2004). *Spiritual aspects of clinical work*. Einsiedeln: Daimon Verlag.

Varga, S. (2011). Winnicott, symbolic play, and other minds. *Philosophical Psychology, 24*(5), 625–637.

von Franz, M.-L. (1980). *Projection and re-collection in Jungian psychology: Reflections of the soul* (W. H. Kennedy, Trans.). La Salle & London: Open Court Publishing Company.

Welsh, T. (2007). Primal experience in Merleau-Ponty's philosophy and psychology. *Radical Psychology, 6*(1).

Winborn, M. (2014). *Shared realities: Participation mystique and beyond*. Skiatook, OK: Fisher King Press.

Winnicott, D. W. (1956). Primary maternal preoccupation. In *Through paediatrics to psycho-analysis: Collected papers* (pp. 300–305). New York: Brunner & Mazel.

Winnicott, D. W. (1971). *Playing and reality*. New York: Basic Books.

Chapter 3

Being psychological

With reference to the history of psychoanalysis, in this chapter I ask what it means to adopt a "psychological" position. In contrast to the close proximity of Freudian discourse to biology, I examine the notion of psychic primacy. I go on to explore how relational analysts have foregone a conceptual emphasis on the psyche in order to recognize the existence and influence of the social. This line of thinking leads to a claim that relationalists have tended to rely upon a secular conception of the social that must be revised if psychoanalytic practice is not to implicitly devalue spirituality.

During the mid-twentieth century, psychoanalysis experienced a form of mainstream recognition in many respects comparable to that which is now enjoyed by neuroscience. In the extent to which the mind has come to be interpreted as a byproduct of the brain, a depreciation of subjective experience often follows. The shift thus implied in our popular conceptions of selfhood might be considered significant. An increasing emphasis on biological models of mind has numerous ostensible causes, not the least of these being the manifold pressures exerted on clinical practice by the pharmaceutical industry. Nevertheless, it might be argued that a share of the responsibility must fall upon psychoanalysis itself. The medicalization of the profession in North America coupled with the field's early concern for questions of purity and fidelity to Freud engendered a constant political maneuvering such as to delimit that which was properly deemed "psychoanalytic." Had this tendency occurred under the banner of some broader and more inclusive signifier, the consequences may have been less adverse. Eugen Bleuler is credited with having coined "depth psychology" [*Tiefenpsychologie*] with just such a view in mind

(Ellenberger, 1970, p. 562). While this designation never gained wide-spread currency,[1] Kohut (1977) later adopted Bleuler's term in an effort to keep his own ideas related to an often hostile psychoanalytic mainstream. More recently, the term has come to be associated particularly with the Jungian community; sometimes to the extent that this notion is mistakenly thought synonymous with analytical psychology itself. Despite the efforts of those diverging from the Freudian orthodoxy, in popular perception *psychoanalysis* remains a far more widely recognized designation than *depth psychology*, and for this reason the less-inclusive term tends to significantly color perception of the field.

Recent efforts to re-evaluate the origins of depth psychology have demonstrated the extent to which Freud and his followers distorted the field's early history so as to reinforce his position as founding father (Shamdasani, 2003; Taylor, 2009). One of the consequences of this tendency has been to forcibly divorce psychoanalytic thinking from the wider history of Western ideas. Because psychoanalysis in the English-speaking world has come to stand for a whole swathe of intellectual activity that psychoanalysts have at the same time often not recognized, the fate of the field has influenced the history of ideas in ways that are complex and not always immediately apparent. It might be suggested that the Freudian legacy has, to a disproportionate extent, carried with it the responsibility for keeping alive the introspective approach to psychology. Pessimistically, it could even be argued that as a consequence of the belligerent fashion in which the early profession handled its affairs, the most significant influence psychoanalysis has had on our perceptions about the nature of mind in the present day lies merely in the role that the field played in hastening the rise of the biological reductionism that it was originally established in distinction to.

Coupled with the shift from a popular interest in psychoanalytic thought and the tropes of the unconscious to that of neurons and chemical imbalances is the emergence of a concern for the notion of *consciousness*. Many of the frustrated and sometimes contrary hopes attendant to the psychoanalytic milieu seem now to be evidenced in the ways in which this term has come to be deployed in academic discourse. For some, the notion of consciousness reflects nothing less than the final field of inquiry waiting to be demystified by scientific positivism. A *New York Times* opinion piece by Princeton psychologist Michael Graziano typifies this attitude. Graziano (2014) confidently claims that there are three great scientific questions pertaining to the human condition: [1] what is our place in the universe? [2] what is our place in life? and [3] what is the relationship between mind and matter? He argues that Copernicus and Darwin have answered the first and second of these questions, while contemporary neuroscience is on the verge of answering the third by disproving the existence of consciousness altogether. Although this supposed dissolving of the idea of consciousness is certainly nothing new, Graziano's particular framing of the question is telling. He seeks to establish the notion of consciousness as the ground upon which Western science is to claim its final victory. What is particularly striking about Graziano's way of phrasing things is that the form of his argument is an unattributed reworking of a claim that suggests something quite different – not that science is about to settle matters but, quite to the contrary, that humanity's place in the universe has been thrown into radical doubt. While the names of Newton and Darwin typically figure in this appraisal, just as they do for Graziano, the question of consciousness is in fact a substitute for the name of Freud. With this amendment the whole matter is given an altogether different cast. Where Copernicus, Darwin, and Freud are often invoked as a trio so as to question our pretensions of knowing, with Graziano's substitution of the subject of consciousness an inversion occurs by means of which the three "big questions" are made to seemingly lock down and confirm the truth claims of contemporary science.

It was in fact Freud himself who first made the connection between his own endeavor and that of Copernicus and Darwin. This association was ostensibly forged so as to explain why psychoanalysis was failing to gain widespread scientific approval. Freud (1917) contended that in recognizing the existence of the unconscious:

> Human megalomania will have suffered its third and most wounding blow from the psychological research of the present time which seeks to prove that the ego is not even master in its own house, but must content itself with scanty information of what is going on unconsciously in its mind.
>
> (p. 285)

While the kernel of this observation may well be of fundamental significance, it often seems that for Freud and his early followers the apparent recognition of the ego's having been de-seated was itself sometimes made basis for its very reinstatement upon the throne of reason – in the field's early history, the initiatory nature of a classical training analysis coupled with a technical emphasis on the role of interpretation served to promote the notion that the elect few had achieved a form of special insight not otherwise available to the general public. It might be thought ironic that in taking aim at the "megalomania" of others, Freud was nevertheless quite ready to associate his own genius with that of Copernicus and Darwin – while such a comparison might well be substantially warranted, Freud's willingness to promote this claim personally (and in context of a point being made about narcissism) still rings a little strangely. The relationship between self-humbling insight and a resultant tendency towards self-aggrandizing inflation has significantly marked the wider discourse of depth psychology. The latter trend has tended to be expressed with particular force wherever the field has sought to portray itself as an objective science associated with the practice of medicine.[2] Yet from the outset psychoanalysis has also exhibited an emancipatory sensibility reflecting a fundamental concern for the value of the individual.

Despite the field's early association with medicine and more recent attraction to the perceived legitimations of neuroscience, psychoanalytic theory and practice has always been in essence *psychological*. The meaning of this assertion is complicated by virtue of the fashion in which the definition of "psychology" has been shaped by institutional forces. The practice of psychology has been forged on the basis of a scientific ideal maintained by means of an emphasis on empirical research. Owing to the fashion in which scientific standards have tended to favor quantitative research over more qualitative approaches, the field of psychology has historically favored externally verifiable data (i.e. behavior) over the products of introspection. With advances in brain imaging, the desire for consensual validation has sometimes resulted in a belief that we can objectively establish what's going on "inside" of the mind with reference to neuroscience – the evidence of external behavior can now be supplemented with that of internal brain states. While the vast popularity of neuroscience among contemporary psychologists is understandable, it contributes to a further blurring of the distinction between a psychological outlook and a biological one. If psychology is understood to be the study of the mind, then a psychological position is one that would posit the immediacy of experience as its foundational point of reference. Demoting the role of introspection in favor of physical observation seems to imply that the field of psychology is merely a temporary lean-to in the quest for material understanding. Thus, in its very effort to secure legitimacy the profession of psychology is in danger of registering itself obsolete.

The emphasis on biology often implies some fixed and often unexamined beliefs concerning the relationship between mind and matter. Fundamentally, this emphasis tends to presuppose that the former is a byproduct of the latter. It also suggests that by means of human endeavor it is possible to transcend the conditions of mind in order to objectively grasp matter. That is, despite the fact that the field of psychology takes as its object the human subject, it is assumed that our subjectivity can somehow be transcended by means of itself so as to subsequently explain itself.[3] That the profoundly religious nature of such an undertaking goes largely unrecognized is unfortunate, for it often results in saddling the adherents of other belief systems with some rather heavy baggage (e.g. Dawkins, 2008; Dennett, 2007).

It is widely acknowledged that Freud modeled himself as a positivist, and that a significant reason for his doing so was as a means of distancing psychoanalysis from philosophy. Tauber (2009) writes:

> Freud's embrace of scientism and positivism followed the fashion of his time. By the end of the 19th century, the natural sciences, left to their own technical pursuits, ascended to great heights of technical mastery of nature. That success required an epistemology, which seemingly built from commonsensical notions of empirical knowledge, and by successfully responding, positivist philosophy assumed its hegemonic hold on the scientific community. When Freud entered the scientific community, investigators began to refer to themselves as "scientists" instead of "natural philosophers" [. . .] positivism, which seeks radically neutral and objective knowledge (frequently omitting to account for its own values and self-refuting assumptions), organized Freud's ever-present desire to legitimize psychoanalysis by linking its theories and the clinical data upon which they were based with those sciences that he thought had achieved a kind of objectivity he admired.
>
> (p. 34)

Yet Freud's wish to establish psychoanalysis on the terms of positivistic science were never realized. Freud's *Project for a Scientific Psychology* (1895) was abandoned precisely as a consequence of his being unable to find neurological support for his speculative approach.[4] The endogenous physiological force of Q postulated by Freud in 1895, returns as the boundary concept of libido in his later work. While this notion continues to be conceptualized in the mechanistic/hydraulic terms of the *Project*, this style of thinking is now apparently to be understood as metaphorical. Nevertheless, we are hard-pressed not to come away with a sense that Freud is still speaking literally.[5]

Freud's adoption of a psychological position appears to be required not on principle but as a consequence of the limits of early twentieth-century brain science.[6] By contrast, Jung professes to adopt this position in the cause of upholding a fundamental philosophical stance. His assertion as to the "reality of the psyche" (1952, para. 1507) reflects a commitment to the immediacy of subjective experience – that is, the quality of being "real" is defined in terms of the immediate experience of the individual. Any question of invoking a world "external" to the psyche is to be treated with some measure of circumspection. While this is certainly not to the active *denial* of consensual realities, it does suggest that these realities should never be treated as a basis from which to annul subjective experience. Postulates such as "matter" or "society" are to be approached in terms of the problems of adaptation that they present for the individual, and not as arbitrators of ultimate truth.

In articulating this distinction between the experienced needs of adaptation and the active acceptance of collective truths, Jung's psychology differs fundamentally with conventional psychoanalytic assumptions. For Freud, words are the markers of mature psychic functioning precisely because they are oriented towards the external world. Freud contrasts *word-presentations* with *thing-presentations*. Word-presentations are associated with the secondary process and reflect a linkage between verbal stimulus and conscious idea. Thing-presentations, by contrast, are images of objects. The preconscious comes into existence by means of a hypercathexis linking thing-presentations to word-presentations. It is this process that enables the emergence of higher mental functioning as the secondary process comes to gain ascendency over the primary process. In the absence of the structure imposed by language, thing-representations are pulled down into the service of the Id and thus rendered unconscious. Freud (1915) states: "A presentation that is not put into words, or a psychical act which is not hypercathected, remains thereafter in the *Ucs.* in a state of repression" (p. 202).

For Freud, consciousness is thus fundamentally dependent on language. Jung, by contrast, does not tie conscious experience exclusively to language. In asserting the primacy of the psyche, Jung implies that what is referred to in Freudian terms as "primary process" is not entirely alien to consciousness. Jung asserts the experiential primacy of the maternal realm of images over the paternal realm of language, stating that "the psyche consists essentially of images" (1926, para. 618) and that "image *is* psyche" (1929, para. 75). Thus, while in a classical Freudian context upholding a psychological position is reflective merely of adopting a metaphorical position that is assumed to ultimately correlate with a material reality (brain anatomy), in a Jungian frame of reference to adopt a psychological stance is to emphasize that all forms of directed thinking (including, we must assume, neuroscience)[7] are always subtended by unconscious fantasy.[8] A similar idea is forwarded by Melanie Klein, who extends Freud's drive concept to be inclusive of the idea of an external object. This shift reflects a sense that the drive is not only more integrally related to the world but also to the functioning of the mind; a sensibility that would inform Bion's theory of thinking, wherein the capacity to dream (which, for Bion, subtends all conscious activity) is dependent on the capacity to synthesize the raw data of experience (beta elements) to form pictograms (alpha elements). For Bion, a preconception of a thing is necessary in order that the individual should be able to formulate a conception of it. A conception emerges where a preconception coincides with a realization. The Oedipal myth, for instance, is considered to reflect a preconception that enables a certain kind of knowledge about the parents.

It is noteworthy that just as Jung's later work tended to emphasize the spiritual rather than instinctual pole of the archetype, in developing his notion of preconception, Bion similarly moved away from a phylogenetic perspective (Luzes, 2005).[9] Sullivan (2009) observes that Jung's emphasis on the primacy of psychic reality reflects a significant line of commonality with Bion: "Jung and Bion both begin with the psyche itself" (p. 35).[10] Bion goes so far as to suggest that the proper material of the analytic encounter is the immediate emotional experience of the analytic hour, and that information purporting to concern matters in the outside world constitutes what he terms *hearsay evidence*:

I have learnt from this sort of thing that the evidence made available to you by any patient who actually turns up is far and away of greater consequence than anything you hear said – hearsay evidence, evidence the patient gives you about other people. When I have interpreted these facts – that so-and-so had written a letter, descriptions about the relationship of this patient with somebody else, but nothing whatever about the patient – that was really falling for it and treating hearsay evidence as being of real importance. I suppose it is of real importance with patients who are less disturbed, or with whose lesser degree of disturbance one is dealing, but I do put it in a very, very low category of analytic evidence.

(Bion, 1976–1979, pp. 59–60)

Antonino Ferro has subsequently argued that this emphasis on the here-and-now emotional experience of the field needn't be understood as an injunction to ignore what Bion refers to as hearsay evidence, but rather that it implies understanding all references to events external to the field as a form of commentary on it – more specifically (reflecting Ferro's particular take on Bion), as a commentary on the analyst's role as a container. Ferro (2009) endorses a form of listening that assumes "a zero degree of external reality in any communication by the patient" (p. 211). Such an outlook is of course not to deny the reality of events occurring outside the analytic encounter, but to assume that any reference to such events occurring within the therapeutic situation should be heard as a response to the recent functioning of the analyst in their role as container. Ferro is suggesting that the analytic relationship provides a crucible in which the patient's presentation is assumed to reflect an expression of their intrapsychic relationship to the analyst's interpretive activity. Ferro (2009) speaks of transformations in dreaming, "in which the analyst precedes every communication by the patient with a kind of 'magic filter' comprising the words 'I had a dream in which . . . '; this represents the highest possible level of positive functioning of the field – namely, when the field itself dreams" (p. 214).

This challenging position naturally invites criticism. While offering a sympathetic engagement with Ferro's work, Donnel Stern (2015) argues: "To understand everything the patient says as a dream makes the external world into nothing more than a means of expression and deprives trauma of a meaningful place in the genesis of human problems" (p. 95). For Stern, the notion that events external to the analytic situation would only be raised as a form of commentary on it is equated with a denial that the outside world can meaningfully impact the intrapsychic. This line of criticism is offered in response to Ferro's clinical approach, which itself depends on the particular definition of the analytic field Ferro adopts. Ferro's outlook appears to require that the individual psyche is only transcended in some respect in the special case of the container-contained relationship. Thus, to remain committed to an intrapsychic position entails that the analyst should interpret all events transpiring within the analysis in terms of their role as a container.[11] What links the imagination of the clinician with that of the patient is the projective-identificatory dynamism of the container-contained relationship. The imaginative field is co-constructed, and not in any respect preexistent. In contrast to this strictly intrapsychic position, Stern suggests that more relationally oriented analysts tend to emphasize a dialectical approach reflecting the mutually constitutive yet distinct nature of internal and external worlds.

In delegitimizing the analyst's role as an arbitrator of final truth, relationalists have drawn attention to how fundamentally problematic the relationship between inner and outer reality actually is:

> What has been on offer from contemporary psychoanalytic theory in general and relational theory in particular, is that we can never be entirely satisfied with sharply differentiated determinations about the extent to which our patient is elaborating his relationships to unconscious internalized objects or the other within the interpersonal setting of analysis.
>
> (Cooper, 2018, p. 193)

This uncertainty also extends to the clinician. Thus, from a relational perspective, the post-Bionian outlook is suspect not only because it fails to address the impact of events external to the treatment but also because it fails to account sufficiently for the analyst's unconscious participation. Ferro's thinking reflects an apparent belief that the analyst can function as a self-contained container.[12] For relationalists this position is inadequate, for it fails to account for the enacted dimension of the treatment. Despite the extent to which Bion's work endorses psychic primacy, the notion of a self-contained container suggests that the permeability of the analyst's mind can be modulated in a very controlled way – an approach to practice that implies that the analyst can gain sufficient mastery over the unconscious as to be able to suspend personal needs and motivations.

In responding to this perhaps excessively enclosed conception of the analyst's psyche, we might suppose that the relational challenge to this outlook points to a more transpersonal conception of psychic life. This is not so, however, for the significant reason that most relationalists do not "begin with" the psyche. Instead, relational thinking has often tended to start from a conception of *the social*. For some relationalists, the intrapsychic may appear to reflect nothing more than the causally determined internalization of prior social experience. Thus, the apparently more "balanced" approach relationalists seek to offer is sometimes misleading. While it is certainly true that relational thinkers have done much to problematize hard distinctions between the interpersonal and the intrapsychic, the psyche itself is often implicitly treated as a product of social conditioning.

Grasping the implications of this emphasis on the social is important if we are to appreciate the potential shortcomings of contemporary psychoanalysis as a spiritually receptive discourse. Rather than locating the origins of psychic life in the unconscious – a principle that can readily be interpreted in accordance with its original philosophical sense as a spiritual ground – relational thinking is prone to posit a secular (i.e. *disenchanted*) conception of the social field as primary, thus tending to implicitly conceptualize the soul as a socially conditioned byproduct. Resultantly, the psyche is not allowed creative autonomy – this being reflected quite clearly wherever relationalists treat conceptions of selfhood and agency as necessary fictions.

If we are to uphold the primacy of the psyche, must we forego the relational emphasis on the social? My response to this question is an unequivocal "no." However, meeting this challenge requires a radically different way of thinking about the environment. Should we insist on maintaining a secular/disenchanted understanding of the social field, then we will be hard-pressed to uphold a relational approach to treatment that is not implicitly demeaning of both the human subject and spirituality. If the psyche is to come first without surrendering our emphasis on the social, then we must consider that the external world is in some respect psychic. Such an idea enables the possibility that the external world might be considered creatively expressive of psychic life, and not merely causally determinative. This would imply that there is some degree of personally meaningful intentionality in events seemingly external to the person. In the following three chapters I seek to give some sense of how a re-enchanted worldview might shape clinical practice.

Notes

1 Freud (1914) briefly acknowledges this appellation only to state that it is directly equatable with "psychoanalysis" (p. 41).

2 While the medicalizing of the profession has historically reflected the most obviously normative influence on practice, with the relational shift a new normative tendency has perhaps started to emerge in terms of a more explicit *politicizing* of the field (see Brown, in press).

3 In a related sense, as though *wired for it*, human beings invented computers only to subsequently think of themselves *as* computers.

4 Lothane (1998) states: "The amount of genuine brain science in the *Project* is small compared to the preponderance of brain mythology, that is, a restatement of common psychological phenomena, such as thought, perception, memory, dreaming, and speech, in the language of brain anatomy and physiology" (p. 63).

5 As Bishop (2010) observes, it is Freud's retention of this style of expressing himself (despite no longer dealing in physiology) that pushes his work closer to vitalism (p. 51). Barratt (2016, 2018) argues that Freud's concept of *Trieb* subverts Cartesian mind/body dualism by positing an intermediate term that is neither reducible to biology (for it is not equivalent to *Instinkte*) nor mental operations (since, while it fuels representation, it cannot be represented in itself). Barratt relates Freud's thinking in this regard with Eastern ideas concerning subtle energy.

6 It is on this basis that recent proponents of neuropsychoanalysis (e.g. Northoff, 2011; Schwartz, 2015; Solms, 2015) seek justification in attempting to reclaim the Freudian project along neurological lines.

7 Shamdasani (2003) goes so far as to suggest that "Jung held that psychology constituted the fundamental scientific discipline, upon which other disciplines should henceforth be based. In his view, it was the only discipline which could grasp the subjective factor that underlay other sciences" (p. 15).

8 This implies a fundamental limitation in terms of the dominant empirical research paradigm as a means to doing psychology (cf. Smedslund, 2009, 2016).

9 For an examination of significant areas of overlap in the work of Bion and Jung, see Sullivan (2009) and Winborn (2018).

10 With particular reference to recent post-Bionian scholarship, Connolly (2018) speaks of an "aesthetic turn" in psychoanalytic thinking such as to reflect an increasing compatibility with Jungian discourse.

11 In agreement with relational thinking, Ferro does not work with a view to uncovering historical truth. Instead, he is concerned with the transformation of experience and the development of mind. The analyst's role is to assist the patient in symbolizing emotional experience. In this context, the analyst is not invested in the reality (or otherwise) of external events

raised by the patient, but considers any statement made by the patient to be reflective of his or her current position in relationship to the analyst's function as an interpreter/metabolizer of the patient's experience. The analyst never gets so far as being concerned with the analysis of events external to the treatment, since to do so would entail surrendering the analyst's proper function. An approach of this nature does not consider external events to be irrelevant to the life of the patient, but it does consider that if the analyst adopts a correct technical approach then these events will only be relevant *to the treatment* as material for the analyst's metabolizing function.

12 Supervisory considerations notwithstanding.

References

Barratt, B. B. (2016). *Radical psychoanalysis: An essay on free-associative praxis*. New York: Routledge.

Barratt, B. B. (2018). On the otherwise energies of the human spirit: A contemporary comparison of Freudian and Jungian approaches. In R. S. Brown (Ed.), *Re-encountering Jung: Analytical psychology and contemporary psychoanalysis* (pp. 47–67). New York: Routledge.

Bion, W. R. (1976–1979). The Tavistock seminars. In *The complete works of W. R. Bion* (Vol. 9, pp. 1–92). London: Karnac Books.

Bishop, P. (2010). The unconscious from the storm and stress to Weimar Classicism: The dialectic of time and pleasure. In A. Nicholls & M. Liebscher (Eds.), *Thinking the unconscious: Nineteenth-century German thought* (pp. 26–56). Cambridge, UK: Cambridge University Press.

Brown, R. S. (in press). Relational normativity in the politics of North American psychoanalysis: Some clinical reflections on the notion of privilege. *Psychoanalytic Dialogues*.

Connolly, A. (2018). Sea changes: The iconic and aesthetic turns in depth psychology. In R. S. Brown (Ed.), *Re-encountering Jung: Analytical psychology and contemporary psychoanalysis* (pp. 68–82). New York: Routledge.

Cooper, S. H. (2018). The things we carry: Finding/creating the object and the analyst's self-reflective participation. In L. Aron, S. Grand, & J. Slochower (Eds.), *De-idealizing relational theory: A critique from within* (pp. 191–208). London & New York: Routledge.

Dawkins, R. (2008). *The God delusion*. New York: Mariner Books.

Dennett, D. C. (2007). *Breaking the spell: Religion as a natural phenomenon*. New York: Penguin Books.

Ellenberger, H. F. (1970). *The discovery of the unconscious: The history and evolution of dynamic psychiatry*. New York: Basic Books.

Ferro, A. (2009). Transformations in dreaming and characters in the psychoanalytic field. *International Journal of Psychoanalysis, 90*(2), 209–230.

Freud, S. (1895). Project for a scientific psychology. In J. Strachey (Ed.), *The standard edition of the complete psychological works of Sigmund Freud* (Vol. 1, pp. 281–391). London: The Hogarth Press.

Freud, S. (1914). On the history of the psycho-analytic movement. In J. Strachey (Ed.), *The standard edition of the complete psychological works of Sigmund Freud* (Vol. 14, pp. 1–66). London: The Hogarth Press.

Freud, S. (1915). The unconscious. In J. Strachey (Ed.), *The standard edition of the complete psychological works of Sigmund Freud* (Vol. 14, pp. 159–215). London: The Hogarth Press.

Freud, S. (1917). Introductory lectures on psycho-analysis. In J. Strachey (Ed.), *The standard edition of the complete psychological works of Sigmund Freud* (Vol. 16, pp. 241–463). London: The Hogarth Press.

Graziano, M. (2014, October 12). Are we really conscious? *New York Times*.

Jung, C. G. (1926). Spirit and life. In *Collected works* (Vol. 8, pp. 319–337). Princeton, NJ: Princeton University Press.

Jung, C. G. (1929). Commentary on "the secret of the golden flower". In *Collected works* (Vol. 13, pp. 1–56). Princeton, NJ: Princeton University Press.

Jung, C. G. (1952). Religion and psychology: A reply to Martin Buber. In *Collected works* (Vol. 18, pp. 663–670). Princeton, NJ: Princeton University Press.

Kohut, H. (1977). *The restoration of the self*. New York: International Universities Press, Inc.

Lothane, Z. (1998). Freud's 1895 project: From mind to brain and back again. *Annals of the New York Academy of Sciences, 843*, 43–65.

Luzes, P. (2005). Preconception. In *International dictionary of psychoanalysis*. New York: Thomson Gale.

Northoff, G. (2011). *Neuropsychoanalysis in practice: Brain, self and objects*. New York: Oxford University Press.

Schwartz, C. (2015). *In the mind fields: Exploring the new science of neuropsychoanalysis*. New York: Pantheon Books.

Shamdasani, S. (2003). *Jung and the making of modern psychology: The dream of a science*. Cambridge, UK & New York: Cambridge University Press.

Smedslund, J. (2009). The mismatch between current research methods and the nature of psychological phenomena: What researchers must learn from practitioners. *Theory & Psychology, 19*(6), 778–794.

Smedslund, J. (2016). Why psychology cannot be an empirical science. *Integrative Psychological and Behavioral Science, 50*(2), 185–195.

Solms, M. (2015). *The feeling brain: Selected papers on neuropsychoanalysis*. London, UK: Karnac Books.

Stern, D. B. (2015). *Relational freedom: Emergent properties of the interpersonal field*. Hove, UK & New York: Routledge.

Sullivan, B. S. (2009). *The mystery of analytical work: Weavings from Jung and Bion*. New York: Routledge.

Tauber, A. I. (2009). Freud's philosophical path: From a science of mind to a philosophy of human being. *The Scandinavian Psychoanalytic Review, 32,* 32–43.

Taylor, E. (2009). *The mystery of personality: A history of psychodynamic theories.* San Francisco, CA: Springer.

Winborn, M. (2018). Bion and Jung: Intersecting vertices. In R. S. Brown (Ed.), *Re-encountering Jung: Analytical psychology and contemporary psychoanalysis* (pp. 85–112). New York: Routledge.

Part II

Clinical reflections

Chapter 4

Panpsychism and psychotherapy

Drawing from Jung's work on synchronicity, I articulate a "panpsychic" approach to treatment and begin to articulate a range of clinical benefits. I suggest that this outlook complements recent efforts to outline a teleological approach to enactment, and that the notion of enactment suggests a uniquely psychoanalytic approach to disenchantment.

As an attitude towards clinical work, psychic primacy can be understood as an interpretive commitment to the soul's telos.[1] Such an approach contrasts with a focus on material causes – whether expressed in terms of biological reductivism or a disenchanted conception of the social field. In emphasizing that the soul comes first, we assume an outlook that is concerned with the emerging meaning of the individual's experience. It is important to emphasize that psychic primacy does not entail rejecting causes, but rather assumes a causal outlook to be incomplete. If the role of biology and environment are not to be neglected in this scheme of thinking, they must be understood as related to, and expressive of, the soul.

Panpsychism is a philosophical school of thinking which suggests that consciousness or soul is a universal quality of the natural world. In his last major work, Jung (1955–56) writes: "It may well be a prejudice to restrict the psyche to being 'inside the body.' In so far as the psyche has a non-spatial aspect, there may be a psychic 'outside-the-body'" (para. 410). Key to understanding how Jung comes to make this assertion is his notion of synchronicity. Jung (1952) defines synchronicity as "the simultaneous occurrence of a certain psychic state with one or more external events which appear as meaningful parallels to the momentary subjective state" (para. 850). Jung came to this notion via his interest in paranormal phenomena, his observation of dreams, and through his work with patients.

The quintessential example of synchronicity offered from Jung's clinical practice is given with the incident of the scarab beetle:

> My example concerns a young woman patient who, in spite of efforts made on both sides, proved to be psychologically inaccessible. The difficulty lay in the fact that she always knew better about everything. Her excellent education had provided her with a weapon ideally suited to this purpose, namely a highly polished Cartesian rationalism with an impeccably "geometrical" idea of reality. After several fruitless attempts to sweeten her rationalism with a somewhat more human understanding, I had to confine myself to the hope that something unexpected and irrational would turn up, something that would burst the intellectual retort into which she had sealed herself. Well, I was sitting opposite her one day, with my back to the window, listening to her flow of rhetoric. She had an impressive dream the night before, in which someone had given her a golden scarab – a costly piece of jewelry. While she was still telling me this dream, I heard something behind me gently tapping on the window. I turned round and saw that it was a fairly large flying insect that was knocking against the window-pane from outside in the obvious effort to get into the dark room. This seemed to me very strange. I opened the window immediately and caught the insect in the air as it flew in. It was a scarabaeid beetle, or common rose-chafer (*Cetonia aurata*), whose gold-green color most nearly resembles that of a golden scarab. I handed the beetle to my patient with the words, "Here is your scarab." This experience punctured the desired hole in her rationalism and broke the ice of her intellectual resistance. The treatment could now be continued with satisfactory results.
>
> (para. 982)

Jung's first recorded use of the term "synchronicity" was in 1930 (Jung, 1957), but it was another 22 years before he treated this subject systematically (Jung, 1952). Although Jung came to formulate his ideas about synchronicity through personal and clinical experience, his approach to talking about this notion in print emphasized trying to link his thinking with quantum physics (see Jung & Pauli, 2000). He sought to establish synchronicity as a scientific principle at the expense of examining this question more extensively in terms of clinical work and human affairs.

This reflects Jung's concern to establish his challenging ideas about synchronicity in a manner that might enable them to be accepted and understood by a broad audience.

In the extent to which Jung sought to illustrate synchronicity with reference to personal experience, Progoff (1973) suggests that Jung focuses on the more "dramatic" examples of this phenomenon in order to underscore his point. This emphasis may have been at the expense of a broader recognition of the relevance of this principle in our daily lives. Progoff argues that this tendency can give the misleading sense that synchronicity is only an occasional phenomenon: "We shall very likely find that the events in which the principle of Synchronicity is expressed are much more numerous than we have realized. They occur in small, unobserved ways all through our lives" (p. 166). This perspective is also supported by Jung's close colleague Marie-Louise von Franz who, in citing a statement of Jung's concerning the relationship between atomic physics and psychology, states:

> At first sight, "mirrorings" of psyche and matter that have the same meaning can be empirically established only in the relatively rare and irregularly occurring synchronistic events. It seems likely to me, however, that Jung's observation that the reconstruction of psychic processes in the microphysical world probably occurs as continuously as the psyche perceives the external world is to be understood in the sense that this mirror-relation exists *continuously* in the deeper layers of the unconscious but that we become aware of it only in certain exceptional situations in which synchronistic phenomena become observable. That would mean that in the deepest layer of the unconscious the psyche "knows" itself in the mirror of the cosmic world and that matter "knows" itself in the mirror of the objective psyche, but this "knowledge" is "absolute" in the sense that for our ego it is almost completely consciousness-transcending. Only in those rare moments when we are impressed by synchronistic phenomena do we become conscious of fragments or points of the mirror-relation.
>
> (von Franz, 1980, pp. 194–195)

The significance of Jung's notion of synchronicity and its place in the wider scheme of his psychology is readily underestimated. This is partly consequent upon the fact that Jung only formally introduced the concept and its broader implications in his late work. However, the shift heralded by the emergence of the synchronistic worldview can be understood as a response to theoretical tensions that can be traced throughout Jung's career. These tensions are reflective of the Cartesian basis upon which Jung grounded his ideas about typology.

In *Psychological Types* Jung first introduces the notions of introversion and extraversion. It should be noted that the typological distinction Jung establishes has considerable relevance for psychoanalytic thinking about the relationship between inner life and the external world. Jung's work offers a significant way of understanding the different emphases that come through in our divergent approaches to this question. In the extent to which a clinician's theory of personality privileges factors conventionally considered to be external to the individual, the approach thus suggested can be thought fundamentally extraverted in nature. Likewise, clinicians who tend to approach the patient looking through a more internal or intrapsychic lens adopt a more introverted frame of reference. Thus efforts to reconcile the attitudes or consciousness without reducing one to the other have direct relevance for contemporary debates in psychoanalysis (for example, the dispute between relational and Bionian field theorists).

In Chapter 1, I argued that Jung's earlier work was significantly shaped by his efforts to avoid betraying a paranoid outlook. This resulted in him emphasizing the role of introspective fantasy (via active imagination) as the means to directly access the unconscious, and thus privileging introversion. The extravert, by contrast, always encounters the unconscious at a remove – i.e. projectively. Jung privileges introversion by asserting the primacy of the subjective factor while appearing to assume that this factor resides *within* individuals. At the same time, however, Jung is very much concerned with attempting to articulate a psychology that transcends "the personal equation" as expressed in the biases of a theorist's own typology (see Shamdasani, 2003). As such, the implicit privileging of introversion reflected in the emphasis that the clinical application of Jung's psychology places on the retraction of projections could not afford to go unchallenged.

Jung's work does come to address this question, but in a manner that lacks significant clinical elaboration. In his later work, drawing from the alchemist Gerhard Dorn (1530–1584), Jung's engagement with the idea of the *unus mundus* [one world] reflects his philosophical adoption of a dual-aspect monism wherein the internal world on the one hand, and the interpersonal/cultural/environmental on the other, are considered expressions of the same underlying reality. This position enables the possibility both of recognizing the ways in which our everyday experience tends to register these two domains as distinct, and to make sense of participatory experiences of meaning – experiences of intimacy, synchronicities, and non-ordinary states that can occur both spontaneously or via spiritual practice. As the individual moves forward in his or her individuation, it seems possible that extraversion no longer serves only the needs of a person's adaptation to society, but rather society's adaptation by means of the individual to the evolving demands of the collective unconscious. Additionally, since with this new model the unconscious can express itself through matter, attending to outer events can directly serve the individuation process – the collectivity of the unconscious offers a bridge not just to other people but to all things external. In this way, the synchronicity principle can be understood as an attempt to identify and describe the participatory relationship between self and world.

Teleology and enactment

The idea that events in the external world are inherently meaningful in their relationship to the individual is clearly challenging. Such an idea is perhaps liable to be dismissed by many clinicians as fanciful and off-puttingly New-Agey. However, recent developments in psychoanalysis would appear to point in this direction. The seed of this radical perspective is to be discerned in the phenomenology of enactment.

The concept of enactment emerged so as to describe the fashion in which one party's acting out (usually the patient) elicits a complementary acting out in the other (usually the analyst). Patient and analyst thus join to play out a shared drama that is reflective of their past experiences, and of which both remain unconscious. Enactment was initially understood to reflect episodic disruptions to the treatment wherein patient and analyst collude to create a therapeutic impasse out of their mutual resistances. This episodic conception of enactment has been increasingly challenged, however, with a recognition that patient and analyst alike are *constantly* influencing each other in ways that are unconscious. It has therefore been suggested that rather than approaching enactment in episodic terms, we might more correctly think of enactment as a constant factor in therapeutic work. In this light it seems sensible to suppose that enactment is by no means inherently destructive, but only becomes problematic at certain moments where treatment can fall into an impasse so that the parties must somehow become aware of the unconscious dynamics that have gotten them stuck. Contemporary relational analysts are increasingly coming to assume that there may be something healing about the enactive process itself – that while some forms of enactment are destructive, others can be creative.

A significant step has recently been taken by Galit Atlas and Lewis Aron in seeking to bring our attention to the teleology of enactive process. Drawing from Ferenczi, Jung, Bion, and Searles; Atlas and Aron (2018) argue that we should consider enactment to be inherently creative:

> We are suggesting [. . .] that the flow of enactive engagement, the enactive dimension of analysis, may at times be fecund and transformative in and of itself, not only by working one's way out of it. Our argument for generative enactment is tied to and builds on our assumption that enactments dramatize, bring to life, not only the individual's conflicts but the intersubjective field, allowing for its growth and transformation through dramatic dialogue.
>
> (p. 13)

How is this teleological dimension of enactment to be conceptualized? From a classical transference-based perspective, a teleological attitude considers that the re-actualization of past experience is not driven merely out of reactive repetition but is also expressive of the psyche's drive towards a different sort of outcome. In this light, the patient doesn't behave in a particular way simply because it's what they know but out of a creative impulse that works towards a different conclusion. This notion is already evident in "Remembering, Repeating and Working Through," wherein Freud (1914) suggests that the compulsion to repeat is in the service of the patient's unconscious attempts to remember. Building on this point of view, the teleology of enactment might be understood to reflect a creative impulse understood to reside "within" both analysand and analyst so that their actions in the treatment can be considered (in some degree) performative of a change that both members of the dyad seek to realize both outwardly and within themselves. This understanding of events entails an additive approach to the respective contribution of both participants.

However, if we are to adopt a field-focused outlook then our conceptualization of the teleology of enactment cannot be confined to the respective contributions of the two participants. In attributing a teleology to the field itself, we find ourselves moving towards a panpsychic outlook on treatment. In agreement with the position taken in the present work concerning the need of establishing an intrapsychic ground upon which recognition might be founded (see Chapter 2), towards the conclusion of their most recent work, Atlas and Aron state:

> Unconscious communication is simply an expression of minds being inherently intersubjective. Intersubjectivity is not a joining of separate subjects but rather precedes and is the ground for it. On a deep unconscious level, we are always already interconnected and at one.
>
> (Atlas & Aron, 2018, p. 153)

It is in this light that Atlas and Aron go so far as to state: "We are calling for a return of the 'soul,' of the 'psyche,' of soulfulness and spirit back to psychology" (Atlas & Aron, 2018, p. 137). The necessity of their making this claim remains largely implicit in their work. One of the tasks of the present text is to make more explicit why this "return of the soul" is necessary for the evolution of relational psychoanalysis.

While the notion of acting out entails a one way relationship between the intrapsychic life of the patient and its external expression, as a two-person phenomenon enactment complicates things. It is certainly possible to understand enactment as shaped fundamentally by the mutual inducements of patient and analyst. However, in addition to reflecting a rejection of a field-focused approach to the treatment, experience shows that the specificity of the fit between patient and clinician is often uncannily apt (Connolly, 2015; Davoine & Gaudillière, 2004; de Peyer, 2016; Grof, 2006; Mayer, 2001, 2007; Suchet, 2016; Tennes, 2007). As Bass (2001) writes: "Such moments, reflecting deep and sometimes mystifying points of connection and receptivity, have always been part of the experience of being an analyst" (p. 688). If we entertain the idea that the analyst's prior experience often seems to render him or her a carefully (or perhaps even uniquely) matched fit for the process, then the sense emerges of a teleological influence upon the patient that is liable to be understood not only as emanating from within but also in equal measure as emanating in some sense from without in terms of the coincidental fit with the analyst.

Thinking in these terms, it is possible to understand the unconsciously choreographed nature of enactment as a manifestation of synchronicity. This would recall Progoff and von Franz's claims that synchronistic phenomena are probably much more common than we suppose – perhaps even a constant. The psychoanalytic literature on enactment may therefore be understood to reflect a hugely significant clinical supplement to Jung's more speculative work on synchronicity. Meanwhile, situating enactment in terms of synchronicity may prove informative for clinical practice. Understood synchronistically, it might be suggested that the notion of enactment offers a way of conceptualizing and working therapeutically with re-enchantment.

Transpersonal psychologist Michael Washburn (1994) offers an integrative developmental approach that seeks to reconcile psychoanalytic ideas about ego development with Jungian ideas about ego transcendence. He conceptualizes psychoanalytic dualism as follows:

> This dualism is at once an intrapsychic (i.e., egoic-nonegoic) dualism and an interpersonal (i.e., self-other) dualism. The intrapsychic side of the dualism is based ultimately on primal repression, the interpersonal side on primal alienation. Primal repression and primal alienation [. . .] are not two different structures but rather are two different (inner and outer) dimensions of the same structure. Correspondingly, dualism is not divided into separate intrapsychic and interpersonal forms; it is a single *bidirectional* division of the psyche.
>
> (p. 73, emphasis in original)

In illustrating this position, Washburn (1995) offers the example of anxiety/guilt in relationship to achieving independence from the parents. He points out that this phenomenon can be understood both in interpersonal terms as the external struggle with parental others, and in intrapsychic terms as the ego's struggle with super-egoic constraints. He observes that these struggles are two sides of one and the same process (p. 101). In distinction to some contemporary psychoanalytic approaches that would seek to "overcome" Cartesianism by reductively collapsing the individual into their social context, an outlook of this kind considers dualism as in some degree developmentally inevitable. This approach suggests that while the intrapsychic cannot be considered ultimately distinct from the interpersonal, attempting to transcend this dualism is a fundamentally transformative task and not a merely intellectual one.

Efforts to address Cartesian thinking within contemporary psychoanalysis are most closely associated with the intersubjective self psychologists in their efforts to challenge what Stolorow and Atwood (1992) dub "the myth of the isolated mind" (p. 7). A major difficulty that arises with any theoretical approach that would seek to annul or radically minimize the intrapsychic, is that such an approach would seem to require endorsing a kind of behavioral reflexivity. An outlook of this sort can readily imply that personal experience is nothing more than an epiphenomenon of social conditioning. This being the case, it becomes difficult to justify the possibility of meaningful therapeutic intervention.

Gray (2013) asserts that endorsing a distinction between interior and exterior worlds by no means implies a subsequently unbridgeable separation, and draws attention to the ethical problems that arise in refusing this distinction:

> In my view, the interior/exterior trope is an important psychophilosophical, ethical, and phenomenological distinction. The idea that we are autonomous beings who are responsible for our actions and who are in relationship with other autonomous beings similarly thought of, that we are orientated towards those beings, and they to us, is constituted in part by the inner/outer trope. Thus a dissolution of the inner/outer trope would have far-reaching ethical and existential implications simply because we are all in the world, part of the world, yet able to bracket the world and turn in upon ourselves.
>
> (p. 80)

In the context of a psychotherapeutic theory, the absence of a "within" to things collapses difference and seems to cast doubt on what it is that's being worked with. Even the intersubjective self psychologists are required to accept the existence of organizing principles, and have acknowledged that their claims to have transcended dualism were perhaps too hasty (Atwood & Stolorow, 2014, pp. 139–140).

Stolorow, Atwood, and Orange (2002) appear to offer a position that might be considered compatible with the perspective offered in the present chapter when they speak of the notion of a *psychological world*, which they prefer to the Cartesian subject-object distinction: "A knower cannot be an item in the world. Instead, the experiential world seems to be both inhabited by and inhabiting the human individual. People live in worlds, and worlds in people" (p. 34). A passage such as this serves to demonstrate the confusion that can arise in trying to break free from Cartesian thinking. The very terminology adopted in order to delineate this position is itself reliant upon making a distinction between self and world. In stating that people live in worlds and worlds live in people, the authors only reaffirm the felt distinction between the two frames of reference. Furthermore, if the statement that "worlds live in people" is to be meaningful, then the communicative intention here would have to be more than figurative and point to a metaphysical claim about the nature of reality.

Challenging Cartesianism has been a central concern of transpersonal psychology since its inception.[2] In response to such thinking, Ken Wilber (1997) states that subject/object dualism

> is the hallmark, not of Descartes' error, but of all manifestation, which Descartes simply happened to spot with unusual clarity. It is still with us, this gap, and it remains the mystery hidden in the heart of samsara, a mystery that absolutely refuses to yield its secrets to anything less than postformal and nondual consciousness development.
>
> (p. 83)

Attuning ourselves to the phenomenon of enactment suggests an emerging participatory awareness. In order to fully appreciate how this phenomenon might challenge our basic understanding of reality (and the clinical implications which in turn follow), it is necessary to underscore that enactive process is by no means restricted to the therapeutic situation. This perhaps goes without saying, yet the clinical context in which this phenomenon has been identified and explored has tended to obscure the relevance of this idea beyond the consultation room. Emphasizing enactment as a clinical phenomenon tends to reinforce the idea that the intersubjective field is created by the two participants rather than being preexistent, and that "object" relatedness is entirely distinct from authentic relationship.

Some initial examples

Listening to our patients' reports of their experience outside the consultation room (not to mention attending to our own), it is often apparent that events unfolding beyond the clinical setting are indicative of enactive process. The more we attend to this phenomenon, the more bewilderingly complex do these dynamics appear. The difficulty one has in expressing this is consequent upon the rationalism that tends to impose and resolve all but the most extraordinary of circumstances in terms of mutual inducement. Our understanding of enactment has developed to acknowledge that while enactments may appear to take place as discrete events, the "enacted dimension of the analytic process" (Katz, 1998) is a constant. This notion can be further expanded with an acknowledgment of *the enacted dimension of daily living*. Thinking in these terms might lead to a broadening awareness of the phenomenon under discussion, which in turn should further alert us to the inadequacy of explaining this phenomenon additively – i.e. as a material consequence of privately bound intrapsychic influence.

I will now offer four short examples of enacted process occurring outside the treatment. I have arranged the examples in order of synchronistic magnitude – the first example is most easily rationalized in terms of the individual eliciting a response from their environment, whereas the last is most clearly synchronistic. In arranging the material in this way, my intention is to invite the reader to consider that our one-sidedly rational perspective needs to be fairly well hit over the head with an example of synchronicity in order to shake our attachment to a disenchanted worldview. I do not offer these examples as a "proof" of synchronicity or panpsychism – the proof (or refutation) of these ideas can only be furnished by one's own experience. Rather, I wish to stimulate consideration of the possibility that the more obviously extraordinary examples of synchronicity are not merely chance outliers, and that they reveal a more fundamental patterning that remains largely incomprehensible to our everyday consciousness – a style of consciousness that struggles to take a view that is global enough to apprehend the phenomenon in question.

Vignette I

Raj's life circumstances and goals were being dictated almost entirely by his long-standing efforts to ameliorate the anxiety of his mother; a state of affairs of which Raj himself seemed unaware, considering himself to be self-serving and taking pride in his independence and lack of expressed need for support from others. Having graduated from the school of his mother's choosing to enter the profession his mother had urged him towards, he had secured an internship on Wall Street. On his way to work one morning, he got into an altercation with a homeless man. The homeless man had approached Raj in an aggressive manner, and a physical confrontation ensued. Raj was subsequently arrested and charged with assault. While in jail he suffered a series of panic attacks. Following his release he became suicidally depressed and was unable to continue at his internship. This sequence of events culminated in his seeking treatment.

How might we understand these events if we approach them as corresponding to a development in Raj's inner world? When Raj was confronted by this homeless man, he was confronted by the denied sense of his own need and dependency. Disgusted at this image, he responds with aggression and a fight ensues – an attempt to wrestle with the problem in a show of his own force. Before this dispute could be resolved, however, the police intervene and Raj is forced into confinement. Raj's efforts to make contact with his own dependency are interrupted by the law of the established order, and he is forced to acknowledge his confinement. This brings about a visceral experience of his powerlessness, thus overthrowing his sense of independence and resulting in a collapse of his self-image. The work could now begin of integrating an understanding of the ways in which Raj's apparently self-serving independence was itself reflective of a self-sacrifice expressing dependency on his mother.

Vignette 2

Sean's wife took a business trip leaving him to take care of their three children – an event that was quite common, and that tended to leave him feeling resentful and alone. He described having fallen into a depression while she was away, but had managed to partially get himself out of this with a pep talk that he gave himself while out walking. He reasoned that he needed to focus on the good things in his life and be appreciative. Shortly after pulling himself up in this way, he noticed a man on the street who he recognized from church. He hadn't seen this person in quite some time, and it became apparent as he neared that the man was intoxicated. Sean attempted to talk with him, but without much success. In church the following day he expressed his concern about this person to the pastor. The pastor said that he was aware of the situation, and that he had been gently trying to encourage the individual in question to return to services. He also said that if Sean felt so inclined, he might want to reach out to this man himself – perhaps their combined efforts would make a difference. Sean felt reassured by the manner in which the pastor expressed his concern without demonstrating anxiety or an excessive sense of personal responsibility.

Sean's encounter with the man who he knew from church gave performative expression to a suffering part of himself that was difficult to relate to, and which was being numbed or subdued. The initial encounter offered itself spontaneously without any question of Sean having to orchestrate this – it simply happened that just as Sean was attempting to get a hold of his emotions he encountered this person. In his subsequent effort to relate to this man and draw support from elsewhere, he enacted an attempt to draw attention to the suppression of his own loneliness and to find help with it. The church community reflects Sean's immediate field of consciousness, while the pastor's attitude paralleled an emerging awareness and acceptance of Sean's suffering.

Vignette 3

Throughout much of her childhood, Angela, a computer programmer in her early forties, had been made subject to extensive verbal and physical abuse at the hands of her alcoholic mother. In the second year of treatment, Angela expressed a sense that she was coming to realize much more clearly the impact of her father's failure to protect her. This theme had recently been constellated in light of events at work. Her immediate manager, a man ten years her senior, was failing to protect them both from the overbearing demands of the project leader – a woman who also happened to be his wife. Coincident with a growing awareness of the failure of protection, Angela felt an increasing sense of resentment at the ways in which her ex-wife, Sophia, had treated her. Sophia had been a highly regarded clothing designer. She was also alcoholic and frequently unfaithful. Despite this, the relationship had lasted almost ten years – apparently in part owing to Angela's belief that Sophia required her protection and would be unable to survive without her. Things finally ended when Sophia died in a car accident. Though it was now several years since her passing, Angela continued to pay for a storage space that was filled with artifacts from Sophia's career – clothing samples and designs.

Angela was pained by the continued sense of responsibility she felt to Sophia's legacy.

A turning point arrived when Angela was offered a new job. On the evening of the day she gave notice to her manager, Angela had been standing in line waiting to be assigned a table at a restaurant when an older man who had also been waiting online struck up a conversation. It transpired that he was a professor at the Fashion Institute of Technology. Furthermore, to Angela's considerable surprise it emerged that he had extensive familiarity with Sophia's work. He was thus uniquely qualified to help Angela deal with Sophia's possessions, and quite pleased at the opportunity to do so.

The failure of Angela's father to offer protection from her mother might be understood from a conventional intrapsychic perspective as being reflected in Angela's continued failure to protect herself – in this case from her manager. However, this apparent failure had a substantive basis in circumstances. In order to survive, Angela had to continue exposing herself to the working conditions that so much encapsulated her past experience. By challenging her lack of self-belief so as to eventually find alternative employment, Angela was able to create the conditions wherein she was able to enact a different form of relationship with her manager. In a dream-like manner, Angela's chance encounter with the FIT professor gave outward expression to a parallel change occurring within her – in confronting her neglectful manager, this figure was transformed and assumed the face of the helpful professor.

Vignette 4

Yao, a Chinese-American man in his early twenties, had been hospitalized on a psychiatric inpatient unit owing to a persistent state of panic consequent upon his belief that the Chinese authorities had a hit out on him. He believed that he had the power to control governments, and that he was personally responsible for the US government shutdown of early 2019 which was taking place at the time of his hospitalization. Yao's family had moved to the United States when he was a child. He described himself as a "refugee," though records indicated otherwise. His family reported that they had kicked him out of the home owing to his unwillingness to stop smoking marijuana, which they considered to be the cause of his psychosis. Three days after Yao was admitted to the hospital, Brian, a US-born man of Northern European descent in his late fifties, was hospitalized to the same unit. At intake, Brian identified himself as a Chinese hitman who was feeling panicked by his homicidal ideation. Despite his rather imposing appearance, Brian's presentation was good-natured and gentle. Brian stated that he was a regular user of hallucinogenic substances, thus causing staff to question whether his psychotic presentation was merely consequent upon substance use. However, Brian's drug test came back clean. Brian expressed his wish to work with Chinese clinicians who he believed would be better able to understand him, and was disappointed when he was told that there were no Chinese clinicians working on the ward. Despite the startling coincidence between the presentation of these two patients, the bewildered hospital staff's main concern was to keep the two men apart out of a fear that their meeting might result in violence.

That Yao would experience himself as a refugee suggests a sense of being threatened from within the family, as does the fear of being executed by a Chinese operative. In Yao's world, the notion of *government* would appear to stand both for his family, and for the structure of his own personality. To claim responsibility for the government shutdown is thus both to assume responsibility for his family rejecting him, and for his own state of psychosis. Smoking marijuana provided an apparent way out of the family, but while this act draws attention to the family system's hostility (kicking him out leading to his being assigned refugee status) it simultaneously denies it by making "the fault" his own (choosing to smoke and being responsible for the "shutdown"). Meanwhile, Brian considers himself to be a dangerous and drug addled hitman, yet he had willingly admitted himself to the hospital out of concern for hurting others. We might speculate that Brian's identification with the role of a Chinese hitman reflects a sense of himself as an outsider (from a foreign culture) and of his feeling personally responsible for terminating his relationship with others (a hitman). Yao and Brian both identify themselves as powerful and dangerous men, yet they both voluntarily had themselves hospitalized owing to a concern about their powerlessness – Yao to prevent the Chinese government from taking his life, and Brian from being able to resist his murderous nature.

What would the possible enactive consequences be of these two individuals encountering each other? Given the parallel concerns of the two men, we might speculate that their meeting could well be of considerable therapeutic benefit – assuming we endorse an idea that meaningful coincidence exists and has a teleological purpose. It doesn't seem farfetched to assume that Brian's wish to connect with Chinese people (who he feels understand him better) could readily lead to his striking up a friendly relationship with Yao. For Yao, we might imagine the older Brian symbolizing a threatening image of authority (the very hitman he had been expecting) who might nevertheless come to be rendered more relatable. Equally, for Brian, Yao might suggest himself as a relatable embodiment of Brian's own vulnerability and of the tendency he takes to assume responsibility for his own isolation. This would reflect a potential challenge to his sense of himself as ruthlessly self-interested (murderous). However, in rationalistic flight from the craziness of the coincidence itself, the hospital staff *fear violence* and, in denial of the violence perpetrated by the psychiatric system, seek to prevent the two patients from ever meeting. In this way, the imposed order of the hospital system enactively recapitulates the imposed order that both individual's experience in terms of a belief in their own destructiveness.

Applications in clinical practice

For better or worse, a hallmark of North American psychoanalysis in general and relational psychoanalysis in particular is an emphasis on pragmatism.[3] The question is thus liable to be asked: why is a panpsychic outlook on treatment more *useful* than a more dualistic conception of the intrapsychic and external worlds as transactionally related yet fundamentally distinct? In this section of the present chapter, I outline some of the clinical benefits that I consider to be associated with the approach suggested.

A less pathologizing and more empowering approach to clinical work

In a manner that is in significant respects supportive of the position I am offering, Paul Wachtel (2008, 2017) argues that for a theory of personality to be truly relational, the analyst cannot afford to treat the patient's psyche as expressing itself from the inside out. Rather, the clinician must seek to recognize the fashion in which the structure of the personality is constantly being mirrored in the structure of the person's interpersonal relations. Wachtel's argument is in large part an explicit recapitulation of Stephen Mitchell's seminal paper "Object Relations Theories and the Developmental Tilt" (Mitchell, 1984). In this paper, Mitchell argues against notions of developmental fixation that he considers result in conceptualizing patients as passive and infantile. Objecting to such an outlook, Mitchell suggests that we should explore the ways in which the patient plays an *active* role in sustaining the problems that bring them to treatment – this being reflected in their present relationships.

Wachtel argues that contemporary relational analysts have failed to adequately address Mitchell's challenge and do not attend sufficiently to the external world of the patient – relational clinicians tend to focus on the mutually constructive nature of the therapeutic interaction without sufficiently acknowledging that the patient's interactions with others function in a similar fashion. Wachtel wishes to emphasize that he is not seeking to abandon the intrapsychic, but is merely contextualizing it. In order to be able to sustain this emphasis on context without annulling the intrapsychic (i.e. to explain the continuity of one's life experiences), Wachtel (2008) posits the idea of *accomplices*. What he means by this is that we unconsciously seek out other people who will act in conformity with our intrapsychic expectations:

> We do not persist in our old ways of perceiving and experiencing simply because they have been "internalized" (and thenceforth are there because they are there). That persistence requires a repeated set of *transactions* with others, transactions in which one's own behavior – and its role in eliciting particular behaviors from the other – is crucial [. . .] understanding the persistence of the key patterns in people's lives requires an understanding of the ways in which we induce others (usually without awareness or understanding of the process) to play the role of "accomplices" in these patterns. A purely "internal" accounting does not address this dynamic. Rather, a full and adequate account of the individual as a person *living-in-the-world* is an account in which everyday actions and what might be called deep subjectivity are equally present but in which it is acknowledged that we do not really understand either without understanding the other.
>
> (p. 157)

While the particular emphasis Wachtel places on the manner in which one's relationships sustain and parallel personality structure strikes me as essential, I consider his notion of accomplices to be insufficient – both in reflecting experience, and in realizing his desire to articulate a more truly "relational" theory.

The notion of "accomplices" doesn't do justice to the complex, unpredictable, and sometimes uncanny ways in which interpersonal events can come to express internal dynamics. With an attentiveness to the frequency with which these dynamics emerge and the often spontaneous fashion in which they do so, the idea that individuals unconsciously orchestrate their external experience places too much burden on the behavioral efficacy of the individual. With reference to the four vignettes offered in the previous section of this chapter, while the more quotidian forms of enactment reflected in the first two vignettes might conceivably be understood in the fashion Wachtel is suggesting, the more strikingly synchronistic examples of enactment suggested by vignettes three and four are more difficult to explain.

Just noticing and tracking enactments in the carefully circumscribed environment of the treatment is in itself profoundly challenging. If we are to widen our gaze to encompass the world outside of the treatment room, the scope and complexity of the phenomenon we have come to label "enactment" is quite astounding. Indeed, the scale and largely unconscious nature of this phenomenon is such that it can perhaps only be apprehended in occasional moments of intuitive insight. Attempts to rationalize the specifics of this phenomenon for the sake of elucidation in case material will always do an inestimable disservice to it.

An approach that emphasizes the patient's role in directly sustaining their own suffering is itself inherently pathologizing. This tendency is reflected both in Wachtel's notion of accomplices and in the early work of Mitchell from which Wachtel draws. Mitchell (1984) writes: "Psychopathology is not merely a state of aborted, frozen development, but a cocoon actively woven out of fantasied ties to significant others" (p. 494). In this paper, Mitchell takes the position that early experiences "seriously distort subsequent relatedness" (p. 495). Thus, in the effort not to treat the patient like an infant, Mitchell and Wachtel nevertheless continue to adopt an outlook that subtly privilege's the superiority of the analyst's position as an adjudicator of the patient's experience. This is understandable in the context of Mitchell's (1984) earlier paper, but is perhaps surprising in the more recent work of Wachtel who doesn't sufficiently acknowledge that endorsing this more relational approach to the personality nevertheless entails privileging the clinician's perspective and thus surrendering a more relational approach to the treatment itself. Panpsychism encourages us to attend to the external world of the patient not by trying to work out how the patient perpetuates their own suffering, but rather by supporting patients in engaging more effectively with the enacted dimension of daily living.

A reductive/pathologizing tendency emerges wherever the intrapsychic is severed from a transpersonal context and treated as though in some sense *causative* of the relational field. Consider the following clinical example offered by Davies and Frawley (1994):

> Vera's incest ended only when, at age 20, her father tried to murder her one night when she struggled to escape. For years, years that included a number of psychiatric hospitalizations, Vera told no one about the incest. The first time she did disclose, she became acutely suicidal. Violently resisting hospitalization, she required four paramedics to restrain her. For some time, subsequent disclosure of material related to her incest evoked a similar response. Eventually, through repeated interpretation of the repetition of *the trauma invoked through her actions*, Vera was able to see that after she revealed memories of affects associated with her incest experiences, *she behaved in a way that resulted in a terrifying reenactment* of her father pinning her down on the floor to rape her. *In a convoluted and destructive way, Vera was enacting* loyal preservation of her internalized relationship with her father.
>
> (pp. 95–96, emphasis my own)

The outlook offered here fails to acknowledge that the most immediate form of abuse Vera was experiencing during the treatment wasn't being perpetrated by her father but by the mental health care system (see Soros, 2019). It is the violence of "helping" professionals which is now being enactively rationalized as though it were caused by Vera and done for her own good.

Similarly, and as the term itself suggests, Wachtel's notion of *accomplices* would only seem to reinforce that the patient is in a subtle sense being blamed. This seems very much against Wachtel's intentions, yet it is the unavoidable consequence of his seeking to promote a more rigorously relational theory that nevertheless preserves the intrapsychic dimension without allowing for a transpersonal conception of the psyche. Wachtel wishes to uphold a distinction between the intrapsychic and the interpersonal, and yet he might appear to be collapsing the intra-psychic into the interpersonal where he states that "the very nature of those structures and commitments [i.e. the intrapsychic] is contextual" (Wachtel, 2008, p. 69). This statement will only stand if it is modified with an additional recognition that as much as we might consider the intrapsychic to be defined contextually, we must also consider that the nature of the "context" can itself be understood as being in some respect psychic.[4] What Wachtel is almost but not quite suggesting is that the psyche is not constrained to the individual. This claim, however, entails explicitly endorsing a form of panpsychism. Wachtel stops short of this, and is thus forced to rely heavily upon the retrograde idea of induce-ment; a notion that preserves the one-person outlook that Wachtel is oth-erwise so keen to challenge.

Upholding transitional space

As has already been touched upon, the clinician's efforts to uphold tran-sitional space are significantly dependent upon an underlying conception of reality. If our understanding of the psyche is ultimately reducible to the functioning of the brain (i.e. a discrete material object) then, regardless of how relational our theories of clinical interaction may appear, our basic worldview will tend to work against this. Likewise, insofar as we under-stand internal and external worlds either as fundamentally distinct or as entirely reconcilable, our outlook contradicts the transitional ideal. Now it might be argued that in refusing to posit sharp distinctions between the intrapsychic and the interpersonal, relational analysts already make sig-nificant strides towards addressing this problem. But while relationalists do consider the intrapsychic and the interpersonal to be difficult to differ-entiate, the question of uncertainty tends to rest upon the limits of obser-vation rather than reflecting a postulate about the nature of reality itself. Generally speaking, a material conception of the social field is implicitly considered primary while the inner world tends to be treated as though caused by material circumstances. Notions such as personal agency and selfhood are thus frequently posited as adaptive fictions, while social fac-tors are much more likely to be treated as objectively real (particularly if they exhibit a political charge).

While commonsense dictates that we should be willing to recognize an *experiential* distinction between inner and outer worlds, this distinction cannot afford to be confused with a metaphysical assertion concerning the limits of the self. Thinking panpsychically results in an underlying view of reality that encourages us to attend more closely to the personal meanings not only of our interpersonal relations, but also of external events more broadly. In emphasizing the *fact* of the external world in terms that are too much dependent on a materially objective sense of fundamental reality, trauma is barred from transitional space so that our very conception of trauma is itself a traumatized one. The threat of reductivism that emerges in upholding a psychological perspective only applies where we limit our thinking to causal explanations – i.e. how is this person's past experience shaping their present reality. Thinking teleologically we might ask instead: how is the emerging meaning of this person's life currently being actualized in the shape of external events.

With respect to recognition theory, I have suggested that it is problematic to treat recognition as though in some sense operating outside of the psyche. In conceptualizing the intrapsychic as distinct from intersubjective recognition, there is a clear danger that we come to consider our grasp of external reality as though operating in distinction from the unconscious ground of psychic life. Doing so is again liable to break down transitional space. This became apparent to me when a relationally oriented colleague complained that she was having a hard time with a patient who wouldn't "play" with her. As we discussed the case it became clear to us both that the consequences of thinking in terms of the patient not being willing to play was that "playing" and "not playing" were being pushed out of transitional space and forced into patient and analyst as two separate and reified states. Upon further reflection it became apparent that this very problem seems to be built into Benjamin's theorizing. Benjamin (2004) links transitional space (i.e. the space of play) with her conception of thirdness, which she defines as "a quality or experience of intersubjective relatedness that has as its correlate a certain kind of internal mental space" (p. 7). While the creation of intersubjective space would appear to mean being less literal, Benjamin's manner of theorizing this position is itself dependent on what can often seem a reified distinction between the intrapsychic and the intersubjective. In the foregoing quotation transitional space is explicitly bisected into outer and inner reality. This directly contradicts the definition of transitional space offered by Winnicott (1971), for whom play is "neither a matter of inner psychic reality nor a matter of external reality" (p. 96).

As we saw in Chapter 2, Benjamin's influential theory of intersubjectivity rests upon a strict differentiation between an intrapsychic perspective and the capacity to recognize the other in their own right. Benjamin (1995) states: "From the intersubjective standpoint, all fantasy is the negation of the real other, whether its content is negative or idealized – just as, from the intrapsychic view, external reality is simply that which is internalized as fantasy" (p. 45). This outlook leads Benjamin to suggest that our ideal is to be able to sustain a tension between the two positions; an idea which she links to Winnicott's notion that the baby both discovers and creates transitional phenomena. However, it might be argued that the theoretical approach Benjamin adopts doesn't uphold both ends of the bargain. In the foregoing statement Benjamin states that from an intrapsychic perspective external reality is simply that which is internalized as fantasy. As Winnicott's work shows, however, this claim is inaccurate. In fact, with the perspective Benjamin here imputes to an intrapsychic position she merely restates an "external reality" based perspective on the intrapsychic. From an intrapsychic perspective, external reality isn't that which is internalized to become fantasy, but that which is *created* in fantasy. With this it becomes apparent that the tension Benjamin seeks to honor cannot be sustained without addressing the Cartesian worldview that her work implicitly adopts. In respect to Benjamin's opposing fantasy to recognition, Stolorow, Orange, and Atwood (2001) observe: "This definition is a rather dramatic return of the Cartesian subject-object split, the separation of an absolutized external reality from a mind that perceives, distorts, or negates it" (p. 474).

A panpsychic outlook allows us to locate recognition as a process in which transitional space is realized precisely as a consequence of the experienced distinction between internal and external worlds having in some measure been transcended. In conceptualizing the occupation of a complementary position being more about oneself than the patient, this very thought perhaps runs contrary to surrender. In effect, Benjamin's theory inadvertently "does to" the clinician when, in moments of impasse, Benjamin suggests that clinicians should hold themselves accountable for their own role. Rather than fostering awareness of our present state of unconscious relationship to the third, this approach emphasizes a *lack* of relationship. Benjamin (2004) states: "Once we have deeply accepted our own contribution – and its inevitability – the fact of two-way participation becomes a vivid experience, something we can understand and use to feel less helpless and more effective" (p. 11). The emphasis Benjamin places on assuming personal responsibility can certainly be beneficial in moments of impasse where a fight to the death is in the offing, yet it might be argued that the rationale for this approach is itself subtly contributive to the emergence of such moments. Ghent (1990) stresses that surrender is not volitional. This being so, the best that we can hope from our theories of clinical interaction is that they might foster receptivity. Imagining ourselves as being made subject to what Ogden (1994) refers to as the "subjugating third" is itself a freeing gesture. In positing a dream field in the context of which we undergo the experience of being "done to," our attention shifts from feeling done-to by the patient to a *shared* experience of being done-to in the third. Such an outlook might help us to remain mindful that the other person's struggle is also our own.

This has relevance for impasses that are marked not only by an excess of confrontation but also by a lack of it. In contrast with a fight to the death, a different kind of impasse is reflected when one or both of the participants experiences the other as already dead. In such moments – often associated with patients that come to be labeled "narcissistic" – the analyst's efforts to "play with" what they experience as an "unplayful" patient, or the patient's efforts to play with what they experience as an unplayful analyst, can be understood as demanding an increase in affective heat. Here surrender does not entail a movement towards recognition but rather a willingness to enter playfully into conflict.

In the early phases of our work together, I experienced Jonathan as difficult to please. Throughout much of each session he would speak at length allowing, as it seemed to me, virtually no room for my input. Shortly before the end of each hour, however, he would segue into pushing me for my thoughts – demanding that I offer my take on how he was doing, and expressing disappointment with my lack of responsiveness. This felt quite suffocating. I was left with a confounding sense that I couldn't offer what he wanted owing to his pushing so hard for it. At the same time, I couldn't help but feel that there was some measure of truth in Jonathan's perspective that I was failing to engage him – during session I often came to feel quite dissociated, only to find myself blinking in bewilderment as the inevitable moment of reckoning arrived and I was suddenly expected to contribute. Part of me was resentful at not being allowed more room, while another part of me felt vaguely guilty for not being able to engage more effectively. Towards the end of a session in which I had felt particularly excluded/dissociated, Jonathan stated with open derision that he didn't feel this was how therapy should be – he believed that therapy was meant to be more like a game of tennis where you knock the ball back and forth. I experienced this comment both as distinctly entertaining and as an incitement. Managing to find purchase with the metaphor he had offered, I observed that I didn't seem to be a match for his service game. We both laughed and the session ended in a less explicitly oppositional frame of reference than had become usual. The patient would later refer to this moment as having been significant to him in having provided evidence that he would be able to work with me. The apparent success of this interaction depended on us both being able to find ways of playing with the idea that the other person wasn't playing. Through affective engagement some measure of recognition was achieved without either of us feeling that we needed to entirely give up our respective positions in the game.

A more meaningful approach to trauma

In the very effort to validate trauma, our theoretical outlook can inadvertently serve to sustain its status as such. By emphasizing the external reality of trauma, conventional relational models risk pulling trauma out of transitional space. To be quite clear: recognizing the fashion in which trauma is experienced as externally imposed seems to me absolutely essential. However, an emphasis on the external reality of trauma can readily leave the individual feeling powerless. Jung (1955) writes:

> The individual must meet the trauma with a quite definite inner predisposition in order to make it really effective. This inner predisposition is [. . .] to be understood [. . .] as a psychological development which reaches its climax, and becomes manifest, at the traumatic moment.
>
> (para. 217)

While seeking to indoctrinate patients into thinking about trauma in terms of a spiritual meaning is likely to be counterproductive and could quite readily be detrimental, remaining open to this possibility ensures that there is less likelihood of this kind of meaning-making actually being blocked in the treatment.

The difficulties that can arise in the absence of this perspective are particularly evident wherever disavowed trauma might be understood as having influenced an individual's core sense of identity. For example, if a basic sense of who the person is may have been significantly shaped by child abuse, this state of affairs leads to a psychological catch-22 wherein being able to properly remember and acknowledge the abuse as an externally imposed fact is itself liable to undermine the person's basic sense of identity. It can happen that the aspect of themselves upon which an individual has been able to most firmly establish a sense of personhood simultaneously functions so as to conceal the original trauma. Under such circumstances, the sustained internalization of abuse seems necessary in order to preserve one's basic sense of sanity. This tendency is readily exacerbated if, understandably, the clinician feels that they should actively support the person's identification. Fearful lest approaching the trauma be experienced as pathologizing the associated identification, both patient and clinician can readily find themselves "colluding" so as to avoid the abuse.

A panpsychic attitude towards external influence enables the possibility that trauma might be meaningfully linked to the individual as a function of their becoming. If the individual's core sense of identity is to be supported more effectively, then social construction must assume a spiritual basis. Philosopher and theologian Corbin (1969) writes:

> But all of this, it may once again be argued, is "Docetism."[5] Yes. But as we have already stressed, it is docetism that is far from degrading "reality" by making it an "appearance"; on the contrary, by transforming it into appearance it makes this "reality" transparent to the transcendent meaning manifested in it. This docetism attaches no value to a material fact unless it is appearance, that is, apparition. It is in this sense that the Imagination accomplishes at every instant a "new creation" and that the Image is the recurrence of Creation.
>
> (Corbin, 1969, p. 244)

A patient who struggled with the feeling of years "lost" to trauma, shared with me her conviction that she had lived several iterations of the life circumstances into which she was born. With this latest incarnation she had finally been able to master the challenge. By demonstrating interest in this idea and mirroring back the sense of personal accomplishment associated with it, the patient was supported in her ongoing efforts to find meaning in what, from a secular perspective, is liable to be treated reductively as nothing more than an unfortunate childhood. The individual's ongoing efforts to grasp the suffering that had been engendered by externally imposed trauma led to a powerful sense of being called to *consciously* address this theme with compassion in the world.

In the absence of this sense of greater purpose, a more creative recovery from trauma often remains blocked. An overbearing sense of resentment remains, often reflecting the extent to which the individual still struggles with feelings of personal responsibility for what happened to them. It is not uncommon for people in this position to enter the helping professions with the active intent of *righting a wrong*. The struggle to establish a relationship of personal meaning to trauma comes to be reflected in a compromise-formation mixed with largely unconscious guilt, and the meaning that the person finds in his or her experience is confined to affirming the existence of trauma as an externally imposed fact.[6]

To be psychological – to seek to position oneself in conformity with the soul's logic – is to avow that life itself has reasons. Participating in a process that helps enable an individual to create a personally meaningful narrative of their experiences means understanding events seemingly "external" to that person as in some respect being related to the necessary pattern of that person's life. While the external perspective plays an essential role in helping a patient to come into emotional contact with trauma, if the overarching thrust of the therapeutic process often means finding a way to live more meaningfully out of one's past, then this ultimately entails registering traumatic experience as personally meaningful. In working to alleviate the patient's feelings of personal responsibility, care must be taken so as not to lose sight of the potentially creative impetus expressed by this seemingly destructive tendency. Integration requires that events external to the person must ultimately be experienced as in some sense belonging to them. To assume that thinking of events in the world as a means of psychic expression is to rob them of their reality is to assume that this reality is not itself in some respect psychic.

Working with the material at hand

Approaching seemingly external events in terms of an intrinsic personal meaning fosters an attunement to the material at hand. Just as the therapeutic importance of enactment can be understood in terms of the manner in which enactment gives immediate emotional form to the subject matter of the treatment, a sensitivity and responsiveness to the inherent personal meaning of external events helps patient and therapist to engage with the material presently constellated.

Steve was raised in a single parent family. His father had left his mother when Steve was three. The younger of two brothers, upon entering treatment Steve considered himself naturally anxious – something that he credited to his mother's genetics. Now in his early thirties, he remained close both to his mother and to his older brother. His brother, whom he admired, had always encouraged him to be mindful of his mother's perceived emotional frailty. To "be a man" meant to be self-sufficient and to put others' needs ahead of his own. Steve referred to the emotionally demanding side of himself as "the ogre," and berated himself for sometimes acting like a "passive aggressive dick" towards his girlfriend. In treatment, Steve and I were starting to explore Steve's often negative attitude towards his emotional life.

Earlier that morning, Steve and his friend Paul were walking to the subway. They had been in conversation when Paul broke off to help a man who was struggling to open a stroller with one arm while holding a crying baby in the other. Steve hadn't noticed the man until his friend went to help him. In session, Steve reported that his failure to even see this man, let alone offer his support, had left him feeling like a bad person. He harshly rebuked himself for being so selfish and expressed his hope that I might be able to help him address this obvious deficit in his personality. Steve stated: "I want to get out of my head so that I can be more helpful to others." In response, I pointed out that perhaps he too was struggling with what felt like a baby on his arm, and that his impulse to get out of his head was in fact indicative of how lonely it could feel taking care of himself without support. With obvious relief Steve acknowledged that he did feel very much alone in his efforts to improve himself. In thus working with my patient to help "open the stroller," Steve was able to feel less burdened in session with the sense that his emotional demands should be kept under such restrictive control.

Staying close to the imagery presented enables the clinician to more readily access the emotional content of the session. Being too literal in one's relationship to this material can distract from just how much has been said, and often results in the enacted dimension of the treatment becoming merely repetitive rather than transformative. Steve's wish to identify with his helpful and "selfless" friend is indicative both of his need for support and of the very tendency by which he robs himself of the self-care that he yearns for. To approach the patient's wish as merely indicative of the narcissistic withdrawal that it purports to address would only have made me complicit with the status quo. Engaging too literally with the material offered is liable to reinforce the patient's identification with their given role in the scene rather than enabling a perspective in which the image taken as a whole can be understood to express the present state of psyche. Had I been more literal in my response, then in the enacted dimension of the treatment my position would have paralleled his own – i.e. failing to notice the man who needs help – and would thus have merely repeated the same dynamic in the treatment as had earlier been enacted on the street.

Depending on the clinical moment, it may well be helpful to explore the patient's associations to being "selfish" or "in his head," the interpersonal dynamics with his friend, the possible identification of his friend with an internalized image of his brother, etc. However, much of this is already alive in the image with which the patient is at present most directly concerned. Additionally, in following the imagery as given, the analyst is guided in adopting a tone that is attuned to the patient's current experience. For example, I would normally be very cautious in relating a patient's needs to that of a baby. Trusting the imagery that was given to me by the patient, however, I pushed through my clinical squeamishness on this issue and to the apparent benefit of the treatment.

Attunement to the analytic process

A willingness to listen for the possible meaning of external events provides an additional avenue by which clinicians might monitor their own participation. An example of this was offered to me when a patient, Emma, began our session by reporting the following event: As Emma was entering the 5th Avenue building in which my office is located, a little girl had been standing near the entrance. The girl approached Emma with something in her hands. It was a baby bird that she was apparently caring for. Emma had the sense that the girl wanted her to be impressed, but all that Emma could muster was a murmured and lifeless, "Wow." This event led to a memory of her own efforts as a child to care for a sick bird. When she took the bird to show her mother, her mother had severely admonished her. She was told that by touching this bird she had effectively killed it – the bird's mother would want nothing more to do with it. Prompted by the content of this event and its timing, I asked Emma if she had perhaps recently felt criticized by me. Emma denied this, but after a short pause reported that she hadn't brought notes today because she wanted to be more spontaneous. We explored the impact of a recent session in which I had expressed my pleasure that she had seemed able to speak more freely without referring to her notes. The synchronicity thus enabled us to identify and address the disruptive enactment that had taken place. I suggested that it seemed I may have injured the bird myself by inadvertently accusing her of doing the same by taking notes. Like the carefully protected yet vulnerable bird, Emma's note taking was reflective of her fledgling efforts to nurture herself. My prescriptive notion of what spontaneity looked like had naturally caused Emma to feel criticized. In addition to the supervisory function that Emma's synchronistic encounter with the girl had played, further reflection on the themes it raised drew attention both to the ways in which Emma's mother continued to reject Emma's efforts to heal (this being reflected in her mother's recent dismissal of Emma's distress with an assertion that therapy should help you "get over" things) and of the ways in which this form of relatedness currently manifested in Emma's attitude towards herself (as reflected in her sense that anything she brought to therapy felt tainted and unimportant).

Maintaining focus on the patient

Rather than adopting a social justice orientation that would seek to directly engineer more responsible citizens, a panpsychic outlook reaffirms a clinical responsibility to focus on the patient. In tension with the sometimes explicitly activistic sensibilities that can on occasion seem to reflect something of a new norm in North American psychoanalysis, a panpsychic outlook on psychotherapy serves to emphasize the political importance of a clinical approach that is careful not to lose sight of the personal.

Lee was in the early years of his career as a psychiatrist. A white man raised in the Midwest as the only child of evangelical parents, Lee's upbringing had been economically disadvantaged but relatively stable. He had realized his divergence with evangelical Christianity when he was ten, but not feeling able to share this with his parents he had spent the latter half of his childhood acting the part of a believer. Having accrued significant student debt, upon graduating Lee had accepted a relatively well-paid position with a state hospital. Struggling to find meaning in his work, however, he eventually sought treatment for depression. Lee was deeply troubled by the glaring fact that while most of the hospital staff were white, most of his patients were black, and their mental health problems evidently had much to do with economic hardship. Furthermore, the institutional pressures of working in a state hospital often required that he knowingly overmedicate the people he was ostensibly charged with helping. Lee felt guilty at not being able to do more for his patients, and for what he perceived to be his supporting role in upholding basic social inequalities. At the same time, owing to the constraints of his finances he felt trapped in his work. He also felt guilty at what little satisfaction he was actually able to find in his life, asserting that the sense of pleasure he took in being able to call himself a doctor indicated a basic lack of humility.

Lee was out walking in Harlem one morning. Rounding a corner he came upon a young black man who was lying in the street. The man had been shot and was bleeding heavily. The paramedics had just arrived and apparently had things under control, so Lee walked on. Understandably effected by this scene, in the days that followed Lee's thoughts returned to it. He found himself wondering how he might have reacted if he had come upon the scene prior to the ambulance arriving. Would he have been able to help this person? This line of thinking further reinforced his feelings of guilt in relationship to his work.

In hearing this, I responded by stating that this image of the man lying bleeding in the street had me wondering about my patient's own sense of suffering. Lee became thoughtful and then noted that there were two sides to him: the part that has student loans and wants to live a comfortable white collar life, and the part of him that wants to make a change in the world. I suggested that in fearing that he may pass by the man who had been shot, he also feared that he would be passing by the latter aspect of himself – all of that blood spilling to waste. We explored what it might mean to have arrived on the scene earlier. This led to Lee reflecting on the pressures he had felt from his parents to enter the medical field; a decision that he had previously credited solely to his own desire for status. His mother and father had pushed him into medicine, yet his success in this field was not subsequently celebrated. His parents had always placed a particular emphasis on the sinfulness of pride, hence Lee's efforts to please his parents by accomplishing exactly what was asked of him were nevertheless unsuccessful. In fact, it often seemed that Lee's success had merely caused them to resent him.

As we spoke more over the following weeks, it became apparent how much of the parental messaging concerning "pride" Lee still lived with. This messaging was expressed in the sense of incompatibility Lee experienced between the more explicitly "self-interested" parts of himself and those aspects of himself that felt motivated to help others.

In keeping the treatment focused on the patient, even as he raised important socioeconomic concerns pertaining to the wider world, a repetitious enactment of the parental attitude was averted and the treatment was able to create a space for the conflicting aspects of self. In the following sessions we explored the nature of this conflict. As Lee became more able to engage sympathetically with his own needs, he was also able to experience his wish to support the needs of others as an authentic expression of himself rather than as an externally imposed sense of what was right. Over the following months Lee reported feeling less inhibited, both in speaking up for himself and for others. This was reflected in an emerging capacity to advocate more vocally for his patients.

A maxim for aboriginal activism states: "If you have come here to help me, you are wasting your time. But if you have come because your liberation is bound up with mine, then let us work together."[7] Compassion for others is always reflective of self-compassion, and the course of our lives has much to do with the extent to which we are able to grasp the nature of our own suffering. An intrapsychic approach has sometimes been thought to reflect a narcissistic withdrawal from the sociopolitical landscape. Quite to the contrary, panpsychism emphasizes that our participation in the world is not in conflict with attending to our seemingly more private needs, and that recognition of the other is inseparable from recognition of our own otherness.

Deepening engagement in relationship

A panpsychic outlook on treatment complexifies our understanding of the relationship between self and other. This approach emphasizes the individual not at the expense of recognizing the external world, but by finding the individual *in* the external world. The meaning of recognition is thus transformed to take Donnel Stern (2004) at his word where he contends that enactment has to do with "the interpersonalization of dissociation" (p. 213). Additionally, this outlook also suggests the possibility of a more "external" (i.e. transpersonal) perspective on dreams.

My work with Derek focused largely on his efforts to end a relationship with a man named Simon and to follow his long-standing desire to move abroad. Several months subsequent to the end of the relationship and shortly before leaving New York, Derek reported the following dream:

> *I am in an outside place. It feels like a social gathering. I encounter Simon. He appears excited to see me. This surprises me – I had antici-pated that if I ever bumped into him he would be anxious and awk-ward. Simon smiles warmly and seems very open. He tells me that he's ready. "Ready for what?" I ask. "Ready to talk – I know that you've been wanting to talk to me, and now I'm ready." We kiss, and then enter into an interaction wherein it's as though all of the negative feel-ings that had accumulated in my perception of Simon over the course of our relationship seem to slowly fall away. This feels like something Simon is doing to me through his active engagement. I am left with the sense of being able to see Simon for who he really is: an adventurous and brave person.*

Derek described having woken up that morning feeling happy and grounded. Commenting on the dream, Derek indicated that he was tempt-ed to feel that he had really had an encounter with Simon – only Simon wasn't dead, so it seemed to Derek that this wasn't possible. Although Derek's belief system was able to stretch to the possibility of being visited in a dream by someone who had died, the idea of being visited by a living person didn't seem credible. Derek said that since it couldn't have really been Simon who visited him in his dream, then the dream had to have concerned something that was going on "inside of my head" – he touched his temples when he said this. His demeanor changed and, apparently discouraged, he stated that the dream Simon must simply have been what he wanted for himself. He spoke of his uneasiness at the idea – if the dream figure were nothing more than an aspect of his own mind, then he had merely been kissing himself. I reflected that what seemed most striking about the dream was his sense of really "seeing" Simon. Derek seemed encouraged by this, and agreed that the sense of recognition in the dream was what had made it feel so exceptional. Shortly after the session Derek decided to call Simon. He wanted to communicate his sense of pleasure at having had the dream and of being able to see Simon in these terms. Simon responded with marked excitement, for on that same night he had dreamed of driving Derek to the airport; the striking impression that this dream had made upon Simon bore a close correspondence with the experience Derek had described following his own dream of Simon. This exchange reportedly proved helpful in supporting both Derek and Simon through the challenges of the separation.

Grounding overwhelming experiences

When a personal challenge is constellated so powerfully that it emerges simultaneously across multiple life domains, it is not uncommon for patients in the midst of such an experience to report feeling overwhelmed and even crazy. This feeling of craziness can often be understood in terms of an intensification of synchronistic phenomena (or perhaps, more correctly, receptivity or attunement to these phenomena) coupled with the inadequacy of our received sense of reality in being able to make sense of this. Such a state-of-affairs can become destructive if, in an effort to maintain one's sanity, a person either [1] determines that they must be *doing it to themselves* or [2] rationalizes their experience in terms of fixed ideas about external reality while shutting out those who would challenge this. The former approach is typical of neurosis, while the latter is more commonly associated with psychosis.

A panpsychic approach to treatment may cause us to question the ways in which mainstream psychiatry often inadvertently perpetuates what we might term *metaphysical gaslighting* – that is, causing a person to doubt their own sanity by assuming the universally binding nature of one's own reductive views concerning the nature of reality. This tendency is reflected with the diagnostic fervor that clinicians reductively invoke such notions as religiosity, ideas of reference, delusions of grandeur, and magical thinking.

Coda

In this chapter I have attempted to offer some initial sense of what I consider to be the *practical* value of panpsychism for clinical practice. However, what qualifies as "practically" relevant depends greatly on one's expectations of reality. Despite what I believe is its fundamentally emancipatory ethos, psychoanalysis has historically focused on treating pathology while largely bypassing a definition of health or thriving. It is thus worth noting that besides some of the clinical dimensions I have started to outline, there is also the meaning of this outlook as the basis for a more fundamental shift in our sense of relationship to life.

The idea of re-enchantment is only just starting to show signs of entering psychoanalytic conversation – principally by way of recognition theory and the phenomenology of enactment. A Heraclitean dictum states: "You will not discover the limits of the soul by travelling, even if you wander over every conceivable path, so deep is its story." In apparent refutation of this position, psychoanalytic thinking is still prone to imply that in fact the soul's limits can and should be asserted. An intrapsychic perspective must concede to accommodate an external one – a perspective that is conceptualized to reside "outside" of the psyche. But if external reality is in no respect psychic, what is its nature? When analysts seek to implicitly ascribe limits to the soul, is this a theological claim, or is there a tacit understanding that psychoanalysis continues to operate within a secular frame of reference?

Adopting a psychological approach needn't mean denying (or clinically excluding) events in the external world, but rather approaching them in terms of the question of personal meaning – in other words, listening "intrapsychically" doesn't require a reductive narrowing of the analytic field. Rather, it supposes a way of listening that seeks to find in external events a sense of the emerging dynamism of the psyche. This perspective suggests a deepening of the event itself in attempting to account for what the event might ask of us.

In seeking to preserve a conception of the psyche that is fundamentally private yet profoundly contingent on others, relational theories have often inadvertently endorsed an isolated conception of the self which for this very reason is portrayed as an adaptive illusion (Bromberg, 1998; Mitchell, 1993; Stolorow et al., 2001) – an approach to personhood that is at once excessively enclosed *and* excessively contingent on the environment. With an exclusive emphasis on context we might come to feel that we are each *merely* the sum of our relationships to others. Insisting upon the primacy of the psyche, however, the network of relationships out of which the person is posited to have come into being might be regarded as that aspect of reality most immediately available to the individual as the basis for the change they realize in the world – a change that might be actualized precisely as a consequence of the extent to which psychic structure can be considered as the interiorized way of speaking about external relationships. Consider the following statement of Erikson's (1958):

> To be adult means among other things to see one's own life in continuous perspective, both in retrospect and prospect. By accepting some definition as to who he is, usually on the basis of a function in an economy, a place in the sequence of generations, and a status in the structure of society, the adult is able to selectively reconstruct his past in such a way that, step for step, it seems to have planned him, or better, he seems to have planned it. In this sense, psychologically we do choose our parents, our family history, and the history of our kings, heroes, and gods. By making them our own, we maneuver ourselves into the inner position of proprietors, of creators.
>
> (pp. 111–112)

Although accepting a position in the established order is no doubt essential, how we understand the question of authorship has often been treated reductively. It has been observed that the recent tendency to portray personal agency as an adaptive fiction seems fundamentally incompatible with clinical practice (Brown, 2017; Frie & Reis, 2005). This question of agency is directly linked with the problem of creativity – a theme that the relational emphasis on social determination can sometimes minimize. An emancipatory psychoanalysis strives to acknowledge the profound influence of the environment without implicitly disempowering the individual.

Notes

1 I should stress that in speaking of teleology I do not intend to invoke the sense of a singular and already determined goal.
2 The related ecopsychology movement is likewise much preoccupied with the divide between human endeavor and the natural environment (Garrard, 2011, p. 24). At the heart of ecopsychology's agenda is a concern for the Cartesian split between the outside world and the inside of persons. Metzner (1995) characterizes this divide as a "pathological alienation" (p. 55), while Roszak (1992) speaks of the need to question the split as "the great project of our time" (p. 44). See Brown (2016) for related discussion.

3 At its best, pragmatism reflects an attitude of compassionate engagement with the suffering of others; at its worst, pragmatism results in a forceful attitude towards reality having more to do with protecting the established order (in whatever sense that manifests) than with promoting well-being. Contrasting the results-oriented approach of Owen Renik with the more open-ended nature of Thomas Ogden's clinical work, Aron and Starr (2012) argue cogently that psychoanalysis should represent both a countercultural sensibility and a respect for the practical questions of symptom relief (p. 390). They offer an interesting defense of the pragmatic stance by suggesting that taking the analysand's suffering as a serious concern that warrants being addressed directly in itself constitutes a countercultural gesture. This may well be true, though the question still remains as to how we define "taking seriously" suffering.

4 An example of the kind of reductivism that can emerge with a secular emphasis on context is provided by Atwood, Orange, and Stolorow (2002). The authors describe the treatment of a psychotic patient wherein they attempt to interpret the religious content of the individual's experience from what they consider to be a non-pathologizing perspective. While this intent is encouraging, as a consequence of the authors' exclusive emphasis on a disenchanted conception of social context, what this transpires to mean in practice is understanding the religious content of this patient's experience as being reducible to the biographical details of her life. Thus the patient's religious strivings and experiences are understood as merely compensatory, emerging in an effort to protect the patient from a disappearing sense of connection to a "world-sustaining other." On one level this may very well be true, but to understand the patient's presentation *only* in these terms hardly seems sufficient if we are to achieve a perspective that is genuinely non-pathologizing. While this kind of contextual reductivism is certainly a vast improvement on the biological reductivism of the medical model, the authors overestimate the extent to which they have broken away from demanding that the patient conform to the clinician's own assumptions about reality. While attempting to understand the social context in which the patient's religious ideas might be made more comprehensible, the patient's religious striving is apparently not considered in and of itself relevant to the course or final outcome of the treatment (see Brown, 2015).

5 The doctrine that Christ's human/bodily appearance was an illusion.

6 Twelve-step programs offer a related example of this. Members are actively encouraged to find meaning in their experience by helping others struggling with the same problem. However, in this frame of reference helping others entails converting them to the *impersonal* system of meaning offered by the program. Members are welcome to find their own Higher Power, but the definition of addiction is not up for debate. While explicit acknowledgment of a trauma-based perspective is in this case largely rejected, this is in favor of the even more concrete notion of addiction as a "disease." Thus the central

concern of these programs comes to rest upon converting others into a belief in the reality of the supposed disease.

7 Often attributed to Lilla Watson.

References

Aron, L., & Starr, K. E. (2012). *A psychotherapy for the people: Toward a progressive psychoanalysis*. London & New York: Routledge.

Atlas, G., & Aron, L. (2018). *Dramatic dialogue: Contemporary clinical practice*. London & New York: Routledge.

Atwood, G. E., Orange, D. M., & Stolorow, R. D. (2002). Shattered worlds/psychotic states: A post-cartesian view of the experience of personal annihilation. *Psychoanalytic Psychology, 19*(2), 281–306.

Atwood, G. E., & Stolorow, R. D. (2014). *Structures of subjectivity: Explorations in psychoanalytic phenomenology and contextualism* (2nd ed.). London & New York: Routledge.

Bass, A. (2001). It takes one to know one: Or, whose unconscious is it anyway? *Psychoanalytic Dialogues, 11*(5), 683–702.

Benjamin, J. (1995). *Like subjects, love objects: Essays on recognition and sexual difference*. New Haven, CT: Yale University Press.

Benjamin, J. (2004). Beyond doer and done to: An intersubjective view of thirdness. *Psychoanalytic Quarterly, 73*, 5–46.

Bromberg, P. M. (1998). *Standing in the spaces: Essays on clinical process, trauma, and dissociation*. Hillsdale, NJ: Analytic Press.

Brown, R. S. (2015). An opening: Trauma and transcendence. *Psychosis: Psychological, Social and Integrative Approaches, 7*(1), 72–80.

Brown, R. S. (2016). Disadapting to the environmental crisis. *Psychoanalysis, Culture & Society, 21*(4), 426–433.

Brown, R. S. (2017). *Psychoanalysis beyond the end of metaphysics: Thinking towards the post-relational*. London & New York: Routledge.

Connolly, A. (2015). Bridging the reductive and the synthetic: Some reflections on the clinical implications of synchronicity. *Journal of Analytical Psychology, 60*(2), 159–178.

Corbin, H. (1969). *Creative imagination in the ṣūfism of ibn 'arabī*. Princeton, NJ: Princeton University Press.

Davies, J. M., & Frawley, M. G. (1994). *Treating the adult survivor of childhood sexual abuse*. New York: Basic Books.

Davoine, F., & Gaudillière, J. (2004). *History beyond trauma*. New York: Other Press.

de Peyer, J. (2016). Uncanny communication and the porous mind. *Psychoanalytic Dialogues, 26*(2), 156–174.

Erikson, E. H. (1958). *Young man Luther: A study in psychoanalysis and history*. New York: Norton.

Freud, S. (1914). Remembering, repeating and working-through (further recommendations on the technique of psycho-analysis II). In J. Strachey (Ed.), *The standard edition of the complete psychological works of Sigmund Freud* (Vol. 12, pp. 145–156). London: The Hogarth Press.

Frie, R., & Reis, B. (2005). Intersubjectivity: From theory through practice. In J. Mills (Ed.), *Relational and intersubjective perspectives in psychoanalysis* (pp. 3–33). Lanham, MD: Jason Aronson.

Garrard, G. (2011). *Ecocriticism*. New York: Routledge.

Ghent, E. (1990). Masochism, submission, surrender: Masochism as a perversion of surrender. *Contemporary Psychoanalsis, 26*, 108–136.

Gray, F. (2013). *Cartesian philosophy and the flesh: Reflections on incarnation in analytical psychology*. London & New York: Routledge.

Grof, S. (2006). *When the impossible happens: Adventures in non-ordinary realities*. Boulder, CO: Sounds True.

Jung, C. G. (1952). Synchronicity: An acausal connecting principle. In *Collected works* (Vol. 8, pp. 417–531). Princeton, NJ: Princeton University Press.

Jung, C. G. (1955). The theory of psychoanalysis. In *Collected works* (Vol. 4, pp. 83–228). Princeton, NJ: Princeton University Press.

Jung, C. G. (1955–56). Mysterium coniunctionis: An inquiry into the separation and synthesis of psychic opposites in alchemy. In G. Adler & R. F. C. Hull (Eds.), *Collected works* (Vol. 14). Princeton, NJ: Princeton University Press.

Jung, C. G. (1957). Richard Wilhelm: In memoriam. In *Collected works* (Vol. 15, pp. 53–64). Princeton, NJ: Princeton University Press.

Jung, C. G., & Pauli, W. (2000). *Atom and archetype: The Pauli/Jung letters, 1932–1958* (D. Roscoe, Trans. C. A. Meier, Ed.). Princeton, NJ: Princeton University Press.

Katz, G. (1998). Where the action is: The enacted dimension of analytic process. *Journal of the American Psychoanalytic Association, 46*, 1129–1167.

Mayer, E. L. (2001). On "telepathic dreams?": An unpublished paper by Robert J. Stoller. *Journal of the American Psychoanalytic Association, 49*, 629–657.

Mayer, E. L. (2007). *Extraordinary knowing: Science, skepticism, and the inexplicable powers of the human mind*. New York: Bantam Books.

Metzner, R. (1995). The psychopathology of the human-nature relationship. In T. Roszak, M. E. Gomes, & A. Kanner, D. (Eds.), *Ecopsychology: Restoring the earth, healing the mind* (pp. 55–67). San Francisco: Sierra Club Books.

Mitchell, S. A. (1984). Object relations theories and the developmental tilt. *Contemporary Psychoanalsis, 20*, 473–499.

Mitchell, S. A. (1993). *Hope and dread in psychoanalysis*. New York: Basic Books.

Ogden, T. H. (1994). *Subjects of analysis*. Northvale, NJ & London: Jason Aronson.

Progoff, I. (1973). *Jung, synchronicity, and human destiny*. New York: Julian Press.

Roszak, T. (1992). *The voice of the earth: An exploration of ecopsychology*. New York: Simon & Schuster.

Shamdasani, S. (2003). *Jung and the making of modern psychology: The dream of a science*. Cambridge, UK & New York: Cambridge University Press.

Soros, E. (2019). I call this institutionalized rape. In M. Brown, & M. Charles (Eds.), *Women and the psychosocial construction of madness*. Lanham, MD: Lexington Books.

Stern, D. B. (2004). The eye sees itself: Dissociation, enactment, and the achievement of conflict. *Contemporary Psychoanalysis, 40*(2), 197–237.

Stolorow, R. D., & Atwood, G. E. (1992). *Contexts of being: The intersubjective foundations of psychological life*. New York: Routledge.

Stolorow, R. D., Atwood, G. E., & Orange, D. M. (2002). *Worlds of experience: Interweaving philosophical and clinical dimensions in psychoanalysis*. New York: Basic Books.

Stolorow, R. D., Orange, D., & Atwood, G. E. (2001). Cartesian and post-Cartesian trends in relational psychoanalysis. *Psychoanalytic Psychology, 18*(3), 468–484.

Suchet, M. (2016). Surrender, transformation, and transcendence. *Psychoanalytic Dialogues, 26*(6), 747–760.

Tennes, M. (2007). Beyond intersubjectivity. *Contemporary Psychoanalysis, 43*, 505–525.

von Franz, M.-L. (1980). *Projection and re-collection in Jungian psychology: Reflections of the soul* (W. H. Kennedy, Trans.). La Salle & London: Open Court Publishing Company.

Wachtel, P. L. (2008). *Relational theory and the practice of psychotherapy*. New York: The Guildford Press.

Wachtel, P. L. (2017). The relationality of everyday life: The unfinished journey of relational psychoanalysis. *Psychoanalytic Dialogues, 27*(5), 503–521.

Washburn, M. (1994). *Transpersonal psychology in psychoanalytic perspective*. Albany, NY: State University of New York Press.

Washburn, M. (1995). *The ego and the dynamic ground*. Albany, NY: State University of New York Press.

Wilber, K. (1997). An integral theory of consciousness. *Journal of Consciousness Studies, 4*(1), 71–92.

Winnicott, D. W. (1971). *Playing and reality*. New York: Basic Books.

Chapter 5

Imaginal action[1]

Following on the previous chapter's examination of the ways in which evolving conceptions of enactment might challenge clinicians to adopt a panpsychic approach to treatment, in the present chapter I explore this theme from a more explicitly Jungian frame of reference. I argue that while Jung's interest in synchronicity ultimately resulted in his developing a worldview that might address the introverted biases of his psychology, the clinical implications of this shift have not been sufficiently clarified. With reference to several examples, I outline a conception of relational synchronicity wherein the intrapsychic emerges non-projectively within the interpersonal field itself. Comparing and contrasting these occurrences to the more introverted practice of active imagination, it is claimed that such a notion is implicit in Jung's work and is needed as a corrective to his emphasis on interiority. I suggest that what I am here terming "imaginal action" might be conceived as a distinctly Jungian approach to the psychoanalytic notion of enactment. I also show how the idea outlined might find further support from recent developments in the field of transpersonal psychology.

"But the kingdom is inside you and it is outside you."

(Gospel of Thomas)[2]

As Donald lay prone on the sidewalk waiting for the ambulance to arrive, a middle-aged Asian woman held his hand and asked questions. *What is God? Who was Jesus?* His answers were deemed too abstract: the woman insisted that he be more literal. Jesus, for instance, should not be understood as a symbol, but as a man who really lived and was God. Donald hadn't thought to question the veracity of this strange experience until, months later, he mentioned it to a pastor. The pastor, appearing somewhat concerned, noted quietly, "You must have lost a lot of blood." Donald took this observation to imply that the conversation with the Asian woman might not have actually occurred – that he had imagined it. For Donald, the possibility of his having made the event up was of considerable interest. What had previously seemed merely strange now became worthy of more serious consideration. The episode with the Asian woman only became potentially meaningful to Donald when it was suggested that it may have been imagined. Ironically, however, the message of the woman herself had been quite to the contrary – that he should take the flesh and blood experience more seriously.

In Winnicott's (1971) conception of the transitional object, the acceptance of paradox is required in that it should remain unclear whether the object was created by the child, or whether it existed prior to the child's discovery of it. This insight has profound implications for the question of meaning-making in the analytic situation. Although the child's development is seemingly determinant upon a gradual process of disillusionment, it might also be noted that the caregiver's experience of engaging with the child is perhaps optimally one of re-enchantment; the child uses their capacity for play to discover the world, and the adult uses the work of childcare to re-discover their capacity for play. While from the perspective of the caregiver it is the child who is accommodated in sustaining the illusion of infantile omnipotence, it remains fundamentally uncertain who is accommodating to whom – all the more so when we consider Winnicott's (1945) explicit assertion that "fantasy is more primary than reality" (p. 153). The analyst's capacity to enter into the space of play requires an ability to suspend his or her beliefs concerning what is real and what is not. The nature and force of the beliefs that are to be suspended depends on the basic assumptions of the clinician concerning the underlying nature of reality. These beliefs are liable to be expressive of the wider culture.[3] In the secularized West, the creative imagination is generally assumed only to arise as a function of an individual's private experience. Donald's encounter with the Asian woman only started to assume personal meaning when the possibility was introduced to him that the experience had been "in his head."

Introverted bias

Jung's delineation of the attitudes of consciousness expresses a unique contribution to our understanding of the experienced split between self and world. As explored exhaustively in *Psychological Types*, the notions of introversion and extraversion suggest that we each have a predisposition towards interpreting life either in terms of our experience of ourselves or of the world around us. The intuitive appeal of this idea has been reflected in the extent to which both terms have been incorporated into common parlance.[4] If we accept that each of us has a natural predisposition towards one of the two attitudes, then it follows that we each have a natural tendency to resolve the split between self and world by privileging one of the two terms. As clinicians, our fundamental approach to the field of psychology will be shaped by this underlying assumption. Seeking to determine an attitudinal bias within any particular approach to psychology is complicated, however, by virtue of the fact that the discipline of psychology is in and of itself inherently introverted – its object of study is the Cartesian subject. Yet some approaches to psychology are more clearly introverted than others. An extraverted outlook is indicated wherever the study of the psyche seems in danger of being collapsed into the study of biology, behavior, or social relations. Under such circumstances it becomes questionable whether the introverted crux of the matter (i.e. the interior life) has been forgotten altogether.

In light of Jung's emphasis on correcting one-sidedness, his thinking concerning the attitudes of consciousness might give rise to a number of questions:

- If the notion of "psychology" as an academic discipline privileges introversion by definition, how might we start to address this one-sidedness without falling into a reductivism that loses sight of the individual?
- Recognizing that the sense of a living meaning has come to be constrained to the domain of personal experience, how might our metaphors of *interiority* or *depth* be mobilized in the wider world without recourse to the idea of projection?
- To what extent does Jung's psychology succeed in overcoming its own typological biases with respect to the attitudes of consciousness?
- What are the clinical implications of all this?

I have argued that Jung's work demonstrates a consistently introverted bias. I see this reflected in the emphasis that Jung's thinking places on the retraction of projections, and the consequent sense that an extraverted perspective always encounters the psyche at a remove. I have suggested that it was only with the full impact of synchronicity on Jung's thinking, as expressed in terms of his interest in dual-aspect monism, that the possibility emerged of a view that might refrain from privileging introversion. Summarizing my position in an earlier publication (Brown, 2014), I wrote:

> In his early career, Jung first conceptualizes the introvert and extravert positions, suggesting that the two attitudes constitute the opposites out of which the state of *participation mystique* is made partially conscious. In mid-career, he pits these opposites against each other and brings creative heat to the question. This eventually takes him to the position of his late career, wherein the conflict is transcended through recognition of the psychoid nature of the archetype. [. . .] The significance of this development cannot be overstated. Envisioned as a whole, it is apparent that Jung's work necessarily culminates in the idea of the *unus mundus*, since prior to this move his psychology is out of balance (being biased toward introversion) and hence is inconsistent with one of its most fundamental principles.
>
> (pp. 248–249)

I contended that one way of understanding Jung's late (more explicitly metaphysical) thinking is as an attempt to establish a worldview that better honors his commitment to typological wholeness. However, as Main (2007) observes, despite these developments, Jung's application of synchronicity to the clinical situation remained relatively limited.[5] With this said, how might contemporary approaches to clinical work be informed by Jung's late work? In the previous chapter I explored a range of possibilities that I see associated with a panpsychic approach to practice. In this chapter I attend more directly to the Jungian literature in order to locate my approach in context of analytical psychology.

Imaginal action: an initial definition

The practice of active imagination holds a special place in Jung's psychology. As the means by which Jung negotiated his "confrontation with the unconscious," gaining a talent for this practice has for some Jungians been considered a seal of analytic maturity.[6] Given the importance potentially attached to this practice, it might be noted that active imagination is a distinctly introverted endeavor – even if the creative results are shared with others (hence suggesting an extraverted movement into the world), the practice itself fundamentally concerns an engagement with internal imagery.

A more extraverted possibility for active imagination was first offered by Davidson (1966), who suggests that the transference might be considered "a form of active imagination which is described as the enactment in the here-and-now of a hitherto unconscious drama in which the patient has been held a prisoner" (p. 143). For Davidson, the analyst is drawn into this process in a conscious way by being sensitively receptive to the patient's projections. What distinguishes the transference from active imagination proper is the absence of the patient's conscious mediation. The analyst's awareness of the process enables the assumption of an attitude that stands in for the patient's ego integrating function; the patient's fantasy life is not understood by the patient as such, rather it is played out in terms of the transference. In thus conceptualizing the transference as a form of active imagination, Davidson appears to suggest that doing active imagination needn't mean a turn inwards, but could also be understood in terms of enacting something in the world. However, even if defining active imagination in this fashion is accepted as semantically legitimate (cf. Schaverien, 2005), this approach is still explicitly presented by Davidson as a less mature precursor to active imagination proper.

Adopting a more explicitly radical position, Samuels (1985) argues that the imaginal "functions as a linking factor between patient and analyst and that some of the analyst's countertransferences may be regarded as visons and hence part of this imaginal world" (p. 60). Implying a possible resonance with the idea of projective identification, such an approach suggests that the analyst's own fantasy life can in some respect be stimulated by that of the patient – thus might the internal world of the patient be thought of as being not only communicated in terms of the transference but also in terms of a direct communication via the unconscious (Jung, 1946). This line of thinking ultimately causes Samuels to challenge the distinction between the interpersonal (which he defines as relationship) and the intrapsychic (which he defines as image):[7]

We must regard the interpersonal in terms of psyche speaking, and the imaginal in terms of an avenue of communication between two people, a relationship. Persons may carry imagery, imagery may originate in persons. It is necessary to see our field of reference in analysis as seamless and continuous so that ostensible "images" and ostensible "interpersonal communications" do not get separated, nor one gain ascendency over the other on the basis of a pre-conceived hierarchy of importance.

(Samuels, 1985, pp. 67–68)

If we consider that the interpersonal perspective generally reflects a more extraverted conception of the personality, while an intrapsychic outlook is more reflective of introversion,[8] then the foregoing passage reflects an intriguing attempt to bring typological balance to our conceptualizations of the clinical situation. Samuels appears to be suggesting that we might see the interpersonal and the intrapsychic as two sides of the same coin. In practice, however, it is important to emphasize that the distinction between these two domains is first and foremost an *experiential* one – the distinction is an expression of the experienced loss of *participation mystique* as reflected in the Cartesian split between self and world. It is as a consequence of this split that some forms of experience lend themselves more explicitly to an intrapsychic formulation while others suggest an interpersonal one. Clearly it is not possible to collapse the experienced distinction between these two domains merely through an act of theoretical assertion.

Keeping in mind the intent to correct one-sidedness, how might consciousness be modulated so as to enable an intrapsychic experience to be interpersonalized, or an interpersonal experience to be brought more into the realm of the intrapsychic? It seems to me that the former challenge is precisely what Jung seeks to address by way of active imagination. In outlining his approach, Jung states that: "A chain of fantasy ideas develops and gradually takes on a dramatic character: the passive process becomes an action" (Jung, 1955–56, para. 706). The practice of active imagination can thus be understood as a "personifying" of the intrapsychic.

But what of the reverse formulation? We might start by recalling that Jung's notion of active imagination is established in distinction to more quotidian forms of fantasy:

A fantasy is more or less your own invention, and remains on the surface of personal things and conscious expectations. But active imagination, as the terms denotes, means that the images have a life of their own and that the symbolic events develop according to their own logic – that is, of course, if your conscious reason does not interfere.

(Jung, 1935, para. 397)

Clearly not all forms of imagining are conducive to being interpersonalized. A symbol is required such as to cathect the latent possibility of animation and thus dialogue. Similarly, it might be supposed that special conditions would also apply in order for an interpersonal situation to be shifted by means of conscious participation towards the intrapsychic. These "special conditions" might be conceived as hints of the intrapsychic emerging directly within the interpersonal field as synchronicities. Main (2011) writes:

With his concept of the unconscious, especially the collective unconscious, and its challenging relationship to consciousness, Jung theorised both the inevitability and the desirability of such a buffered state [of the self] being undermined as the psyche expressed its natural propensity to develop towards a state of greater wholeness in which more unconscious content was integrated into a widening field of consciousness. In this understanding, however, the main challenge to the self's boundaries comes from within, from the unconscious. A more radical challenge was introduced by the concept of synchronicity. For this concept draws attention to experiences in which content seemingly belonging to the self can, acausally and non-projectively, find expression also in the external world.

(Main, 2011, p. 150)

What I am intending by imaginal action then is not simply the occurrence of a coincidence in the interpersonal world that enables suitable material for projection. In order for our thinking not to fall back into introverted bias, it is necessary that we conceptualize such charged moments in terms of the intrapsychic disclosing itself in a radically unmediated sense, not simply within the interpersonal field, but *as* the interpersonal field – that is, as Main puts it, non-projectively. Two or more individuals thus find themselves immersed in the imaginal dynamics of the moment, with both playing roles in a shared manifestation of psyche.

Two short examples

It has become a commonplace to insist that one cannot speak out of a position of privilege. If a woman tells me that she resents the privileges afforded to men as a consequence of the society we both live in, as a man my possible wish to express a divergent position is potentially stymied as an example of male privilege at work. It might come to seem that the only acceptable response is passive agreement. One way of understanding this dynamic is in terms of projective identification; that is, the woman's intolerable sense of powerlessness is split off and put into me, the man, so that I now feel forced into the experience of being silenced and unable to act.

I formulate the foregoing train of thought standing in line at a Whole Foods[9] waiting to pay for a sandwich. I am dressed professionally in a blazer and tie. Having paid, I go to the seating area with the intention of eating my sandwich. As I sit down, a middle-aged and casually dressed white woman approaches me holding her own lunch (also ostensibly purchased from Whole Foods). She has a somewhat wild look in her eyes. She asks me, "Greed or shark?" I look at her quizzically, and she states that she's doing a survey. Mildly confused and with the sense that this woman is trying to put something on me, I turn the tables and ask her which does *she* choose. She replies, "Innocent." Feeling by now somewhat provoked, I observe "It seems like there might be a veiled message here." The woman smiles coyly and nods. With the sense of being attacked, I return her smile and ask what she supposes that this message might be. At this point in the proceedings the woman appears to become uncomfortable, and withdraws from conversation. Feeling unwelcome, I decide to leave the Whole Foods.

Eating my sandwich in a nearby park, I become aware of how the unexpected interaction with this woman seemingly bore a strange connection with the substance of my reflections moments before I encountered her. My first take on this was to perceive what had transpired as a direct confirmation of my thinking – that this seemingly psychotic woman had taken exception to me on the basis of my appearance, and sought to saddle me with her own greed, aggression, and powerlessness. Upon further reflection, however, I started to think more about my own response and the way in which I had turned the woman's "survey" question back at her. This led to my reflecting on the way in which women's inequality might itself be framed in terms of a history of men projecting their own sense of power-lessness onto women. Whose powerlessness is at stake here?

Schwartz-Salant (1988) recommends thinking of the analytic situation as an interactive field, the dynamics of which are best understood by conceptualizing projective identification in terms of the aspects of an unconscious couple that structure the third – "For then one moves out of a sphere of omnipotence [. . .] and into a domain in which both people can discover how they have, so to speak, been acting out a mutual dream, or how they have been being dreamed" (p. 50). Such an approach is fostered by refraining from interpreting in terms of projection, and instead focus-ing on the quality of the field itself. This outlook is complementary to the notion of imaginal action I am outlining, and perhaps offers some clue as to how these events might be worked with more intentionally.

In the example just offered, my awareness of the synchronistic coin-cidence between my internal discourse and the interpersonal interaction immediately following it only emerged after the fact. This needn't be the case however. A supervisee reported the following experience: Following a period of several months during which her patient had, on multiple occa-sions, failed to appear for sessions, the analyst resolved that she needed to establish a firmer boundary. Previous requests that the patient be more consistent had proven ineffective. In session, the analyst informed the patient that they would not be able to continue working together if there was to be another no-show. The analyst explained her rationale for tak-ing this position, and the patient appeared receptive. As the issue seemed to be reaching a point of closure, however, the patient inexplicably seg-ued into a hateful diatribe concerning her boyfriend's brother. The content of this diatribe focused on the fact of this person being a drug addict – the patient raged self-righteously that, despite having suffered a history of childhood trauma, *she* had never resorted to drugs. In this fashion the patient expressed her profound disgust at the perceived "weakness" of her boyfriend's brother.

It so happened that the analyst had, in her early adulthood, suffered extensively with challenges pertaining to drug addiction (this had not been shared with the patient). Unsurprisingly, the topic thus held considerable charge in terms of the analyst's feelings of shame and professional compe-tency. When the patient's diatribe first began, the analyst became scared. She reported a sense that the patient was able to "see into her soul," and struggled to convince herself that the attack on the boyfriend's brother was not in fact a particularly vicious attack on her personally. Further compli-cating matters, the patient in question also happened to be a clinician in training. In the midst of her rage the patient paused, self-consciously, to state that if she were to be treating someone presenting with similar issues (i.e. pertaining to drug addiction) then as a clinician she believed she would be able to put her personal feelings about this subject to one side and treat the person compassionately. My supervisee perceived that the patient felt judged by her. Furthermore, she believed that this was prob-ably to some extent true, and that judging her patient had enabled my col-league to feel more secure in her professional role as clinician.

When the patient appeared for the following session she had dyed her hair the same color as the analyst's. Without seemingly acknowledging this, the patient then spent much of the session complaining about how others were always copying her. In the months that followed the patient attended treatment consistently.[10] Meanwhile, my supervisee experienced an increasing sense of comfort around sharing her history of addiction with others in the field – a shift which she attributes to something about the experience of this session. She also reports having subsequently been able to engage more deeply with her own experiences of suffering through addiction, and that accessing these feelings more directly has been of direct value in enabling her to engage more empathically with the specific struggles of her patient.

Relationship to the concept of enactment

Before commenting on the two examples just given, I would like to locate the idea I am outlining in relationship to the psychoanalytic concept of enactment. The term "enactment" started to gain popularity within the psychoanalytic world during the 1980s and has been adopted with vari-ous connotations to suggest an increasing interest in the role of unspoken communication.

Jacobs (1986) is credited with having introduced the term, with an ini-tial definition of enactment being further worked out in a 1989 panel dis-cussion convened by the American Psychoanalytic Association (Johan, 1992). The four participants on this panel (Dale Boesky, Judith Chused, Theodore Jacobs, and James McLaughlin) presented papers (McLaughlin, 1991) and agreed upon a shared definition of enactment conceived as dis-crete moments of variable duration wherein unconscious components of the transference and countertransference interact so that theses dynamics are performed as action in the treatment.[11] These dynamics are conceptualized as mutual resistance, yet in being performed the opportunity is presented of identifying the dynamics concerned and bringing them to conscious awareness.

Problematizing Freud's (1914) fundamental distinction between speech and action,[12] an increasing emphasis has been placed on the idea that countertransference must inevitably be performed before it might in some respect be recognized reflectively (Renik, 1993). Levine and Friedman (2000) define enactment as a "complex, overlapping, embedded series of often subtle, unconscious, interactive, mutually constructed dramas that are jointly lived out rather than only spoken of" (p. 73). Enactment has come to be understood as a constant aspect of relationship, rather than being used to signify the ways in which the analyst is *on occasion* countertransferentially prompted into conformity with the patient's internal world. Speaking of discrete moments of enactment is liable to lose sight of the ways in which the performance of the transference and countertransference is always taking place. Despite this danger, it is still necessary to acknowledge that there are specific moments in the treatment where the sense of an enactment having taken place becomes much more pressingly apparent. Anthony Bass (2003) writes:

> We can usually discern a difference between ordinary, quotidian enactments that form the daily ebb and flow of ordinary analytic process and what I had named [. . .] Enactments (capital E), the highly condensed precipitates of unconscious psychic elements in patient and analyst that mobilize our full, heightened attention and define, and often take hold of, our analytic activity for periods of time. These processes frequently are fundamental to psychic change.
>
> (Bass, 2003, p. 660)

Margaret Black (2003) has conceptualized the transformative power of enactment as having to do not so much with the content of such events as with an energizing of the analytic field:

> Much as ionically configured molecular structures, stable in isolation, begin disassembling in the presence of a polarized liquid, so may patient and analyst be thought of as interactively destabilizing

established but not fully resolved unconscious patterns in one another; as a result, unbound energy becomes available for what we might call an energic analytic interweaving that empowers change. In this process, brittlely configured rigid patterns that have imprisoned the patient's psyche may gain destabilizing energy from the similarly con- figured structures in the analyst, which while conflictual, are not so rigidly bound.

(Black, 2003, p. 646)

The distinction Bass makes between quotidian enactments and those more heightened or "energized" moments (to use Black's language) points to a qualitative shift in the relational field, which, in its uncanny nature, is dif- ficult to account for in conventional psychoanalytic terms. Drawing from Jung's ideas concerning synchronicity and active imagination, the notion of imaginal action offers a means by which to engage more seriously with the strangeness of such experiences. By conceptualizing these co-created moments as the quickening of psyche in the world,[13] the tendency to sub- tly retreat from such experiences by conceptualizing them in terms of mutual projections/transferences is diminished.[14] This line of thinking might also offer some clues as to how such moments can be transforma- tive, and what approach might be adopted to better effectuate this.

To return to the example I gave concerning my unexpected encounter in Whole Foods, I turned the question "Greed or shark?" back on the woman who asked it – in effect, I inwardly assumed a conventionally "clinical" perspective on what was happening by imagining something that was "put into" me and then, in what would have constituted a fail- ure of containment had this interaction occurred in a clinical context, I sought to put this something "back inside" the other person. While ostensibly remaining self-aware and avoiding the woman's attack, I failed to recognize the personal relevance of what was taking place in the moment. My colleague, by contrast, assumed a different kind of response. She became explicitly paranoid, and struggled with the idea that her patient could see into her soul. It is my contention that this atti- tude may have enabled the imaginal action to deepen in a way that was not apparent in terms of my encounter with the woman at Whole Foods. I suggest that the difficulty in becoming conscious of an enactment has at least something to do with not having the right conceptual tools to foster a suitably paranoid style of consciousness such as to enable some degree of recognition without foregoing the vitality of one's subjective participation in the moment. This might be compared to the experience of lucid dreaming, wherein the awareness that one is dreaming needs to be balanced with a belief in the importance of remaining in the dream on its own terms. Jung speaks of active imagination as "a deliberate weakening of the conscious mind and its inhibiting effect, which either limits or suppresses the unconscious" (Jung, 1941, para. 320). Perhaps a similar attitude could fruitfully be maintained in responding to enactments. Jung's notion of not acting on an emotion in order that it might give rise to an image entails suspending an attribution of explicit meaning. A similar challenge is posed in terms of resisting the urge to interpret instances of imaginal action in terms of transference/countertransference dynamics. To "recognize" an enactment on such terms is roughly equivalent to rationalizing an active imagination as something artificially contrived or "made up" by the individual. Maintaining the balance in transitional space that was alluded to at the start of this chapter requires the possibility that the person "made it up" be given co-equal weight with the idea that it was "real." In the transitional experience of active imagination,[15] the prerequisite balance is between the rationalistic belief in having contrived the experience oneself, and the psychotic belief that the experience is more real than the person. In the case of imaginal action, the balance suggested is between taking responsibility for one's projections versus a sense of participatory enmeshment in the moment.

Complementary developments in transpersonal psychology

The "participatory turn" in spiritual and religious studies (see Ferrer & Sherman, 2008) offers some further parallels with the notion of imaginal action thus far outlined.[16] Building on the work of Donald Rothberg (1993, 1994, 1996, 1999) and Ken Wilber (1995), Jorge Ferrer (2002) critiques what he refers to as the "experiential" emphasis in transpersonal thinking. He sees this demonstrated wherever spirituality is understood in terms of intrasubjective phenomena or states of consciousness. Ferrer writes: "Ever since Brentano, Husserl Sartre, and others, all experience and states of consciousness are said to be always "of something" and usually "by someone." As a result, whenever we hear the word *experience*, we immediately want to know who had what experience" (p. 33).

Ferrer observes that the idea of spirituality being confined to the interior experience of individuals is a recent development, and is expressive of modernity's trifold division of life into the natural, social, and inner worlds. While transpersonal psychology has historically sought to reclaim the epistemic value of spiritual phenomena, it has done so without challenging the basic assumptions of the modern worldview. Ferrer notes that the challenge for transpersonal thinking is not to collapse the three worlds by endorsing a romantic return to a prior state of affairs, but rather to work towards an integration.

Ferrer suggests that the experiential outlook in transpersonal thinking was informed both by the transpersonal movement's origins in humanistic psychology, and by an understandable desire to uphold what measure of mainstream academic credibility the field might yet sustain given its already challenging subject matter. By conceptualizing spiritual phenomena along experiential lines, Ferrer argues that transpersonal thinkers have often perpetuated a form of *subtle Cartesianism* that is fundamentally incompatible with the nature of most spiritual phenomena, which, by their very nature, tend to challenge the split between self and Other. Ferrer thus wishes to conceptualize transpersonal phenomena as multilocal participatory events. Such events can be understood to occur not only in the context of individuals but also in terms of personal relationships, groups, communities, and even in relationship to the nonhuman environment. Rather than assuming shifts in personal consciousness give rise to spiritual experiences, Ferrer suggests that it is the occurrence of transpersonal events that in turn elicit transpersonal experiences in individuals. This implies that the ostensible subject can in some fundamental sense participate transformatively in the ostensible object such that the distinction between the two is challenged. Ferrer writes:

In other words, aspects belonging to the structures of subjectivity can reach out and become, in a way, objects for consciousness in the external world. Of course, the defense mechanism of projection comes rapidly to mind in this regard. However, psychodynamic accounts of projection are not helpful in explaining the idea to be grasped here, because they depict this external objectification of the subjective as an intrapsychic phenomenon: The projection of our repressed feelings or unconscious personality traits upon people or events does not really transform them; what changes is only our experience of them. By contrast, in transpersonal and spiritual development [. . .] new worlds of corresponding objects and meanings *actually* emerge as consciousness evolves and identifies itself with new structures of subjectivity. This idea receives support from many contemplative traditions such as Vajrayana Buddhism or Kabbalah, which maintain that inner spiritual practices are not merely aimed at changing the self, but at the actual transformation of the world.

(Ferrer, 2002, p. 31)

Jung's transpersonal approach to the psyche perhaps goes some way towards challenging Ferrer's assumption that an emphasis on "experience" rather than "events" is necessarily prone to the subtle Cartesianism that he seeks to challenge. As Ferrer (2002) himself seems to acknowledge, his critique of the experiential emphasis in transpersonal thinking depends on a relatively restricted conception of "experience" and the realm of the subjective (p. 194). Such a critique is problematized by the fashion in which Jung's conception of the psyche challenges assumptions concerning the limits of the subjective (see Brown, 2018b). If speaking in terms of "experience" is liable to reinforce the idea that spiritual phenomena are restricted (in a reductive fashion) to the realm of individuals, speaking in terms of participatory "events" is perhaps equally liable to give the impression that the subject is merely acted upon from without. For the notion of participation to be registered fully meaningful seems to require that both orientations be honored. Nevertheless, the essential thrust of Ferrer's critique clearly remains significant, and his emphasis on events seems like an important corrective to the one-sided (introverted) emphasis on inner experience.

If active imagination is more readily conceptualized as an experience, perhaps instances of imaginal action are better understood as events. In making this heuristic distinction we might briefly consider the two main dangers Ferrer associates with the experiential approach to transpersonal phenomena: *spiritual narcissism* and *integrative arrestment*. Recalling Chögyam Trungpa's (1987) notion of *spiritual materialism*, Ferrer defines spiritual narcissism as the misappropriation of spirituality in the service of egocentric self-centeredness. The notion of integrative arrestment, meanwhile, signifies difficulties in translating spiritual realizations into lasting transformations of self, relationships, and world. By thinking in terms of transpersonal events rather than experiences, Ferrer suggests that these twin dangers of spiritual narcissism and integrative arrestment can be better avoided. Where the underlying assumption is of the ego's participation in an event, spiritual phenomena are less prone to being grasped at narcissistically and more likely to be integrated. I have suggested that a related process might be evident in the fashion that becoming conscious of an enactment tends to pose a danger that we retreat from the event – particularly where our conceptual tools emphasize disentangling transference from countertransference and thus taking ownership of that which we perceive to be ours.

Conclusion

The notion of imaginal action potentially offers a useful supplement to the working ideals of maintaining a symbolic attitude and acknowledging the reality of the transferential field. The "as if" capacity of the analyst is furthered with appropriate metaphysical support and hindered in its absence.[17] Efforts to collapse our understanding of the intrapsychic and the interpersonal, while theoretically satisfying, remain psychologically truncated. Jung's attitudes of consciousness have exerted so much interest precisely because they speak to our everyday experience and not simply to the conceptual systems of philosophers and psychologists. Any attempt to address Cartesianism as a theoretical problem must acknowledge that the theoretical challenge gives voice to an ontological one – that of re-enchantment.

I will close this chapter with the following passage from Jung:

> No, the collective unconscious is anything but an incapsulated personal system; it is sheer objectivity, as wide as the world and open to all the world. There I am the object of every subject, in complete reversal of my ordinary consciousness, where I am always the subject that has an object. There I am utterly one with the world, so much a part of it that I forget all too easily who I really am. "Lost in oneself" is a good way of describing this state. But this self is the world, if only a consciousness could see it. That is why we must know who we are.
>
> (1954, para. 46)

Notes

1 An earlier version of this chapter was published as a paper in the *Journal of Analytical Psychology* (Brown, 2018a).
2 Thomas (2003, p. 45).
3 Winnicott (1953) states of the transitional object: "Its fate is to be gradually allowed to be decathected, so that in the course of years it becomes not so much forgotten as relegated to limbo. By this I mean that in health the transitional object does not 'go inside' nor does the feeling about it necessarily undergo repression. It is not forgotten and it is not mourned. It loses meaning, and this is because the transitional phenomena have become diffused, have become spread out over the whole intermediate territory between 'inner psychic reality' and 'the external world as perceived by two persons in common,' that is to say, over the whole cultural field" (p. 91).
4 Albeit with a somewhat different valance than Jung had intended.
5 Jung's thinking in this respect is restricted to limited allusions concerning the fashion in which synchronistic phenomena can be stimulated by the transference, and to the idea that the occurrence of synchronicities in the analytic situation can provide information about the patient and the progression of the treatment. Two relatively recent papers that seek to expand upon the clinical implications of synchronicity are offered by Bright (1997) and Hogenson (2009).
6 Particularly for those analysts influenced most directly by Marie Louise von Franz and/or James Hillman.
7 In the early history of psychoanalysis, the clearest expression of an extraverted clinical perspective has been reflected in the work of Harry Stack Sullivan and the interpersonal tradition's emphasis on the role of present relationships over and against classical conceptions of the intrapsychic. Jungian thinking has not tended to focus on this distinction nearly so explicitly as have post-Freudian psychoanalysts (particularly in the United States). While Jung's emphasis on the here-and-now coupled with his face-to-face approach to clinical work suggests considerable affinity with an interpersonal approach, his theoretical language emphasizes the intrapsychic. The distinction between the intrapsychic and the interpersonal is a fundamental feature of debates across theoretical orientations in the wider psychoanalytic world.
8 Let it be stressed that a direct equivalence is not intended here – for example, Ronald Fairbairn's thinking demonstrates a fundamentally extraverted sensibility in associating interiority with pathology, but while his developmental theory is correspondingly an interpersonal one his work nevertheless emphasizes the intrapsychic.
9 An upscale American supermarket chain.
10 While, from a more skeptical perspective, an objection might be made that the patient's hair coloring and subsequent compliance in the treatment could in fact signify an adhesive gesture initiated out of fear of retaliation for the patient's anti-addiction rant, it can only be said that such a reading does not appear congruent with the subsequent development of the treatment.

11 Joseph Sandler had already introduced the notion of role-responsiveness, wherein he suggested that the patient subtly pulls for the analyst to play out a part that is reflective of the patient's intrapsychic life. Sandler (1976) suggests that the patient achieves this by way of a fit between the patient's own unconscious life and that of the analyst. He considered this a helpful element of the treatment in bringing to light repressed wishes that came to be expressed directly in the relationship with the therapist. Hirsch (1998) has argued that the notion of enactment brings Freudian thinking into closer alignment with the interpersonal tradition, for it implies a perspective that is resonant with Sullivan's (1953) portrayal of the clinician as a participant-observer. Having started down this road, it is easy to see how a more relational conception of the analytic relationship is liable to emerge as a consequence (just as it had already in the history of interpersonal thinking). Yet for more classically oriented analysts, the fact that enactments do take place needn't imply that this is unavoidable or, for that matter, even therapeutically valuable (see Ivey, 2008). An example can be offered in terms of the post-Kleinian container-contained model. In such a context enactment is liable to be conceptualized as compliance with the patient's projective identifications. This approach assumes that the analyst can somehow get out of their own way – it is the clinician's capacity to place their personal equation to one side that enables them to function as a container. The instance of an enactment thus signifies a collapse of the analyst's role as container, with this being registered as a failure in the analyst's capacity to think (see Bonovitz, 2007).

12 Edgar Levenson (1983) can be considered an early influence in having argued that all speech is a form of action.

13 "Bringing in the dreamer," as Bromberg (2006) puts it.

14 "It is not good form to keep the left hand in your pocket or behind your back when shaking hands" (Jung, 1940, p. 17).

15 For a discussion of transitional phenomena and their direct relationship to active imagination, see Fordham (1985, chapter 4).

16 It is beyond the remit of the present chapter to examine the wider nature and implications of participatory thinking. In previous publications I have argued for the value of a participatory approach both to clinical practice and as a means to reading Jung (see Brown, 2016, 2017a, 2017b).

17 Much of my previous engagement with Jung's work has concerned the ways in which Jung's archetypal thinking supports the idea that a metaphysic is always implied in clinical practice, whether stated explicitly or otherwise (Brown, 2016, 2017a, 2017b).

References

Bass, A. (2003). "E" enactments in psychoanalysis: Another medium, another message. *Psychoanalytic Dialogues, 13*(5), 657–675.

Black, M. J. (2003). Enactment: Analytic musings on energy, language, and personal growth. *Psychoanalytic Dialogues, 13*(5), 633–655.

Bonovitz, C. (2007). Whose who in the psychoanalytic situation: Subject, object, and enactment in the relational and contemporary Kleinian traditions. *Psychoanalytic Dialogues, 17*(3), 411–437.

Bright, G. (1997). Synchronicity as a basis of analytic attitude. *Journal of Analytical Psychology, 42*, 613–635.

Bromberg, P. M. (2006). *Awakening the dreamer: Clinical journeys*. Mahwah, NJ: The Analytic Press.

Brown, R. S. (2014). Evolving attitudes. *International Journal of Jungian Studies, 6*(3), 243–253.

Brown, R. S. (2016). Spirituality and the challenge of clinical pluralism: Participatory thinking in psychotherapeutic context. *Spirituality in Clinical Practice, 3*(3), 187–195.

Brown, R. S. (2017a). Bridging worlds: Participatory thinking in Jungian context. *Journal of Analytical Psychology, 62*(2), 284–304.

Brown, R. S. (2017b). *Psychoanalysis beyond the end of metaphysics: Thinking towards the post-relational*. Abingdon, UK & New York: Routledge.

Brown, R. S. (2018a). Imaginal action: Towards a Jungian conception of enactment, and an extraverted counterpart to active imagination. *Journal of Analytical Psychology, 63*(2), 186–206.

Brown, R. S. (2018b). Where do minds meet? Intersubjectivity in light of Jung. In R. S. Brown (Ed.), *Re-encountering Jung: Analytical psychology and contemporary psychoanalysis* (pp. 160–179). Abingdon, UK & New York: Routledge.

Davidson, D. (1966). Transference as a form of active imagination. *Journal of Analytical Psychology, 11*(2), 135–146.

Ferrer, J. N. (2002). *Revisioning transpersonal theory: A participatory vision of human spirituality*. Albany, NY: State University of New York Press.

Ferrer, J. N., & Sherman, J. H. (2008). The participatory turn in spirituality, mysticism, and religious studies. In J. N. Ferrer & J. H. Sherman (Eds.), *The participatory turn: Spirituality, mysticism, religious studies* (pp. 1–78). Albany, NY: State University of New York Press.

Fordham, M. (1985). *Explorations into the self*. London: The Academic Press.

Freud, S. (1914). Remembering, repeating and working-through (further recommendations on the technique of psycho-analysis II). In J. Strachey (Ed.), *The standard edition of the complete psychological works of Sigmund Freud* (Vol. 12, pp. 145–156). London: The Hogarth Press.

Hirsch, I. (1998). The concept of enactment and theoretical convergence. *The Psychoanalytic Quarterly, 67*(1), 78–101.

Hogenson, G. B. (2009). Synchronicity and moments of meeting. *Journal of Analytical Psychology, 54*, 183–197.

Ivey, G. (2008). Enactment controversies: A critical review of current debates. *The International Journal of Psychoanalysis, 89*, 19–38.

Jacobs, A. N. (1986). On countertransference enactments. *Journal of the American Psychoanalytic Association, 34*, 289–307.

Johan, M. (1992). Panel report: Enactments in psychoanalysis. *Journal of the American Psychoanalytic Association, 40*, 827–841.

Jung, C. G. (1935). The Tavistock lectures. In *Collected works* (Vol. 18, pp. 5–182). Princeton, NJ: Princeton University Press.

Jung, C. G. (1940). Psychology and religion. In *Collected works* (Vol. 11, pp. 3–105). Princeton, NJ: Princeton University Press.

Jung, C. G. (1941). The psychological aspects of the kore. In *Collected works* (pp. 182–203). Princeton, NJ: Princeton University Press.

Jung, C. G. (1946). The psychology of the transference. In *Collected works* (Vol. 16, pp. 353–537). Princeton, NJ: Princeton University Press.

Jung, C. G. (1954). Archetypes of the collective unconscious. In *Collected works* (Vol. 9i, pp. 3–41). Princeton, NJ: Princeton University Press.

Jung, C. G. (1955–56). Mysterium coniunctionis: An inquiry into the separation and synthesis of psychic opposites in alchemy. In G. Adler & R. F. C. Hull (Eds.), *Collected works* (Vol. 14). Princeton, NJ: Princeton University Press.

Levenson, E. A. (1983). *The ambiguity of change: An inquiry into the nature of psychoanalytic reality.* New York: Basic Books.

Levine, H. B., & Friedman, R. J. (2000). Intersubjectivity and interaction in the analytic relationship: A mainstream view. *Psychoanalytic Quarterly, 69*, 63–92.

Main, R. (2007). Synchronicity and analysis: Jung and after. *European Journal of Psychotherapy & Counselling, 9*(4), 359–371.

Main, R. (2011). Synchronicity and the limits of re-enchantment. *International Journal of Jungian Studies, 3*(2), 144–158. doi:10.1080/19409052.2011.592723

McLaughlin, J. T. (1991). Clinical and theoretical aspects of enactment. *Journal of the American Psychoanalytic Association, 39*, 595–614.

Renik, O. (1993). Analytic interaction: Conceptualizing technique in light of the analyst's irreducible subjectivity. *The Psychoanalytic Quarterly, 62*, 553–571.

Rothberg, D. (1993). The crisis of modernity and the emergence of socially engaged spirituality. *ReVision, 15*(3), 105–114.

Rothberg, D. (1994). Spiritual inquiry. *ReVision, 17*(2), 2–12.

Rothberg, D. (1996). Toward an integral spirituality. *ReVision, 19*(2), 41–42.

Rothberg, D. (1999). Transpersonal issues at the millennium. *Journal of Transpersonal Psychology, 31*(1), 41–67.

Samuels, A. (1985). Countertransference, the "mundus imaginalis" and a research project. *Journal of Analytical Psychology, 30*, 47–71.

Sandler, J. (1976). Countertransference and role-responsiveness. *The International Review of Psycho-Analysis, 3*, 43–47.

Schaverien, J. (2005). Art, dreams and active imagination: A post-Jungian approach to transference and the image. *Journal of Analytical Psychology, 50*, 127–153.

Schwartz-Salant, N. (1988). Archetypal foundations of projective identification. *Journal of Analytical Psychology, 33*, 39–64.

Sullivan, H. S. (1953). *The interpersonal theory of psychiatry*. New York: Norton.

Thomas, D. J. (2003). The Gospel of Thomas (M. Meyer, Trans.). In W. Barnstone & M. Meyer (Eds.), *The gnostic bible* (pp. 43–69). Boston & London: Shambhala.

Trungpa, C. (1987). *Cutting through spiritual materialism*. Boston: Shambhala.

Wilber, K. (1995). *Sex, ecology and spirituality: The spirit of evolution*. Boston: Shambhala.

Winnicott, D. W. (1945). Primitive emotional development. In *Through paediatrics to psycho-analysis: Collected papers* (pp. 145–156). New York: Brunner/Mazel.

Winnicott, D. W. (1953). Transitional objects and transitional phenomena: A study of the first not-me possession. *International Journal of Psychoanalysis, 34*, 89–97.

Winnicott, D. W. (1971). *Playing and reality*. New York: Basic Books.

Chapter 6

Therapeutic nonaction

Shifting conceptions of enactment pose fundamental questions as to the nature of therapeutic action. What does it mean to be therapeutically effective? In what sense can the enacted dimension of the treatment be meaningfully engaged by the clinician? In this chapter, I explore the Taoist notion of wu-wei and connect this idea with the work of Jung, Bion, and Searles. With reference to clinical material, I attempt to illustrate the fashion in which the becoming of both patient and analyst are synchronistically connected.

The relational movement has reflected a major shift in how we conceptualize therapeutic change. The early history of Freudian psychoanalysis foregrounded the mutative function of interpretation. Emphasis was placed on the analyst being able to maintain therapeutic neutrality, and their success in so doing enabled the proper application of Freud's theory and technique so as to obtain rationalistic formulations pertaining to the patient's inner world. Over time, however, this mentality came to be challenged – largely by way of an increasing recognition of the role played by countertransference. The notion of countertransference was, in effect, the doorway to a recognition of the ubiquity of the subjective factor. Thoughtful engagement with this notion led to a recognition of the epistemological problems thus implied. Psychoanalytic positivism became increasingly difficult to justify (Fusella, 2014; Orange, 2003). At the same time, many of the field's most interesting theoretical developments pointed clinicians to the possible importance of the relationship itself over and above the analyst's function as an interpreter.

One of the most distinctive contributions made by the relational literature lies in a persistent commitment to the idea that conscious mentation
cannot control for the emergence of unconscious dynamics. Relational
thinking suggests not only that our thoughts about the therapeutic interaction are incommensurate with our experience, but also that we are always
at least a step behind what is currently taking place; that in order for us to
be able to offer a verbal formulation of our experience, what we are speaking of must already be happening or have happened.

The "classical" conception of countertransference has been contrasted
with the so-called totalistic conception (Kernberg, 1965). Classically
understood, countertransference is conceptualized as the unconscious
reaction of the analyst to the patient's transference and is always assumed
detrimental to the treatment. The totalistic viewpoint considers countertransference as the total emotional response that the analyst has to their
patient, this including both conscious and unconscious dimensions. The
totalistic viewpoint enabled the emergence of the idea that the conscious
dimensions of the countertransference might be therapeutically useful.
However, it is only with the emergence of the notion of enactment in the
1980s and the parallel development of the relational movement that analysts started to explore how the clinician's unconscious participation might
also be therapeutically beneficial. Reflecting the centrality that this notion
has assumed within the field, Atlas and Aron (2015) state: "Enactments
may well be a central means by which patients and analysts enter into
each other's inner world and discover themselves as participants within
each other's psychic life, mutually constructing the relational matrix that
constitutes the medium of psychoanalysis" (p. 316). What implications
does this line of thinking have for technique? Jody Messler Davies (2004)
forwards the significant idea that it is possible for a treatment to get stuck
not only when an enactment goes unrecognized but also when an enactment is in some sense resisted or avoided:

> I have come to think of certain impasses in psychoanalytic work not as
> enactments one can't get out of, but rather as nascent enactments that
> one can't fully enter and get into, because occupation of the counter-
> transference component of the enactment is blocked by the analyst's
> dissociated, shame-riddled self-states.
>
> (p. 730)

In a related sense, Grossmark (2012a, 2012b) talks about entering the flow of enactive process and sees this as a contemporary form of free association. To operate "unobtrusively" in the treatment is to engage in this enactive flow: "The work of the treatment is to allow the enactment to tell its story, to emerge in a fully felt way" (2012a, p. 288).

Owen Renik is a well-known proponent of the importance that lies in fully embodying one's subjective responses when working with patients:

> What are the practical implications of a conception of analytic technique that accepts the analyst's constant subjectivity? For one thing, it means we discard a widely accepted principle of technique which holds that countertransference enactment, so called, is to be avoided. While emotional satisfaction for the analyst is clearly not an objective to be pursued, in and of itself, in making technical decisions, neither does recognition that a given course of action will serve the analyst's personal purposes constitute a contraindication to going forward.
>
> (Renik, 1993, p. 564)

Taking issue with this approach, Katz (2014) makes a significant argument that our participation in enactment cannot sensibly be enfolded within questions of technique, since enactment is by definition unconscious. He writes:

> Enactments will occur, without awareness or intent, regardless of what you think you are doing or are intending to do, regardless of the analytic theory you profess, regardless of whether you are scrupulous or free-wheeling in your approach to technique. No analytic practitioner is immune. You will become aware that an enacted process has occurred in retrospect, generally at a dynamically meaningful juncture in the treatment.
>
> (p. 66)

It is important to note both the theoretical basis upon which a claim of this kind rests and the technical problems that arise if one is to challenge it. The notion that enactive process exists beyond the purview of conscious awareness and/or influence rests upon a Freudian conception of consciousness. This line of thinking recalls Freud's assertion that "preconscious" processes are entirely barred from consciousness (see Natsoulas, 2001), and thus suffers from the problem of explaining how something conscious can be related to something unconscious if the two states are irreconcilably different – a question that ultimately reflects the basic problem of mind-body dualism. Throughout the present text I have sought to question the idea that the unconscious is inaccessible to conscious experience, thus my position on this matter is that while enactments will indeed occur without awareness or intent, the analyst does nevertheless have a role to play in guiding this process.

The great difficulty that emerges with a conception of enactment that allows for the analyst being able to in some sense steer the process lies with the question of how a clinician is to determine or sense when a movement "up" is required vs a movement "down" – when does the furtherance of the treatment require shifting towards a more self-conscious attitude, and when does it require allowing oneself a greater degree of emotional freedom. The great advantage of endorsing a Freudian approach to enactment is that doing so obviates this significant problem. For Katz (2014), upholding a technical conservatism is "the dialectical counterpart to the patient's press toward transference actualization" (p. 39). Having thus established this baseline ideal, the analyst's task is to maintain a reserved technical approach while taking note of their inevitable failures to do so and adapting accordingly. However, if we do not consider such an attitude to always be therapeutically optimal then we are left with the messy task of justifying how one is to "know" how to function in the treatment. I will argue that the justification for a relational approach of this sort is best realized in transpersonal terms.

Some clinical material

In a memorable paper concerning the use of the analyst's hate, Frederickson (1990) interprets his felt sense of hatred in the countertransference as an empathic response to his patient. He suggests that at moments in the treatment he came to experience himself as if he were the abused child that his patient had been. Frederickson delineates how, with the use of here-and-now questions and statements, he responded to his patient not by using his experience of the countertransference to offer interpretations of the patient's past, but rather by offering realistic responses that were expressive of the analyst's in-the-moment experience. A particularly charged moment in the treatment is described as follows:

> In the sixteenth month of our work he raged at me because he could not have his old hour back after we had made a change at his request. He finally stood up and towered over me screaming. He had become increasingly provocative but this was the worst. I quickly stood up with my face only three inches from his. In as loud a voice as I could muster I yelled, "Shut up!" I sat down. Jolted, he sat down too as I continued: "I can't take it. I can't take your screaming. I can't take your kicking the furniture. I don't know if people did this to you in your past or what. I just know I can't take it." "Good," he replied, "The first human response I've gotten from you." He was pleased he had made an impact on me but then wondered if this had been staged. In a low voice I tried to make it absolutely clear to him: "Believe me, this was not staged."
>
> (p. 483)

Frederickson uses what he understands to be his induced feelings of hatred as a basis from which to describe what he infers the patient must have felt as a child. By ostensibly standing up for himself with his patient, Frederickson argues that he in fact serves as a proxy to his patient so that the conflict experienced in the past is relived in the present. Voicing his direct experience of being placed in the position of the abused child is reasoned to enable the patient to connect with his own experience. Frederickson writes:

> Premature interpretations attempt to bypass the preliminary phase of feeling the child's position and making here and now interpretations. Premature interpretations which bring in the past may serve the purpose of helping the therapist escape from the painful countertransference feelings in the present. Yet, these are the feelings that allow us to be empathic – to speak for that abused child. In such a case, if we refuse to feel the child's feelings such as hate, we refuse to be empathic. Our hatred becomes empathic when it is used to elaborate and describe the patient's early experiences.
>
> (p. 489)

As the example offered illustrates, this process of elaboration is often implicit – Frederickson voices his own experience in the moment, with this experience only being explicitly related to the patient's past when the patient begins to make this connection for himself. This approach depends upon Frederickson's reported capacity to distinguish between the different transference-countertransference configurations of the analytic dyad. It is necessary that the therapist be able to distinguish between being placed in the position of the abused child (a position that he links with Racker's (1957) notion of concordant identification, wherein the therapist identifies with an aspect of the patient's self), as opposed to being induced into the position of the abusing parent (a position he associates with Racker's notion of complementary identification, wherein the therapist identifies with a patient's internal object). In the former case Frederickson endorses voicing his countertransferential hate as therapeutically useful, while in the latter case Frederickson suggests that the appropriate response is to sit with the feelings and use them as the basis to imagine into the experience of the patient.

Frederickson's paper, published in 1990, offers no reference to the notion of enactment – a term that had yet to develop the kind of widespread currency that it has today. Instead, Frederickson relies upon a distinction between acting from a position of "neutrality" and "acting in." He suggests that where the treatment reflects an exact repetition of the past, we should speak of "acting in," but where the treatment reflects a transformation of past events, we can speak of maintaining "neutrality" – an approach that recalls Winnicott's (1949) idea that it is possible to hate objectively. This rationale is used to show how classical notions of what neutrality looks like may actually promote subtle forms of acting in, this being the case when the original trauma was marked by the apparent "inaction" of one or more of the protagonists.

As compelling as Frederickson's ordering of the material is, I am sympathetic to Hoffman's (1992) suggestion that Frederickson's explanation of the treatment perhaps places too much emphasis on the therapist *knowing* ahead of time when he was positioned as the abused child and when as the abusing adult. As Hoffman puts it:

> This formulation amounts to a post hoc explanation for what seems to have been a more spontaneous personal reaction. Such personal reactions may include inklings of where they fit in relation to the patient's

history and intrapsychic world, but those inklings may be rather faint at the moment of action. At that moment the analyst feels impelled to speak up for himself or herself, knowing that the action may turn out to mean any number of things and also that what follows is not fully predictable.

(p. 296)

With that said, surely there is still something to the distinction Frederickson draws between moments where it feels appropriate to act versus those when it does not. Hoffman admits as much when he speaks of the faint inklings that guide us. What are we to make of these inklings? How are we to articulate a theoretical basis for this?

Considering Frederickson's case in terms of enactment, we might reframe the concordant countertransferential moment in which Frederickson told his patient to "shut up" as expressive not merely of an induced response to his patient but as reflecting a transformation on Frederickson's part as he succeeded in standing up to whatever it was that his patient had come to embody for him personally. This moment of transformation in the analyst was at the same time mutative for his patient. A moment of this kind would therefore conform with the idea that enactment can be creatively generative. Meanwhile, the complementary identification Frederickson argues he sometimes struggled with in experiencing himself as the abusing father would apparently suggest the possibility of an enactment that was simply a repetition of the past.

That a clinical need might sometimes arise that we should in some sense more actively "get in" to an enactment can be understood in at least two ways depending on whether enactment is considered potentially transformative in its own right: on the one hand we have the idea of "getting in" with the sense of maintaining a creative emotional participation which is in and of itself mutative and, on the other hand, we have the idea of "getting in" so that we can get out – a role-responsive willingness to risk making a destructive mistake such that we can then identify and acknowledge this to the ultimate advantage of the treatment. Perhaps these two approaches aren't entirely distinct. The conscious recognition seemingly required in the latter approach still carries with it an enacted dimension – the clinician adjusting his or her role in parallel with the question of a more conscious recognition is in itself performative. Likewise, in the former approach some measure of semi-conscious adjustment can always be assumed a factor, even if the self-conscious appraisal of one's role isn't always evident.

Another example

An example of how the analyst occupying a complementary position with respect to the patient can be mutative without need of an overtly conscious adjustment is offered in my work with Sarah. A socially isolated and marginally housed woman in her early sixties, Sarah had been forcibly hospitalized for a period of a week. The police had been called after she was found to be disturbing customers at a bookstore by talking under her breath.[1] When she returned to treatment in the week following the hospitalization, I sought to explore the experience with her. Sarah appeared sheepish and embarrassed. She was dismissive of her time in the hospital and stated that she would prefer not to talk about it. Despite my trying to encourage Sarah to express her feelings about being forcibly hospitalized (an experience which I had good reason to suppose was distressing), Sarah sought to focus on how much she missed a fantasied boyfriend. My efforts to gently link the content of Sarah's speech to the experience of being hospitalized were unhelpful. Without directly challenging the patient on the existence of the fantasized partner, I attempted to connect the boyfriend's absence with a sense of vulnerability in relationship to the hospital stay. Sarah flatly denied this and stated that I should be more concerned with recent developments in her church requiring members of the choir to wear a uniform. Though Sarah was not a member of the choir, she hoped to eventually become one. In a gossipy tone she expressed her belief that forcing members of the choir to wear a uniform wasn't right, but that it's *what the world has come to*. As Sarah continued to talk about the choir without obvious emotional investment, I was struck with an unusually pronounced feeling of sadness. Just as Sarah was dismissively expressing her sense of the unavoidable nature of the problem that members of the choir should now be required to wear uniforms, I took it upon myself to interject with some vehemence – *yes, perhaps things are this way, but I don't think that it should be to the exclusion of* . . . I had been about to say "self-expression," when Sarah interrupted: *Individuality! Yes! I'm glad you said that.* The remainder of the session was spent with Sarah expressing her sense of displeasure at the fashion in which members of the choir were forced to sacrifice their individuality. Her expression of displeasure felt unusually alive, this standing in clear contrast with her previous attitude of bland acceptance.

In seeking to encourage Sarah to talk about her experience, I was inadvertently re-capitulating the very feeling of being "forced" that I anticipated Sarah needed to talk about. My efforts to directly interpret the patient's speech in terms of the experience of hospitalization, though perhaps not without basis, were nevertheless unsuccessful. By joining Sarah where she was, however, I was able to communicate more effectively. This encounter could *retrospectively* be understood as perhaps having evoked in me a sense of my own experience growing up in a family atmosphere that was characterized by the careful avoidance of strong emotions – a state of affairs that was reflected in a pervasive sense of normotic deadness (Bollas, 1987). Sarah's reticence to talk directly about her experience of being hospitalized had recapitulated the sense of emotional avoidance I had experienced in my own family as a child. However, in this particular moment the anxious urgency of my efforts to access the patient's feelings had come to reflect a bid to make sure that "everything was ok" which placed *me* in the position of being overbearing and poorly related – a resonance not only with the patient's own experience of her mother, but also with the wider mental health care system. Sarah firmly rejected the demand I made upon her that she allow me to care for her in what was more accurately a misguided attempt to care for myself, and helpfully gave me a fresh metaphor to work with in switching from speaking of the boyfriend to the choir. At the enacted level of the treatment, Sarah had performed a service to both herself and me in standing firm against my anxiety so as to remain more related to her own latent emotional experience. I was able to make use of this and return the favor in standing firm with the idea that things shouldn't be this way, thus facilitating further access to her feelings.

The principle of nonaction

The outlook under consideration carries analytic practice to an intuitive position wherein reason may, at times, become a possible obstacle to the process. Acting effectively within the treatment would appear to entail aligning oneself with an appropriate form of responsiveness uniquely defined by the unconscious fit between analyst and analysand. We are left with a sense that the therapist should not be too consciously effortful in their approach, yet we continue to recognize that in the absence of such an awareness the clear danger arises of our acting in ways that are detrimental. How might we better understand our efforts to mediate between performative growth and repetitious destructiveness? What is the decisive factor in determining between these possible outcomes? If good practice requires a submission to the process, in what extent is it possible to submit willfully? These questions have been a long-standing concern of Chinese philosophy. The principle of *wu-wei* is typically translated as "nonaction," or "doing nothing." Reflecting upon this concept offers a fruitful point of reference for recent developments in relational psychoanalysis.

Wu-wei is particularly associated with Taoism.[2] A representative passage from the *Tao Te Ching* runs as follows:

> If everybody knows what beauty is,
> then beauty is not beauty [anymore];
> If everybody knows what goodness is,
> then goodness is not goodness [anymore].
> Therefore,
> Being and nothing give birth to one another,
> Hard and easy are mutually formed,
> Long and short shape each other,
> High and low complement each other,
> Music and voice are harmonized with each other,
> Front and back follow one another.
> Hence,
> The sage focuses on non-action [*wu-wei*] in his works,
> Practices not-saying in his speech,
> The myriad things arise but are disregarded
> The sage produces but does not own
> Acts but does not claim
> Accomplishes work but does not focus on it
> Does not focus on it, and thus it does not go [is lasting].
>
> (Wikisource, chapter 2)

Taoists underscore the value of *tzu-jan* (spontaneity) in our relations with others. At the same time, Taoism emphasizes that there is no benefit to be gained from actively intervening in other people's lives. Interfering causes withdrawal, creates resistance, and obstructs growth. Taoists hold that the ego is frequently misapprehended as something absolute, so that one's own mind comes to be treated as a teacher. Following the dictates of their minds, people are naturally prone to experience a discrepancy between their own will and that of Heaven. Any such discrepancy leads to a sense that the law of Necessity is something imposed externally. To resolve this struggle, we are encouraged to identify ourselves with the *Tao* – the Necessity of the natural order. In thus becoming unified with the *Tao*, that which from the standpoint of the ego is experienced as the absolute restriction of Necessity is transformed to become an experience of absolute freedom – nothing feels externally imposed. Humans are uniquely able to become conscious of the *Tao*, yet the capacity for self-awareness seems intrinsically tied with the possibility of revolting against what Chuang-tzu refers to as *t'ien li* (the natural course of things as determined by Heaven):

Only Man, of all existents, can and does revolt against the *t'ien li*. And that because of his self-consciousness. He tends to struggle hard to evade or change it. And he thereby brings discordance into the universal harmony of Being. But of course all his violent struggles are vain and useless, for everything is determined eternally. Herein lies the very source of the tragedy of human existence.

(Izutsu, 1983, p. 421)

In thus emphasizing the dangers attendant to approaching human relations according to fixed laws of conduct and appropriate behavior, Taoism clearly renders itself distinct from Confucianism. Within Confucianism, the notion of *Jen* reflects the external expression of the Confucian ideal – the term is often translated as "benevolence," "love," "goodness," or "man-to-man-ness." Achieving this ideal requires the application of reasoned discernment and discrimination:

In it is implied the measuring out of one's love. How much love, the Confucianist asks, does one owe to relatives, other men, and all things? [. . .] The gradation of sympathy creates positions of superiority and inferiority and relations of nearness and remoteness. As a man becomes more superior, he becomes more remote. Superiority and remoteness are in a positive correlation.

(Chuang-yuan, 1963, pp. 22–23)

Given the extent to which Taoism emphasizes the value of spontaneity, Taoists do not typically correlate spiritual advancement with remoteness. To the contrary, the spiritual ideal reflected in the notion of *wu-wei* suggests that one's alignment with the Tao is reflected in a more related form of conduct. It would thus be a mistake to consider Taoist practice as aloof from everyday affairs, even if it is Confucianism that is more centrally associated with matters of governance. Where Taoism differs on the question of order, is in objecting to the notion that order should be willfully imposed upon nature:

> The sage does not institute forms and names to restrain things. He does not formulate standards of advance so that the degenerate will be discarded. Instead he assists all things in their natural state and does not play the part of their originator. This is why it is said that the sage never discards anyone.
>
> (Wang Pi)[3]

The principle of nonaction is considered to reflect a perfected form of consciousness, and consists of allowing the natural course of events to unfold. Hence *wu-wei* has also been translated: "refraining from action contrary to Nature" (Needham, 1969, p. 68). Nothing is done in the sense that doing something is to act against Nature, while to identify oneself with Nature is to assist it. It is important to underscore, however, that this non-doing bears little resemblance to the classical ideal of analytic neutrality. Such an approach would take the notion of nonaction far too literally. As Chuang Tzu states: "Non-action does not mean doing nothing and keeping silent. Let everything be allowed to do what it naturally does, so that its nature will be satisfied."[4] *Wu-wei* is not concerned with external actions in the world, but rather with the manner in which these actions are conducted: "Nonaction does not mean quiescence after action has ceased, but quiescence forever in action" (Chuang-yuan, 1963, pp. 10–11). One's conduct in the world could conceivably appear quite animated, yet still be in conformity with the natural order:

> The moment a man *does* something, his very consciousness of doing it renders his action "unnatural." Instead, the Perfect Man leaves all things, himself and all other things, to their own natures. This is the meaning of the term Non-Doing (*wu wei*). And since he does not *do*

anything, he leaves nothing undone. By virtue of his Non-Doing, he ultimately does everything. For in that state, his being is identical with Nature. And Nature accomplishes everything without forcing anything.

(Izutsu, 1983, p. 437)

Parallels in depth psychology

Jung's engagement with Taoist thought is often quite direct. Perhaps the most often cited example is given in his relating of a story told to him by the sinologist Richard Wilhelm:

> There was a great drought where Wilhelm lived; for months there had not been a drop of rain and the situation became catastrophic. The Catholics made processions, the Protestants made prayers, and the Chinese burned joss-sticks and shot off guns to frighten away the demons of the drought, but with no result. Finally the Chinese said, "We will fetch the rain-maker." And from another province a dried up old man appeared. The only thing he asked for was a quiet little house somewhere, and there he locked himself in for three days. On the fourth day the clouds gathered and there was a great snow-storm at the time of the year when no snow was expected, an unusual amount, and the town was so full of rumours about the wonderful rain-maker that Wilhelm went to ask the man how he did it. In true European fashion he said: "They call you the rain-maker; will you tell me how you made the snow?" And the little Chinese said: "I did not make the snow; I am not responsible." "But what have you done these three days?" "Oh, I can explain that. I come from another country where things are in order. Here they are out of order; they are not as they should be by the ordinance of heaven. Therefore the whole country is not in Tao, and I also am not in the natural order of things because I am in a disordered country. So I had to wait three days until I was back in Tao and then naturally the rain came."

(Jung, 1955–56, pp. 419–420)

Jung goes so far as to suggest an equivalence between Tao and what he intends by synchronicity (Jung, 1935, para. 143). Elsewhere he links Tao with his notion of the transcendent function:

From a consideration of the claims of the inner and outer worlds, or rather, from the conflicts between them, the possible and the necessary follows. Unfortunately our Western mind, lacking all culture in this respect, has never yet devised a concept, nor even a name, for the *union of opposites through the middle path*, that most fundamental item of inward experience, which could respectably be set against the Chinese concept of *Tao*.

(Jung, 1953, para. 327)

A compatibility with the notion of *wu-wei* is also very much evident in the work of Bion. This can best be understood in terms of the fashion in which Bion's thinking was significantly shaped by his relationship to India. In particular, Bion's work was influenced by his reading of the Bhagavad Gita, this being expressed most explicitly in his approach to practicing without memory or desire. The Karma yoga of the Bhagavad Gita teaches nonattachment in a fashion that clearly parallels the principle of *wu-wei*. Krishna instructs Arjuna to perform his duty without concern for the results: "Set thy heart upon thy work, but never on its reward. Work not for a reward; but never cease to do thy work" (The Bhagavad Gita, 2:47). This outlook happens to coincide with Freud's (1923) claim that cure should be considered a byproduct of analysis and not its final aim. Bion (1965) writes:

In my experience I find nearly always that the wish to remember what the patient said, or any desire to cure the patient, invariably seems to me to crop up in the situation, and in a formulation, that is intended to keep at bay and to keep out of mind certain other feelings.

(p. 12)

Bion's approach is thus intended to enable a more emotionally engaged way of being in the treatment. Reflective of a basic attitude of faith towards unconscious process, his notion of reverie can be linked with a particular interpretation of *wu-wei* – one that reflects a shamanistic form of engagement. Offering an obvious parallel with Bion's notion of reverie, some Taoist forms of yogic practice suggest that *wu-wei* can be approached "as a sort of psycho-physiological state – similar to trance or hypnosis" (Slingerland, 2003, p. 93).

Despite his emphasis on emotional involvement, Bion's take on nondoing clearly errs on the more literal side, this being expressed with an outlook on clinical practice that still lies very much within a classical frame of reference. Interestingly, in keeping with relational ideas about enactment, the Bhagavad Gita makes a particularly strong case for the futility of such an undertaking:

No man shall 'scape from act
By shunning action; nay, and none shall come
By mere renouncements unto perfectness.
Nay, and no jot of time, at any time,
Rests any actionless; his nature's law
Compels him, even unwilling, into act;
[For thought is act in fancy.] He who sits
Suppressing all the instruments of flesh,
Yet in his idle heart thinking on them,
Plays the inept and guilty hypocrite

(Arnold, 1885, lines 13–22, chapter 3)

Emphasizing the impossibility of our avoiding action altogether, the karma yoga of the Gita is clearly complementary to the Taoist notion of *wu-wei*. Nonaction is not inaction, but acting in conformity with the life principle. As with the rainmaker example offered by Jung, one's efficacy in promoting the necessary change is inseparable from the change we must realize in ourselves. It is because the rainmaker has been affected in relationship to "external" circumstances that his seeming withdrawal is meaningful. The rainmaker's hut, like the analyst's consulting room, is a sacred space that promotes an intentional receptivity to transformation. This intention is a fundamental paradox of Taoism, for it is both an intentionless form of intention and intentional way of being without intention.

Similarly, the emphasis implied when relationalists speak of a "two-person psychology" suggests that if a change is to occur in psychotherapy, then it will be apparent not only with the designated patient but also with the designated analyst. M. O. Slavin and Kriegman (1998) seek to explain why the analyst needs to change. They suggest that the analytic relationship naturally gives rise to conflicts between the needs and identities of both patient and analyst. They conceptualize the transference as a "probe" that sets about its task in the spirit of play, but that should ultimately result in the analyst's own subjective participation being more fully realized within the treatment. When the analyst shows a willingness to confront their own conflicts and change in light of interactions with the patient, the authors argue that this malleability and willingness to be affected provides the essential therapeutic experience. In witnessing the example offered by the therapist, the patient is in turn able to change. This process can be understood in terms of the patient's experience as an effective participant in life. Having tangibly been able to impact the analyst, the patient is able to experience a sense of agency. Thus empowered, the patient is then able to effectuate a change in themselves (J. H. Slavin, 2007).

This approach shares parallels with Jessica Benjamin's ideas about intersubjectivity (see Benjamin, 1998). In the notion of mutual recognition, the rationale for why the analyst must change has always been clear – in moments of impasse, it is the analyst's capacity to surrender (Ghent, 1990) that enables the possibility that patient and analyst might be able to restore recognition of each other as independent subjects. Benjamin (2004) considers this act of surrender on the part of the analyst as a form of offering to what she terms *the moral third* – "accepting the necessity of becoming involved in a process that is often outside our control and understanding" (p. 41). Just as M. O. Slavin and Kriegman argue that the analyst's willingness to change enables that of the patient, Benjamin speaks of the value in the analyst seeking to "go first" in an effort to move into a position of mutual recognition. No doubt this ordering of events can also be reversed. The point I wish to make here, however, is that this model of understanding argues that one party's capacity to change is apparently in some degree causative of the change potentially experienced in the other.

For Jung, if the treatment is to be successful both patient and analyst must be actively involved in the transformation of the third. In an often-cited statement on this matter, Jung writes:

> For two personalities to meet is like mixing two different chemical substances: if there is any combination at all, both are transformed. In any effective psychological treatment the doctor is bound to influence the patient; but this influence can only take place if the patient has a reciprocal influence on the doctor. You can exert no influence if you are not susceptible to influence.
>
> (Jung, 1931, para. 163)

Reflective of the question of the analyst's emotional participation, in speaking of the attainment of Tao, Jung writes: "Not only consciousness, but life itself must be intensified: the union of these two produces conscious life" (Jung, 1967, para. 29). Our growing understanding of enactment helps supplement the sometimes more abstract stance offered by Jung, so that we can examine these ideas at a more granular level. In doing so, the work of Harold Searles seems of particular value. Searles (1975) is perhaps most well-known for offering the intriguing idea that we are all born with an innate psychotherapeutic instinct – a striving to heal those close to us. He contends that the extent to which a patient might be considered psychologically ill is reflective of the extent to which their innate striving to cure significant others went unrecognized and was unsuccessful. In the context of treatment, the patient is thus driven by an unconscious drive to cure the analyst.

Approached transpersonally, the notion of enactment allows us to understand that the psychotherapeutic striving of the patient to heal others is at one and the same time a striving to heal oneself, for the analyst as a person in the world cannot be separated from the analyst as an image residing "inside" the patient. In previous chapters I have attempted to articulate a way of thinking about the relations between inner and outer worlds such that enactive process can be understood not only in terms of two independent persons influencing each other but, on another level, as being reflective of the ways in which we live within what might be thought of as a shared dream field – an imaginal reality that belongs neither to one person nor the other. This imaginal dimension subtends both patient and analyst. According to this view, as much as we might think of ourselves as dreaming, we are also dreamed of. At this level the analyst's capacity to "go first" is reminiscent of the idea that for an interpretation to be accepted as "true" then the change it articulates must already have taken place. The analyst going first is not causative of a change in the patient, but *is* the change in the patient.

Searles suggests that therapeutic impasses are frequently reflective of the patient offering a form of therapeutic support to the analyst of which both are unaware. The patient seeks to encourage the analyst to engage in ways that cause pathological anxiety for the analyst, but which the patient feels more at ease with. For Searles, a transferential shift in the patient's mode of relationship to the analyst is always dependent on the analyst having had to change. If the patient starts to relate to the analyst on different

terms, it is because the analyst has been able to benefit from the therapeutic support offered by the patient and in some sense been able to show
this: "Ironically, the crucial issue is, rather, whether *we* can become and
remain conscious of the symbiotic (preindividuation) dependency which
we inevitably and necessarily (for the successful outcome of "his" treatment) develop toward *him* [the patient]" (Searles, 1975, p. 444). Thus the
movement of the treatment is for Searles dependent on the analyst being
able to spontaneously accept and work with the forms of support offered
by the patient.

Case of Camila

Camila was born blue – the umbilical cord wrapped around her neck, she
had been unable to breathe. The child of Guatemalan parents, she grew
up in the Bronx with a sister two years her senior. Throughout her childhood Camila suffered with severe asthma attacks for which she was frequently hospitalized. She recalled that on such occasions her mother, who
"lived for her children," would sit through the night by her bedside until
Camila was well enough to return home. Camila portrayed her mother as
a picture of maternal provision; functioning without apparent objection
to the patriarchal constraint to which she was subjected, she was devoted
to maintaining the home for her two daughters and her husband. Camila
described her mother as pure and saintly – even to the point of being
somewhat naïve. As Camila got older it became apparent that her mother
knew almost nothing about sex. She recalled her mother's confusion at
reference to a "blow job" on television, and her father communicating to
Camila with a meaningful look that she should not explain to her mother
what it was she was missing.

Camila described her father as a good provider with a short temper, and
intensely protective of his children. When she and her sister were young,
if the doorbell sounded he had trained them to hide under their beds where
they were to wait until their father indicated that it was safe for them to
come out. Why he felt it necessary to do this had never been made clear.
Camila's sister, Gabriela, was the black sheep of the family, and it was
a more or less openly accepted fact that Camila was the favored child.
Gabriela tended to distance herself from family life while Camila enjoyed
a close bond with both of her parents. Around the age of ten, Camila discovered a book on martyrs. She was transfixed by the gruesome stories

of self-abnegation, and considered that to live such a life would be quite wonderful.

Though she was brought up Catholic, in her late teens Camila developed a precocious interest in Mormonism and was baptized into the church. A strong student, Camila moved out-of-state to attend college. She hoped to become a doctor, but her father ardently opposed this. The time away from her family proved challenging. Despite making it most of the way through her required courses, Camila left college without graduating. Shortly thereafter she met the man who would become her husband. As members of the Mormon church, the couple were "sealed" – a marriage ceremony in which husband and wife are bound together for eternity. The marriage itself lasted ten years, during which time Camila's husband fell into alcoholism and became violent. On one occasion he tried to choke her, and she came to fear for her life. Though they were subsequently divorced, for the sealing to be officially cancelled her ex-husband had to give consent – something which he refused to do. Since ending the relationship Camila had struggled to trust men, and in the 25 years that had since passed she had been unable to establish a lasting romantic connection with someone new.

After Camila's father died, Camila's mother became increasingly reliant on her as she began to show obvious signs of Alzheimer's. Camila decided to purchase a house outside of the city in order to provide her mother with a home. Not long after purchasing the house Camila lost her job in the 2008 financial crash. She was forced to take a significantly less well-compensated position, and was unable to keep up with mortgage payments. Camila returned to the city with her mother and they were housed out of charity by a married couple who were lifelong friends of hers. The couple's marriage had long since grown loveless, and Camila found herself acting as something of a buffer between them. In return for being housed, Camila was also expected to take care of the cooking and cleaning. With her mother's condition deteriorating, Camila had felt that she was forced to stop working a nine-to-five in order to provide full-time support as a caregiver. This state of affairs continued for five years, until her mother's health declined to the extent that she was finally placed in a nursing home. With this burden lifted, Camila had expected to be able to return to living a more "normal" life. This had not happened. She struggled to find work, her depression worsened, and she suffered from anxiety when going out in public.

Now in her late fifties, Camila began therapy hoping to find support in her efforts to re-enter the world. From the outset, I found Camila engaging and likable. Despite the obvious difficulty of her circumstances, she was able to articulate the challenges of her daily life with humor. While exhibiting a talent for identifying the absurd in human affairs, her attitude towards other people was nevertheless generous and supportive. It became evident to me that I was not alone in my positive response to her, and that she was well-liked by others. While her efforts to endear could on occasion strike me as perhaps overly ingratiating, Camila's interest in making herself entertaining was not at the expense of other forms of emotional engagement. She was prone to tears and would move fluidly between more animated ways of being and using the treatment as a place to talk meaningfully about her fears and deep-seated feelings of failure and personal inadequacy. She attended therapy reliably, and quickly showed signs of an idealizing attitude towards me.

I will share some reflections on a period of several months approximately two years into my work with Camila. The presentation begins, however, with some personal material of my own. Subsequent to spending several days with my parents, from whom I am semi-estranged, I had the following dream:

I am arguing with my family in my parents' home. My father is physically threatening towards me and tells me that the family will not accept my version of reality – there is a finality to this. My mother and siblings will not support me. Feeling crestfallen, I state that in that case I will have nothing further to do with them. I pack my things and leave with my wife. Outside I find myself on the street where I lived immediately after leaving home in my late teens. I realize I've forgotten something, so I go back while my wife goes on ahead. I return to my parents' home and my brother seems upset – I pat him on the back to let him know that it's not his fault. I call my wife on the phone and an unfamiliar voice answers telling me that she is unconscious in a hospital in Brooklyn having taken a bad aspirin. I'm immediately worried and feel that I need to ask my family to take me there, yet to do so would feel like a self-betrayal. I'm worried about my wife, and about her thinking that I don't care if I can't get to her and perhaps losing touch with her as a result. I see my patient, Camila, who is wanting to make a connection with me, but I feel distracted by my concern for my wife.

Though the time I had recently spent with my parents had been outwardly uneventful, the dream portrayed a state of high emotions pertaining to the matter of my felt sense of exclusion. Several hours subsequent to waking from this dream, I was scheduled for a session with Camila. In the session she informed me that she had dreamed about me that night, and proceeded to offer the following account:

I see a number of computers running Microsoft-DOS. A prospective employer tells me that the computers need to be networked, and that I'm the woman for the task. I don't believe this is true – I have no idea how to deal with these outdated computers. The manager insists, however, and I find myself sitting in front of a panel who will interview me for the job. My therapist [i.e. the author] is on the panel, as well as a friend of mine [a woman Camila had recently mentioned in session who had dismissively told her: "If it wasn't for bad luck you'd have no luck at all"]. I try to say "Hi" to my friend, but she stares me down unsympathetically. To my surprise it is my therapist who smiles at me and waves. I feel pleased that at least someone is rooting for me, and also ironically surprised that it is my therapist of all people who turns out to be the one who is willing to break professional protocol in order to be more familiar. The interview proceeds with members of the panel asking me questions, but each time I'm asked a question another member of the panel cuts me off before I can reply. This happens several times until my friend eventually asks in withering tones, "Can you open your mouth?" "Yes," I manage to respond. "Then, without wasting anymore of our time, can you tell us why you should have the job?" As soon as I begin to speak my friend snorts derisively and interrupts: "No! You can't!" At this point my therapist gets up from the table and announces that he has had enough, and that the way I am being treated is unacceptable. "Come on," he tells me, "We are leaving." My therapist goes to take my hand, but I protest demurely saying that it's not allowed – that it's against the rules to have physical touch between a therapist and their patient. My therapist tells me that this is a special case and that, "Rules are made to be broken." I take his hand and we leave together.

Clearly there is a significant amount of thematic overlap between my dream and that of my patient. In addition to us both having had dreams featuring the other person on the same night, both dreams depict the dreamer being silenced by a hostile coalition that seeks to pass rule on the dreamer's experience of themselves. My dream ended with Camila wanting to make a connection with me – a connection which in Camila's dream is seemingly realized.

My dream perhaps speaks in part to the challenge of maintaining a healthy relationship to life (as personified by my wife) when doing so seems to depend on enduring an attack on one's basic sense of selfhood. Similarly, Camila's dream portrays a situation in which the task of personal advancement appears to be intrinsically allied with a diminution in the sense of self-worth that she would seek to develop. The problem of separation from the family at a personal level – breaking away from a situation that nevertheless continues to exert a hold over us – is reflected at another level in terms of the problem of consciousness breaking away from its unconscious ground. To be cast out of the garden, or cast down from heaven, is to become earthly and to fully enter life. It is also to be saddled with the task of redemption. To be redeemed is to achieve freedom through delivery from sin. To sin against the family is to defy the family law, thus deliverance from sin means initiating a shift in the law. A great challenge is expressed in the need to distinguish between this work of redemption, as against what is demanded of us by our family in order to maintain the status quo. These tasks may even look outwardly the same, with the decisive factor perhaps being the manner in which we approach them.

In session with Camila, I was able to identify several instances of the dynamics seemingly indicated in her dream. For example, when Camila expressed her sense of the emotional toll exerted on her in respect to a difficult friend, this observation was immediately succeeded with the self-admonishment that she had no right to say such a thing and that she should be more grateful for this person's support. Similarly, when Camila stated, "People say life is short, but to me it often feels long," she exhaled with a sigh of apparent relief at having been able to articulate this, but immediately reprimanded herself: "I should appreciate the fact that I'm alive." In each instance I drew attention to the fashion in which her shifting experience reflected the dynamic in her dream between her efforts to support herself and the critical panel of voices that acted so as to immediately silence her. In so doing I thus found myself enacting in session the role assigned to me in Camila's dream.

At the same time, in offering this particular form of responsiveness to my patient it is possible to see how this interaction might be considered therapeutic not only for my patient but also for me. In responding to the problem Camila was facing, I was also engaging with this challenge as it manifested in my own experience. Speaking from my own position of familial estrangement, I was able to support Camila in her position of enmeshment. Insofar as my participation impacted Camila, her responsiveness can be understood as reflecting a form of engagement with my own position of estrangement. In my dream, my family remained unmoved by my efforts to challenge the family law, but there was a suggestion that a connection with Camila might somehow address the consequent sense of stuckness.

Regarding the question of "boundary violation" evoked by Camila's dream, my understanding is that, in this particular context, this imagery reflects a shift in emotional engagement with the treatment – that is, the sense of a boundary being crossed expresses a deepening of psychic investment in the work. Because patients often do not anticipate experiencing a significant level of emotional investment in the person of the therapist, a deepening of the relationship can readily be experienced as inappropriate. This issue is distinct from, and additional to, the complications that can arise from harmful forms of enactment such as have often been linked with the Oedipal situation. It is of course critical to recognize that destructive boundary violations are a real danger, but there is also a danger that the clinician withholds from meaningful engagement under the guise of maintaining an appropriate distance. In the context of therapeutic work, perhaps the most explicitly destructive aspect of enactment is readily identified in the concrete actualization of sex. However, the creative dimension of enactment requires that the avoidance of such violations not be at the expense of intimacy. This state of affairs is paralleled in the Oedipal situation where children can be injured not only by a parent having an excessively eroticized tie to the child, but also by an excessively rejecting attitude influenced by the fear of incest.

For about six weeks subsequent to the aforementioned session, Camila had a series of dreams in which I featured as a small child who had lost his mother.[5] In these dreams Camila would offer comfort to me, and I to her. The question of physical contact between us continued to be a feature – this apparently being made possible as a consequence of my now appearing as a child. A theme that arose during our sessions over this period was

Camila's apparently shameful wish to feel special in my eyes, a wish that she forcefully dismissed as dangerously unreasonable while at the same time flirtatiously complimenting me on my own capacity to hold boundaries; she referred to me as "the king of boundaries." I drew attention to the ways in which this apparent talent on my part left her feeling that she wasn't special. I also drew attention to my sense that with the anxious manner in which she offered this wish, there was a sense that she might believe that she did in fact have the power to induce me to break boundaries – a fear that I was going to let her down. During this phase of the treatment I continued to encourage reflection on the ways in which Camila experienced attacks from within and without on her right to express anger and disappointment.

Meanwhile, over the course of the weeks that Camila was dreaming of me as a child, I had several dreams in which I was negotiating in order to make room and/or find time for Camila. This question of "making room for" might be thought reflective of an undertaking to be able to establish a different form of emotional availability to my patient. This would entail allowing more of what my patient represents to me into conscious awareness, which in turn would potentially figure a shift in my waking relationships.

Over this same period of the treatment, the health of Camila's 96-year-old mother showed signs of deteriorating – this eventually culminated in her death. In the weeks following her mother's passing, Camila spoke in glowing terms of her mother's faultless success as a parent. I had the sense of this characterization being offered to me with a certain measure of mawkish forcefulness; as though Camila were challenging me to contradict her. I drew attention to the extent to which her mother's sense of personal meaning had come to depend on an identification with motherhood, and of the ways in which her efforts to be a "perfect" mother might be reflective of her refusal to relinquish this role. I also drew a parallel between her idealization of her mother and her idealization of me. She said, "Oh I know you're not perfect!" but immediately proceeded to offer an extended soliloquy on my excellence as a therapist. I pointed this out to her as the session closed. She responded by telling me in a seemingly playful manner that I couldn't "take a compliment." As she left my office, in response to my, "See you Friday," she offered a coy "Maybe" – a response that was not quite typical of her. However, she immediately retracted this as a joke and said she would see me at the appointed time.

Passing through the doorway she swooned slightly and said that she felt faint, but after a moment gathered herself and indicated that she was ok – a moment that I privately associated with the circumstances of her birth and her subsequent asthma attacks, and which I considered perhaps noteworthy in that she was able to right herself unaided.

Winnicott's (1953) notion of good enough parenting finds clear parallel in Taoist teaching. Stensrud and Stensrud (1979, p. 80) write:

> Taoists recognize that we cannot live without structure. Physical laws are necessary or we would inhabit a chaotic entropic universe. We can differentiate, however, between two kinds of structure. The first type of structure is oppressive. Oppressive structure is designed in such a manner as to elicit compliance from its inhabitants. The intent behind this structure is to exert control with little regard for individual interests. The second type of structure, which is authentic, is designed in such a manner as to enhance the development of individual discipline and responsibility. The intent behind this type of structure is to provide a framework from within which people can experience control as coming from within themselves rather than from their environment.

In the following session Camila returned cautiously to the subject of what I had interpreted as her idealization of me. I reframed my approach to this, and shared my genuine sense of appreciation for how supportive I felt she was of me in my efforts to support her. She reported at that moment suddenly feeling very moved at the idea of her being supporting of others, yet struggled to understand why.

This interaction perhaps suggests the possibility of realizing a more relationally nuanced conception of idealization. Whether considered as a defense or a naturally occurring growth process, idealization is typically thought of as a one-person phenomenon that obscures the "reality" of the other person. Significant relational contributions on this subject have been offered by Stephen Mitchell and Joyce Slochower. Mitchell (1997) situates idealization in relationship to the psychoanalytic devaluation of romantic love and, referencing Loewald, suggests that idealization can be considered *constructive* in the sense of offering an animating force that enlivens reality rather than obscures it. Mitchell challenges the idea that a waning of romantic idealization reflects a grasping of the realistic truth about the other person, and reverses this claim to suggest that romantic disenchantment is often indicative of a misleading reduction of the beloved in the interests of achieving a false-sense of security. Meanwhile, Slochower (2011) draws our attention to the ways in which idealizations are often co-constructed, with analysts inevitably participating in this process so as to elicit narcissistic gratification from patients. What might also be emphasized is the potential therapeutic value *for the patient* in the analyst actually being able to benefit from the experience of being idealized, with this being confirmed in the analyst's capacity to recognize without guilty collapse that this benefit has occurred. If Kohut's (1971) emphasis on being able to accept the patient's idealizations is considered in light of Searles's ideas about the patient's efforts to heal the analyst, it becomes apparent that when an analyst thinks of idealization as not being "about them," this may often reflect a potentially repetitious enactment of the ways in which caregivers were unable to accept the care of their own children.

All of this is of course not to suggest that the clinician should actually *identify* with the patient's idealization of them – this can only be expected to lead to an inflation, the sustenance of which depends upon continued idealization. Rather, it seems to me that there is a happy medium in being able to accept idealization (I exist in relationship to something great), which reflects a tension between the extremes of identification (I am this great thing) and outright rejection (this greatness has nothing to do with me). There is a world of difference between identifying with another's idealization and being able to accept and be touched by the fact that it is indeed one's own person that another person has found suitable as an intermediary for this process.

In this case, the response to Camila's idealization that seemed mutative was neither to ignore it nor challenge it, but rather to acknowledge that I had indeed benefited from it. The support Camila gave me in allowing me to support her was recognized by us both, thus partially freeing us from a relational pattern that was reflective of the ways in which both our mothers had remained excessively identified with their roles as mothers. This shift in the relationship entailed us both adopting less "regressively" dependent attitudes with respect to the question of our respective roles as caregivers.

Within a week of her mother's passing, Camila found work with an elderly woman who was looking for a personal assistant. At their first meeting the woman grandly announced: "*I* will be your mother now." A dynamic rapidly developed between Camila and this woman that entailed the woman taking care of Camila in ways which felt constrictive and unwanted, but to which Camila consented so as to avoid hurting her new employer's feelings – the woman would offer her various treats that required that Camila stay beyond the end of her scheduled work hours. The emergence of this relationship helped Camila in her growing recognition of the ways in which she had supported her mother; particularly as her new employer's behavior became more explicitly demanding and hostile.

Meanwhile, the therapeutic relationship came to focus more centrally on Camila's father. I experienced a greater degree of relational freedom (Stern, 2015), thus allowing for a more reciprocal form of playfulness to emerge. Camila had a dream in which I featured as Robin Hood leading a band of Merry Men. She was partly Maid Marion and partly not. She was supposed to marry her father. Upon realizing this she became distressed. She knighted me with a very heavy sword that was difficult to lift. In the following session I encouraged her to explore the ways in which she was indeed psychologically wed to her father – I connected this with the ways in which her father had sought to protect her from men, and the ways in which she now protected herself. Camila expressed considerable distaste towards this suggestion, but on the three nights subsequent to our session she dreamed repeatedly of being told that she had to marry her father. On the third night she actually went through with it. In the dream she saw herself in a mirror wearing a bridal gown. She was impressed at how much weight she had lost and felt good about the way she looked. However, this sense of things vanished as she realized who it was she was supposed to marry. Filled with dread as she was forced to walk down the aisle, she saw her father waiting at the altar. She was betrothed to her father, and they were taken to a hotel where they were to spend the night together. Lying on the marriage bed with her back to her father, the lights went out and she turned in terror to confront him. To her great relief she discovered it was now me in bed with her. She was starting to get undressed as she woke up.[6]

Shortly after having this dream Camila took some tentative steps towards dating – the first time she had approached doing so in many years. She also came to realize that the emotional demands being made upon her by the older woman she was assisting were excessive and, despite considerable guilt, terminated her employment with her. Over this same period I received an unexpected request from my sister that she be able to visit me, this culminating in her coming to stay – the first time we had seen each other in over a decade. In this fashion, a complementary change occurred as a shift in Camila's enmeshment with her parents corresponded with a subtle shift in my own state of familial estrangement.

Closing reflections

The foregoing case study might serve to underscore the radically incomplete nature of our efforts to encapsulate clinical process. Any detailed evaluation of case material that doesn't include some recognition of the analyst's personal investment is evidently lacking, yet in attending to the analyst's experience it becomes clear that this process cannot be understood merely in terms of the patient in question. All of the significant relationships to which patient and analyst belong have bearing on how a treatment develops. Those we are close to provide "supervision" for us wherever we share a basic commitment to change.

A saying from Chan Buddhism runs: "In carrying water and chopping wood – therein lies the wonderful *Tao*."[7] *Wu-wei* does not suggest an otherworldly transcendence of one's needs and reactions to the environment, but an appropriately weighted expression of them: "All our daily activities – walking, standing, sitting, lying down – all response to situations, our dealing with situations as they arise: all this is Tao" (Ma-Tsu). While the Western mind has tended to associate spontaneity with a reductive conception of subjectivity, the kind of spontaneity suggested in the notion of *wu-wei* reflects an idea of subjective action that can be understood to express "the highest degree of objectivity" (Slingerland, 2003, p. 8). This spontaneous ideal is the principle by which the human subject comes to establish their correct place in relationship to the cosmos. In the extent to which we succeed in conforming with this ideal, enactment functions generatively. In our inevitable lapses, enactment becomes merely repetitious and requires a more conscious approach such as to restore the working ideal. Charles (2003) writes:

> How do we balance the vital importance of our potency with the equally vital importance of our lack of omnipotence? Perhaps there lies the key: that our potency is not omnipotence and our lack of omnipotence is not impotence. In the balance between these two extremes lies a region within which two subjects can meet, can have an effect on one another and be affected, in turn, without losing the self within

the relationship. The type of faith we need in this work is grounded in our ability to touch the other and be touched, without becoming lost in the process.

(p. 698)

In this chapter I have asked what does it mean to be therapeutically effective, and in what sense can the enacted dimension of the treatment be meaningfully engaged by the clinician? Locating these questions in relationship to the notion of *wu-wei*, it is apparent that embracing the telos of enactment pushes analytic practice towards an intuitive sensibility that cannot be justified in any systematic sense. The paradoxical nature of *wu-wei* has been reflected in the various practical interpretations this principle has invited. Thus my intention in this chapter has not been to finally resolve the questions I have posed, so much as to demonstrate that for the furtherance of psychoanalytic thinking these questions might best be approached on a spiritual basis. In the case study I have offered, I hope to have given some sense of the ways in which the clinician's relationship to the enacted dimension of the treatment is always expressive of their own readiness to be transformed.

Notes

1 Subsequent to the closure of her local library, in order to have somewhere to go during the day the patient had come to rely on being able to sit at a table in the bookstore's coffee shop.
2 Taoism can be understood both as a religion and a philosophical system. The fundamental principle of this tradition is reflected in a commitment to live harmoniously with the natural order. This is reflected in the principle of *Tao* – a notion that is considered fundamentally undefinable, but that is variously translated as the way, path, road, or principle.
3 Quoted from his "Commentary on the Lao Tzu" published in Chan (1963, p. 322).
4 Quoted in Needham (1969, p. 69).
5 Searles (1975) writes: "Most important are the primitive, long-unconscious processes of introjection of the analyst's more ill components, and projection upon the analyst of the patient's areas of relative ego strength, whereby the patient attempts to take the analyst's illness into himself and treat the "ill analyst" there, within the patient, so that a healthier analyst can eventually be born out of the patient. This is a dimension of what does, indeed, take place during the course of, and as a result of, the therapeutically symbiotic phase of the treatment" (p. 427).

6 While adequately exploring the clinical implications of this dream extends beyond the scope of the present discussion, it can be noted that the furtherance of the treatment entailed the ongoing elaboration of the more constructive elements figured in this imagery (i.e. Camila breaking away from the hold of her father and establishing a personal relationship with her own analytic stance) from the more regressively incestuous (i.e. her wish to please me and win me over by compliance).

7 Bodde (1953) expands upon this with reference to the statement of Zen master Baizhang Huai-hai (720–814): "What the man does is no different from what he did before; it is only that the man himself is not the same as he was" (p. 284).

References

Arnold, E. (1885). *The Bhagavad-Gita.* New York: Project Gutenberg. Retrieved May 30, 2019, from www.gutenberg.org/files/2388/2388-h/2388-h.htm#chap03. [EBook #2388].

Aron, L., & Atlas, G. (2015). Generative enactment: Memories from the future. *Psychoanalytic Dialogues, 25*(3), 309–324.

Atlas, G., & Aron, L. (2018). *Dramatic dialogue: Contemporary clinical practice.* London & New York: Routledge.

Benjamin, J. (1998). Finding the way out: Commentary on papers by Malcolm Owen Slavin and Daniel Kriegman by Philip A. Ringstrom. *Psychoanalytic Dialogues, 8*(4), 589–598.

Benjamin, J. (2004). Beyond doer and done to: An intersubjective view of thirdness. *Psychoanalytic Quarterly, 73*, 5–46.

Bion, W. R. (1965). Memory and desire. In *The complete works of W. R. Bion* (Vol. 6, pp. 7–17). London: Karnac Books.

Bodde, D. (1953). Harmony and conflict in Chinese philosophy. In *Essays on Chinese civilization* (pp. 237–298). Princeton, NJ: Princeton University Press.

Bollas, C. (1987). *The shadow of the object.* New York: Columbia University.

Chan, W.-T. (1963). *A source book in Chinese philosophy.* Princeton, NJ: Princeton University Press.

Charles, M. (2003). On faith, hope, and possibility. *Journal of American Academy of Psychoanalysis, 31*(4), 687–704.

Chuang-yuan, C. (1963). *Creativity and Taoism: A study of Chinese philosophy, art, & poetry.* New York: The Julian Press, Inc.

Davies, J. M. (2004). Whose bad objects are we anyway: Repetition and our elusive love affair with evil. *Psychoanalytic Dialogues, 14*(6), 711–732.

Frederickson, J. (1990). Hate in the countertransference as an empathic position. *Contemporary Psychoanalysis, 26*, 479–495.

Freud, S. (1923). Two encyclopaedia articles. In J. Strachey (Ed.), *The standard edition of the complete psychological works of Sigmund Freud* (Vol. 18, pp. 233–260). London: The Hogarth Press.

Fusella, P. (2014). Hermeneutics versus science in psychoanalysis: A resolution to the controversy over the scientific status of psychoanalysis. *The Psychoanalytic Review, 101*(6), 871–894.

Ghent, E. (1990). Masochism, submission, surrender: Masochism as a perversion of surrender. *Contemporary Psychoanalsis, 26*, 108–136.

Grossmark, R. (2012a). The flow of enactive engagement. *Contemporary Psychoanalysis, 48*(3), 287–300.

Grossmark, R. (2012b). The unobtrusive relational analyst. *Psychoanalytic Dialogues, 22*(6), 629–646.

Hoffman, I. Z. (1992). Some practical implications of a social-constructivist view of the psychoanalytic situation. *Psychoanalytic Dialogues, 2*(3), 287–304.

Izutsu, T. (1983). *Sufism & Taoism: A comparative study of key philosophical concepts*. Berkley: University of California Press.

Jung, C. G. (1931). Problems of modern psychotherapy. In *Collected works* (Vol. 16, pp. 53–75). Princeton, NJ: Princeton University Press.

Jung, C. G. (1935). The Tavistock lectures. In *Collected works* (Vol. 18, pp. 5–182). Princeton, NJ: Princeton University Press.

Jung, C. G. (1953). Two essays on analytical psychology. In *Collected works* (Vol. 7). Princeton, NJ: Princeton University Press.

Jung, C. G. (1955–56). Mysterium coniunctionis: An inquiry into the separation and synthesis of psychic opposites in alchemy. In G. Adler & R. F. C. Hull (Eds.), *Collected works* (Vol. 14). Princeton, NJ: Princeton University Press.

Jung, C. G. (1967). Alchemical studies. In *Collected works* (Vol. 13). Princeton, NJ: Princeton University Press.

Katz, G. (2014). *The play within the play: The enacted dimension of psychoanalytic process*. Abingdon, UK & New York: Routledge.

Kernberg, O. (1965). Notes on countertransference. *Journal of the American Psychoanalytic Association, 13*, 38–56.

Kohut, H. (1971). *The analysis of the self: A systematic approach to the psychoanalytic treatment of narcissistic personality disorders*. Chicago, IL: The University of Chicago Press.

Mitchell, S. A. (1997). Psychoanalysis and the degradation of romance. *Psychoanalytic Dialogues, 7*(1), 23–41.

Natsoulas, T. (2001). The Freudian conscious. *Consciousness & Emotion, 2*(1), 1–28.

Needham, J. (1969). *Science and civilization in China: Volume 2. History of scientific thought* (Vol. 2). London & New York: Cambridge University Press.

Orange, D. M. (2003). Antidotes and alternatives: Perspectival realism and the new reductionisms. *Psychoanalytic Psychology, 20*(3), 472–486.

Racker, H. (1957). The meanings and uses of countertransference. *Psychoanalytic Quarterly, 26*, 303–357.

Renik, O. (1993). Analytic interaction: Conceptualizing technique in light of the analyst's irreducible subjectivity. *The Psychoanalytic Quarterly, 62*, 553–571.

Searles, H. F. (1975). Patient as therapist to his analyst. In *Countertransference and related subjects: Selected papers* (pp. 380–459). New York: International Universities Press, Inc.

Slavin, J. H. (2007). The imprisonment and liberation of love: The dangers and possibilities of love in the psychoanalytic relationship. *Psychoanalytic Inquiry, 27*(3), 197–218.

Slavin, M. O., & Kriegman, D. (1998). Why the analyst needs to change: Toward a theory of conflict, negotiation, and mutual influence in the therapeutic process. *Psychoanalytic Dialogues, 8*, 247–284.

Slingerland, E. (2003). *Effortless action: Wu-Wei as conceptual metaphor and spiritual ideal in early China.* Oxford & New York: Oxford University Press.

Slochower, J. (2011). Analytic idealizations and the disavowed: Winnicott, his patients, and us. *Psychoanalytic Dialogues, 21*(1), 3–21.

Stensrud, R., & Stensrud, K. (1979). The Tao of human relations. *The Journal of Transpersonal Psychology, 11*(1), 75–82.

Stern, D. B. (2015). *Relational freedom: Emergent properties of the interpersonal field.* Hove, UK & New York: Routledge.

Translation: Tao Te Ching. (2019, May 30). *Wikisource.* Retrieved 12:57, May 30, 2019, from https://en.wikisource.org/w/index.php?title=Translation:Tao_Te_Ching&oldid=9209562 (Attributed to Lao-Tzu, licensed under https://creativecommons.org/licenses/by-sa/2.0/ for CC BY-SA 2.0).

Winnicott, D. W. (1949). Hate in the counter-transference. *International Journal of Psychoanalysis, 30*, 69–74.

Winnicott, D. W. (1953). Transitional objects and transitional phenomena: A study of the first not-me possession. *International Journal of Psychoanalysis, 34*, 89–97.

Part III

Participation

Chapter 7

Towards a participatory psychoanalysis

In this chapter I argue that the secular nature of efforts to establish a philosophical basis for relational psychoanalysis jeopardizes the field's commitment to pluralism. Starting with an examination of the perspectivism of Donna Orange, I move on to consider the hermeneutic approach offered by Donnel Stern. I argue that the theoretical trajectory of both figures' work points towards an emerging "participatory" turn in psychoanalysis. Drawing from corresponding developments in transpersonal theory, I examine the idea that spiritual experiences can be conceptualized as participatory events such that the ontology of spiritual/religious truth can be considered inherently pluralistic. In abstaining from secularizing the experience of meaning, I suggest that this philosophical outlook offers a more receptive philosophical basis from which to approach clinical work.

Throughout the present text I have sought to challenge the idea that psychoanalysis can remain spiritually uncommitted while claiming sympathetic engagement with religion and spirituality. While I believe that there is extensive personal investment in spirituality among relational analysts, relational *theorizing* often delegitimates spirituality in ways that are subtle yet deeply significant. In particular, relational psychoanalysis has often implicitly treated spiritual concerns as though theoretically distinct from the substance of relationship. This is expressed in a conception of the interpersonal field that accepts a disenchanted view of the world as normative. In failing to more directly address disenchantment, relational theorizing is prone to conceptualize spirituality as a fundamentally private matter. Reflecting this state of affairs, Blass (2006) takes issue with the way in which psychoanalytic writing that is apparently sympathetic to religion and spirituality nevertheless tends to portray articles of faith as "transitional objects" and in this way appears to subtly undermine the veracity of religious truth claims. In the extent to which psychoanalysis has been able to accommodate to religious belief, this has typically been accomplished by way of a positive revaluation of fantasy. While reflecting a step forward, this approach nevertheless falls short of genuine acceptance. As Blass writes: "Analytic theories that stress the value of illusion can appreciate religion only in so far as it does not demand our belief that what the religion posits is really true" (p. 28). This tendency is indicative of the challenge psychoanalytic practice still faces in establishing a genuinely hospitable outlook towards spiritual and religious concerns.

Pluralism and perspectival realism

The theme of pluralism has always been a central concern for relational thinking. In emphasizing the role of social context, relationally oriented analysts have sought to promote approaches to practice that are sensitive to the question of difference. This tendency is reflected in the extent to which the field has sought to engage the claims of postmodernity. Lyotard (1984) states: "Simplifying to the extreme, I define *postmodern* as incredulity towards metanarratives" (p. xxv). Such an aversion is naturally compatible with the relational idea that truth is mutually constructed. However, the connotations of postmodernism have often been claimed to result in an untenable basis for practice (Bell, 2009; Eagle, 2003; Mills, 2012b).[1] Despite the pluralistic appeal of postmodern thinking, clinical work requires a philosophical outlook capable of authorizing interpretation.

An influential attempt to meet this epistemological need has been offered by intersubjective self-psychologist Donna Orange. Ringstrom (2010) goes so far as to suggest that Orange's "perspectival realism" is representative not only of the underlying position of her intersubjectivist colleagues but also of the wider relational movement (p. 198). Perspectival realism asserts that reality exists independently of our interpretations, that our interpretations are reflective of this reality, and that our interpretations are always *contextual* and thus incomplete. This attitude is said to evade relativism while enabling multiple points of view. Orange (1992b) explains:

> The notion of perspective includes the idea of something on which someone can have or take a perspective. The viewer, patient or analyst,

stands somewhere in relation to something – a dream, a reported experience, an event in the treatment. The perspective also includes an angle of view, higher or lower, wider or narrower, as the case may be, on whatever is under consideration. For comparison, consider the indefinite number of photographs that could be made of the Brooklyn Bridge from various vantage points. To press the analogy further, consider what effects various kinds of film and lenses could add to the variety. No picture is true, and none is distorted. Or, if you wish, all the pictures are true, and all are distorted in that each takes a point of view. They are simply various views, some more aesthetically pleasing than others. But they are all views of *something*.

(p. 564)

The approach Orange adopts is reflective of an undertaking to save relational epistemology from relativism by endorsing a worldview that will [1] anchor interpretation and [2] enable relationship to the scientific community:

Neither philosophic relativist nor psychoanalytic constructivist can, however, provide any positive account of what constitutes scientific progress or psychoanalytic cure. The measure of a philosophy of science is its ability to provide criteria by which it is possible to say coherently that one scientific theory makes progress over its predecessor or that it does not. Similarly, a theory of psychoanalytic knowledge [. . .] ought to provide us with a basis for choosing one construction over another. A relativistic approach, of course, cannot do this.

(p. 562)

Orange describes her approach as "unabashedly antireductionist" (p. 484). However, from a more wholeheartedly constructivist perspective this claim would likely seem dubious – the philosophical outlook Orange adopts implies a *unitary* conception of reality that is only somewhat tempered with a recognition that context will always limit understanding. Orange (1992a) writes: "a subjective organization of experience is one perspective on a larger reality never fully attained or known but continually being approached, apprehended, articulated, and shared" (p. 196). This notion of approaching a fixed truth that exists distinct from our perception of it illustrates in what extent the perspectival realist outlook rejects the stronger pluralistic claims of constructivism – while subjective truth is still registered as inherently multiple, this multiplicity is negotiated with reference to a fixed and unitary conception of reality considered quite distinct from subjective cognition.

In emphasizing context as a *limitation* on one's capacity to grasp a more encompassing reality, it seems questionable whether a perspectival outlook is compatible with the claims of spirituality. Spiritual experiences often reflect an apparent *transcendence* of immediate context to embrace a wider sense of meaning. By contrast, perspectival realism reinforces Cartesian isolation and underscores our contextually bound smallness. Should one be of an ardently secular mindset, then a recognition of this smallness might be thought appropriate. Even the assertion of our smallness, however, tends to betray larger ambitions – consider Stolorow's (2011) claim that the pursuit of Truth is nothing more than a manifestation of the fear of death, or Hoffman's (1998) similar assertion that meaning is merely a construct snatched from the threat of oblivion. While these existential views no doubt exhibit their own imaginative vitality, they also serve to demonstrate that seeking to dispute any question of foundational truth in itself requires that we invoke it.[2]

Despite her broad emphasis on clinical hospitality, Orange (2010) is surprisingly explicit in betraying her own secular commitment where she writes: "Is there really enlightenment, Buddhist-style? [. . .] I think not, and do not believe Wittgenstein did either" (p. 241). Is a Zen satori experience thus to be considered delusional? How could such an outlook not be considered deeply reductive from the point of view of a patient who reports having undergone such an experience, or who devotes their life towards seeking to achieve this? If clinical receptivity is to be considered paramount, as Orange (2011) herself argues, then we must strive to endorse a maximally accepting way of conceptualizing belief.

Towards participation

Donnel Stern (1997) draws explicit attention to the limits of perspectival thinking:

> The problem with the approach is two-fold. First, it reduces the individual's role in the construction of experience to the selection of an angle of view on a preformulated object, and that, as far as I am

concerned, unreasonably cramps our conception of the constitutive involvement of the individual in the genesis of her own experience. [...] Second, this "angle-of-view" perspectivism leads to a constricted view of reality. Such a view of reality is unitary and unacceptably concrete.

(p. 182)[3]

Centrally influenced by the hermeneutics of Gadamer, Stern endorses the notion that reality should be considered inexhaustible in its interpretive possibilities. He suggests that the given and the made are in dialectical tension, and that fundamental reality can thus be considered both multiple and processual.

In drawing from Gadamer, Stern's work takes the significant step of moving psychoanalytic thinking towards what has elsewhere been termed a *participatory* outlook (Tarnas, 1991). However, Stern does not address this tradition directly. Rather, his participatory sensibility emerges osmotically in the extent to which his thinking has been influenced by Gadamer. Before examining the extent to which Stern's work might be said to embody a participatory sensibility, it is first necessary to offer some sense of what might be intended by participation.

The participatory outlook explained

Participatory thinking seeks to address the relationship between subject and object. This outlook can be traced most directly to the philosophical tradition of romanticism. Richard Tarnas (1991) states that the participatory worldview was initiated by Goethe, and can be traced through the work of such figures as Schiller, Schelling, Hegel, Coleridge, Emerson, and Rudolf Steiner.[4] The participatory sensibility emerges in trying to realize a more satisfying way of thinking about the relationship between self and world. This need can be understood to have emerged as a consequence of the limits associated with both Western science and phenomenalism. On the one hand, positivism expresses a unificatory conception of objective reality that human cognition somehow comes to grasp in absentia having achieving a "view from nowhere" (Nagel, 1986). On the other hand, the phenomenological line of thinking that can be traced to Kant and that culminates in postmodernism is liable to result in a solipsistic and disembodied relativism. Both approaches come to demean the reality of the subject. Participatory thinking offers an alternative approach by suggesting that mind and world are coextensive.

Transpersonal theorist Jorge Ferrer has adopted participatory thinking as a means to initiate a participatory turn in transpersonal psychology. Ferrer's work is helpful in evaluating recent efforts to establish a philosophical framework for relational psychoanalysis. Historically, transpersonalists have often sought to endorse the spiritual claims of divergent wisdom traditions by attempting to reconcile them via an overarching intellectual framework drawn from the philosophy of religion – "perennialism" offers a grand narrative approach to spirituality that holds that while there are many legitimate paths to truth, truth itself is singular. The world's religious traditions are perceived to offer different interpretations of the same spiritual reality. Such an outlook can be considered a form of perspectivism on the sacred.

Although relatively ecumenical, in seeking to reconcile divergent approaches to spirituality with an underlying conception of truth, the perennialist sensibility threatens to impose some rather severe limitations on the variety of religious experience – contradictions are not allowed to stand since divergent positions are required to conform to a pre-given schema, often with the effect that the experience of meaning comes to be categorized and treated developmentally. By extension, this strategy entails not only passing fixed value judgments on individuals but also on the world's religions. As Tarnas (2001) writes:

> Since experience of the ultimate spiritual reality was regarded as one shared by mystics through-out the ages, such experience was, like scientific truth, independent of human interpretations and projections and empirically replicable by anyone properly prepared to engage in the appropriate practices. In turn, this consensually validated supreme reality was seen as constituting a single absolute Truth which subsumed the diverse plurality of all possible cultural and spiritual perspectives within its ultimate unity. This was the essential transcendent Truth in which all religions at their mystical core ultimately converged.
>
> (p. 65)

A significant aspect of Ferrer's revisioning of transpersonal theory concerns an undertaking to address the pluralistic failings of the perspectivism reflected in the perennial philosophy. Ferrer (2017) holds to the participatory notion that spirituality "emerges from human cocreative participation in an undetermined mystery or generative power of life, the cosmos, or reality" (p. 10). Such an outlook allows for the ways in which spirituality is shaped by social and linguistic factors. The spiritual dimensions of experience are understood to be realized co-creatively in the encounter between the individual and the cosmos; any question of transcendence is always to be taken as a particularized expression of the emergent mystery. As Ferrer (2011) states, this outlook "allows the conception of a multiplicity of not only spiritual paths, but also spiritual liberations and even spiritual ultimates" (p. 5).

Ferrer's approach is influenced by Varela, Thompson, and Rosch's (1991) notion of enaction – a term that these authors use to express the idea that embodied activity gives rise to a world of cognitive distinctions that are reflective of the mutual relationship between organism and environment. With particular pertinence to a relational outlook, Ferrer stresses the limited individualistic fashion in which spiritual experiences have tended to be theorized in the transpersonal literature. Rather than assuming a skin-encapsulated notion of interiority limited to particular individuals, Ferrer (2002) emphasizes that transpersonal experiences are participatorily co-enacted so that such events can be understood to manifest in terms of relationships. As Hartelius (2016) explains: "An ontological claim within participatory thought, then, is a claim about the existence of a particular relationship, or relational field, and the dynamic relational processes that arise within it" (p. v).

Knowledge is no longer considered merely reflective of a pre-given reality, but rather the environment as we experience it is brought into existence in an active process that can itself be considered fundamentally transformative. Ferrer argues that the participatory turn reflects an enactive understanding of the sacred, so that religious or spiritual experiences should be understood as co-creative events. The Kantian distinction between the world and our experience of it comes to be problematized in suggesting that cognition is actively implicated in the disclosure of the world itself: "Participatory enaction, in other words, is epistemologically constructivist and metaphysically realist" (Ferrer & Sherman, 2008, p. 35). Such an approach avoids the tendency of reductively perceiving spirituality as "only" a construct of culture, yet safeguards against the threat of dogmatism. A participatory approach is both epistemological *and* ontological. It is this willingness to address a pluralism of being that enables participatory thinking to embrace the best of what postmodernity has to offer without falling into relativism.

The incomplete nature of the participatory turn in psychoanalysis

Having offered a brief overview of participatory theory, we are now in a position to return to the work of Donnel Stern. Stern's work can be understood as an attempt to introduce a participatory outlook to psychoanalysis. As previously touched upon, however, Stern himself does not reference the participatory tradition directly. We will recall, however, that Stern is centrally influenced by the participatory hermeneutics of Gadamer. For Gadamer (2004): "*Understanding is to be thought of less as a subjective act than as participating in an event of tradition*, a process of transmission in which past and present are constantly mediated" (p. 291, italics in original).

Does Gadamer's participatory influence thus render Stern's approach receptive to a deeper engagement with spirituality? A significant sticking point is the exclusive emphasis Gadamer places on the role of language:

> His hermeneutical theory is nevertheless lacking in the extent to which it fails to provide an account of the various aspects of human nature and of the mystery of human existence that inform interpretations both of life and of the written text. Thus, for example, while one searches Gadamer's writings in vain for any systematic account of human nature, the only aspect of man that receives discussion is his linguisticality. Furthermore, Gadamer's philosophical hermeneutics shuns any theological (or ultimately grounding) foundation. This lack of theological foundation raises the question of relativism in Gadamer's hermeneutics.
>
> (O'Reilly, 2012, pp. 842–843)[5]

Stern's work is explicit in supporting what he considers the fundamental postmodern discovery that "All experience is linguistic" (1997, p. 7). He goes so far as to state that words "are the sole means of our engagement with living" (p. 27) and that language "is the sum total of what allows and creates meaning [. . .] no meaning can exist outside it" (2000, p. 762).

To argue that all meaning is bound to language would suggest that experiences of "higher" meaning are fundamentally misguided. Spiritual or mystical experiences often suggest a sense of meaning that *exceeds* language. As with the perspectival emphasis on context, language conceived as a limit on meaning radically undermines the notion of spirituality. This consequence seems diametrically opposed to Stern's hermeneutic concern with enabling multiple perspectives on reality. By placing too much emphasis on language an implicit secularity creeps in. This secular tendency is perhaps further reinforced in the implied model of the unconscious that emerges from Stern's emphasis on the formative nature of the (disenchanted) interpersonal field. As Mills (2012a) writes with reference to Stern's work:

> What we may infer is unconscious is really only *nonconscious* events, such as those regulatory functions belonging to our neurobiology. Here there is no need to postulate a dynamic unconscious. There is no unconscious teleology, no unconscious ego directing such mental actions, no unconscious intentionality of any kind. "Formulations" or "interpretations" that are "avoided" or barred are simply linguistic processes that are either foreclosed or "restricted." What Stern calls the unconscious is merely formed through the repudiation or absence of linguistic construction.
>
> (p. 45)

Stern's approach misses the opportunity of connecting the notion of the unconscious with a broader conception of undetermined reality. The value of Stern's adoption of Gadamer lies in the fashion that language might be understood not as a limit but as a way of giving expression to, and thus transforming, reality. Emphasizing language as a limit inadvertently severs the individual from direct creative participation in the wider reality. It is the concept of the unconscious psyche as a link with the broader collective that enables meaningful interpretive participation.

In contrast to Stern's strict emphasis on language, Reason (1998) suggests that there are at least four different kinds of participatory knowing:

> *Experiential knowing* is through direct face-to-face encounter with person, place or thing; it is knowing through empathy and resonance, and is almost impossible to put into words.

>*Presentational knowing* emerges from experiential knowing, and provides its first expression through forms of imagery such as poetry and story, drawing, sculpture, movement, dance and so on.
>
>*Propositional knowing* "about" something, is knowing through ideas and theories, and is expressed in abstract language or mathematics.
>
>*Practical knowing* is knowing "how to" do something and is expressed in a skill, knack or competence.
>
> (p. 43, italics in original)

Embodied and imaginative forms of knowing can be understood to supplement the more conscious and explicitly linguistic operations of the rational mind, thus grounding conscious experience in the unconscious. Such a grounding is necessary in order to register participation psychologically meaningful. If a shift in the individual's psyche is to bring about a direct change in the collective, this would require that the psyche is meaningfully connected with reality so that reality itself is in some degree psychic. Stern's view appears to suggest that the mind is a social construct which is at the same time essentially private – i.e. while the mind is shaped by (and can shape) the external world, this process is always consciously mediated and bound solely to language. The individual participates only in language, and not in nature.

Stern (1997) argues that novelty is dependent upon "the incommensurability of action and knowledge, and the continuous reworking that goes on within each of these modes of experience" (p. 23). How does Stern understand the nature of "action" here? Having opted to endorse a non-dynamic conception of the unconscious, by implication this statement appears to flirt with an assertion that creative participation emerges as a consequence of the interaction between material events and self-reflection. Yet it is precisely this conception of an objective world standing apart from the act of interpretation that Stern is concerned to challenge. While acknowledging that the distinction between differently encoded forms of experience seems inadequate in accounting for the "raw and nonrational in unconscious life," Stern nevertheless argues that a perspectival-constructivist approach must do without such notions as drive or personal idiom because "there can be no reality that is meaningful apart from our interpretation of it" (p. 20). This again seems unnecessarily restrictive and out of keeping with Stern's otherwise emancipatory outlook. The notion of drive is only problematic if interpreted as a purely objective biological given that is not multiply interpretable and subject to participatory transformation. Adopting a participatory perspective does not require a rejection of drives, but rather enables the possibility that relational thinking might yet *reconcile* with drive theory. In the following chapter I show how such an undertaking might be conceptualized with reference to Jung's theory of archetypes.

Notes

1 Stephen Mitchell is particularly well known for having engaged directly with postmodernism, yet in recognition of the theoretical limitations that emerge in overemphasizing context he had started to distance himself from this sensibility in his later work (Taub, 2009).

2 The notion of spirituality speaks directly to our sense of living meaning – to that which we hold sacred. Wherever a given value exerts a particular fascination for us, a question of spirituality is thus implied. This remains the case whether what is at stake can be considered explicitly religious or otherwise.

3 Perhaps in response to the criticism of perspectival thinking articulated by Stern, in a later publication Orange (2003) makes a significant revision to her own position which seems to bring her approach more in line with Stern's:

> Writing now I would emphasize in addition that what we understand is itself temporal and emergent, not just a preexisting text or "fact." The process of coming to understanding creates more to understand, and this process is not reversible, or reducible to putatively previous "states" and dialectical alternatives. It allows not only expanded but changed organizations of experience.
>
> (p. 481)

Although this amendment is made as a seemingly casual aside, the implications are extensive. Subjective cognition is now directly implicated in a notion of the real which is itself open to change.

4 Sherman (2008) has subsequently suggested that the emergence of participatory thinking in the West can be traced as far back as Ancient Greece, and can be roughly divided into three historical phases: the formal (associated with Plato), the existential (associated with Aquinas), and the creative (a phase still developing, and which coincides with the paradigm identified by Tarnas).

5 Gadamer speaks in interview of his reluctance to disclose his own beliefs (Gadamer & Gehron, 1995).

References

Bell, D. (2009). Is truth an illusion? Psychoanalysis and postmodernism. *International Journal of Psychoanalysis*, *90*(2), 331–345.

Blass, R. B. (2006). Beyond illusion: Psychoanalysis and the question of religious truth. In D. M. Black (Ed.), *Psychoanalysis and religion in the 21st century: Competitors or collaborators?* (pp. 23–43). London & New York: Routledge.

Eagle, M. N. (2003). The postmodern turn in psychoanalysis. *Psychoanalytic Psychology*, *20*, 411–424.

Ferrer, J. N. (2002). *Revisioning transpersonal theory: A participatory vision of human spirituality*. Albany, NY: State University of New York Press.

Ferrer, J. N. (2011). Participatory spirituality and transpersonal theory: A ten-year retrospective. *The Journal of Transpersonal Psychology*, *43*(1), 1–34.

Ferrer, J. N. (2017). *Participation and the mystery: Transpersonal essays in psychology, education, and religion*. Albany, NY: State University of New York Press.

Ferrer, J. N., & Sherman, J. H. (2008). The participatory turn in spirituality, mysticism, and religious studies. In J. N. Ferrer & J. H. Sherman (Eds.), *The participatory turn: Spirituality, mysticism, religious studies* (pp. 1–78). Albany, NY: State University of New York Press.

Gadamer, H.-G. (2004). *Truth and method* (2nd ed.). New York & London: Continuum.

Gadamer, H.-G., & Gehron, C. (1995). Hans-Georg Gadamer: "Without poets there is no philosophy". *Radical Philosophy*, *69*(January/February), 27–35.

Hartelius, G. (2016). Participatory transpersonalism: Transformative relational process, not the structure of ultimate reality [editor's introduction]. *International Journal of Transpersonal Studies*, *35*(1), iii–ix.

Hoffman, I. Z. (1998). *Ritual and spontaneity in the psychoanalytic process: A dialectical-constructivist view*. Hillsdale, NJ: Analytic Press.

Lyotard, J. F. (1984). *The postmodern condition: A report on knowledge*. Minneapolis: University of Minnesota Press.

Mills, J. (2012a). *Conundrums: A critique of contemporary psychoanalysis*. New York & London: Routledge.

Mills, J. (2012b). *Conundrums: A critique of contemporary psychoanalysis*. New York: Routledge.

Nagel, T. (1986). *The view from nowhere*. New York: Oxford University Press.

Orange, D. M. (1992a). Chapter 10: Subjectivism, relativism, and realism in psychoanalysis. *Progress in Self Psychology*, *8*.

Orange, D. M. (1992b). Perspectival realism and social constructivism: Commentary on Irwin Hoffman's "discussion: Toward a social-constructivist view of the psychoanalytic situation". *Psychoanalytic Dialogues*, *2*(4), 561–565.

Orange, D. M. (2003). Antidotes and alternatives: Perspectival realism and the new reductionisms. *Psychoanalytic Psychology*, *20*(3), 472–486.

Orange, D. M. (2010). Recognition as: Intersubjective vulnerability in the psychoanalytic dialogue. *International Journal of Psychoanalytic Self Psychology*, *3*, 227–243.

Orange, D. M. (2011). *The suffering stranger: Hermeneutics for everyday clinical practice*. New York: Routledge.

O'Reilly, K. E. (2012). Transcending gadamer: Towards a participatory hermeneutics. *The Review of Metaphysics*, *65*, 841–860.

Reason, P. (1998). Toward a participatory worldview. *Resurgence*, *168*, 42–44.

Ringstrom, P. A. (2010). Meeting Mitchell's challenge: A comparison of relational psychoanalysis and intersubjective systems theory. *Psychoanalytic Dialogues*, *20*(2), 196–218.

Sherman, J. H. (2008). A genealogy of participation. In J. N. Ferrer & J. H. Sherman (Eds.), *The participatory turn: Spirituality, mysticism, religious studies* (pp. 81–112). Albany, NY: State University of New York Press.

Stern, D. B. (1997). *Unformulated experience: From dissociation to imagination in psychoanalysis*. Hillsdale, NJ: Analytic Press.

Stern, D. B. (2000). The limits of social construction: Commentary on paper by Cynthia Dyess and Tim Dean. *Psychoanalytic Dialogues*, *10*(5), 757–769.

Stolorow, R. D. (2011). *World, affectivity, trauma: Heidegger and post-Cartesian psychoanalysis*. New York: Routledge.

Tarnas, R. (1991). *The passion of the Western mind: Understanding the ideas that have shaped our world view*. New York: Harmony Books.

Tarnas, R. (2001). A new birth in freedom: A (p)review of Jorge Ferrer's revisioning transpersonal theory: A participatory vision of human spirituality. *The Journal of Transpersonal Psychology*, *33*(1), 64–71.

Taub, G. (2009). A confusion of tongues between psychoanalysis and philosophy: Is the controversy over drive versus relational theory a philosophical one? *International Journal of Psychoanalysis*, *90*, 507–527.

Varela, F. J., Thompson, E., & Rosch, E. (1991). *The embodied mind: Cognitive science and human experience*. Cambridge, MA: MIT Press.

Chapter 8

Bridging worlds[1]

In this chapter I offer a participatory approach to Jung's archetypal thinking. With reference to the relationship between analytical psychology and the psychoanalytic mainstream, I consider the ways in which upholding a pluralistic sensibility might be threatened in seeking to maintain scientific credibility. Drawing attention to the process-oriented qualities of Jung's work, it is suggested that the speculative nature of Jung's archetypal thinking offers a more adequate basis for contemporary practice than might be assumed.

How Jung's archetypal thinking is interpreted can be considered critical to the wider reception of his ideas. Challengingly, however, academic perception is effectively split between two quite contrary kinds of objection – the first on behalf of the universal and the second on behalf of the particular. This split reflects a fundamental rift in recent intellectual discourse between scientific realism and postmodern constructivism. For those wishing to establish the universality of Jung's findings, the problem as expressed in the contemporary intellectual climate is of establishing scientific credibility. Despite Jung's protestations, the archetypes are still liable to appear speculative in nature and, for want of a more robust scientific basis, unworthy of attention. Meanwhile, for those seeking to *oppose* grand narratives, Jungian archetypes are registered objectionable not because they lack proven universality but for purporting to claim universality in the first place. What both lines of criticism appear to share is an implicit rejection of that which James Hillman characterizes as "spirit" (in distinction to soul) – that which is concerned with transcendence and a unified conception of higher truth.[2] Thus, in the extent to which Jung's work has been associated with an emphasis on the archetype considered as a spiritual referent having "the functional significance of a world-constituting factor" (Jung, 1952c, para. 964), it should hardly surprise that his psychology has not received wider attention.

We might roughly conceptualize this state-of-affairs further with reference to the distinction made by Samuels (1985) in classifying Jungian thinking in terms of classical, developmental, and archetypal schools. The developmental school, in its association with infant attachment, evolutionary biology, and neuroscience, reflects the strain of Jungian thinking most directly engaged with negotiating the sensibilities of mainstream psychology.[3] Meanwhile, the archetypal approach,[4] with its emphasis on phenomenology, its skepticism towards science, and its explicit rejection of a metaphysical stance, has been the most ostensibly postmodern of the Jungian outlooks. Finally, in remaining loyal to the perceived letter of Jung's work, the classical school maintains a position that, while seeking to preserve the full breadth of Jung's thinking, arguably does so at cost of a more direct engagement with the contemporary intellectual climate.

Adopting a spiritually receptive approach to psychology in the context of the wider ideological assumptions attendant to clinical practice poses an obvious challenge. In apparent recognition, Jung is well-known for emphasizing the numinous[5] as an experience, while often claiming to abstain from drawing metaphysical conclusions concerning the nature of ultimate reality. The problematic nature of this distinction, as made apparent in Jung's work itself, lies in the extent to which those experiences that we tend to ascribe as "spiritual" are intimately associated with gnosis. Under such conditions the proximity of the divine is not experienced as merely conjectural. To subsequently treat the experience only in these terms, while not without value, is nevertheless one-sided. Addressing this one-sidedness remains difficult; although a noncommittal respect for spirituality as a "life domain" may pass muster within the clinical mainstream, engaging the truth content of these experiences continues to be regarded as suspect and beyond the preserve of psychology proper.

Over the last 50 years the field of transpersonal psychology has developed to more directly explore the relationship between Western psychology and spirituality. Counting Jung as a founding father, figures like Abraham Maslow, Stanislav Grof, Michael Washburn, and Ken Wilber have made significant contributions that might be assumed to have direct interest for Jungian debate. The relative lack of interaction between transpersonalists and Jungians is surprising, and certainly warrants fuller attention. In this chapter I will suggest that recent developments in transpersonal psychology might offer a way of thinking about Jung's ideas that recognizes the claims of science without capitulating to them, preserves the pluralistic outlook of the archetypal movement (as reflected in Hillman's anti-essentialist "polytheism") without neglecting to ground this sensibility in a notion of higher truth, and offers a more adequate way of elucidating the creative tensions in Jung's work than is offered by the tendency to emphasize his self-professed Kantianism. In order to convince of the potential importance of this approach I begin by addressing recent debates in relational psychoanalysis before examining the parallels in analytical psychology. I then demonstrate how a reading of Jung's psychology made available via the work of transpersonalists Richard Tarnas and Jorge Ferrer might provide an interesting means of responding to these theoretical challenges. I argue that this approach offers a way of holding Jung's thinking such as to more effectively register the ubiquity of the personal factor. While the line of thinking that follows is ostensibly of a theoretical nature, I wish to suggest that Jung's psychology indicates the short-sightedness of any outlook on practice that would seek to treat our perception of the clinical "facts" as separable from the question of an underlying worldview.

Relational motives

While Freudians classically conceive relationships to develop out of the desire to satisfy innate needs in an effort to maintain homeostasis, the relational outlook points to a reversal of this claim and suggests instead that our motivations for action come to be established in relationships. Going hand in hand with this reversal is a significant reconceptualization of the psychoanalytic relationship – one that has often been alluded to in terms of a shift from "one-person" to "two-person" models of thinking. Rather than striving for clinical neutrality, relational analysts have sought to recognize the inevitability of mutual influence and to develop technical approaches that reflect this. In emphasizing co-participation, relational thinking thus suggests a natural compatibility with Jung's (1946) alchemical approach to the clinical encounter. This coupled with the relational emphasis on dialoging with other disciplines has reflected a significant opportunity for Jungian and psychoanalytic discourses to engage (see Brown, 2018). But while Jungians have shown some interest in exploring overlaps with recent psychoanalytic thinking, relational analysts have perhaps been less quick to engage analytical psychology. Besides reflecting the enduring legacy of Jungian discreditation, this lack of engagement is perhaps also reflective of the extent to which Jung's psychology suggests certain sensibilities that seem not to be in keeping with the forward-looking attitude of the relational field. In particular, Jung's readily criticized tendency to portray the archetypes as timeless and universal ordering principles can appear to betray an essentialist metaphysics that stands in opposition to the loosely constructivist outlook reflected in much relational theorizing.

While classical Freudian analysts have conventionally endorsed an approach having to do with making essentially objective truth claims, in emphasizing the co-construction of meaning relational analysts have come to question the analyst's interpretive authority. While this undertaking is theoretically liberating and seemingly in step with the needs of multiculturalism and a pluralistic approach to clinical practice,[6] the untethering of meaning from Truth appears to threaten clinical authority – perhaps even to the extent that the clinical situation itself may no longer be theoretically justifiable (Mills, 2012). As a consequence of such difficulties, relational theorists have often invoked infant attachment thinking in support of their clinical ideals (Beebe & Lachmann, 2003). Thus Buechler (1997) playfully refers to infant attachment theory as a "secure base" for psychoanalysis, while Fonagy and Target (2007) speak of "rooting the mind in the body." For the more pluralistically committed, however, a concern remains that scientific claims about "normal" development have often been deployed to oppress minority voices (Teicholz, 2009, 2010). As Stern (2008) argues, the decontextualized nature of most psychological research has the effect of implicitly reinforcing the existing social order as natural.[7] Attachment theorists are generally not concerned with exploring questions of epistemic pluralism – attachment theory is firmly grounded in the assumptions of scientific discourse thus registering a basic incompatibility with postmodern-constructivist sensibilities (Fajardo, 1993; Strenger, 1991). As such, where contemporary psychoanalysis comes to rely on theories of motivation that seek justification in attachment studies, there is a clear danger that recent thinking only pushes the field closer to the scientific worldview that the more postmodern elements of relational theory would have us believe is being questioned. While it should be stressed that drawing from attachment thinking can no doubt offer the basis for important clinical insights, the objection I am presently raising is not with the value of the ideas themselves but with the underlying philosophical assumptions thus invoked where relational theory seeks to *justify* its claims with recourse to the science of attachment studies.[8]

Elsewhere I have argued (Brown, 2017b) that the relational movement's more radical and emancipatory tendencies have been restricted in consequence of [1] the need of establishing a philosophical basis that will authorize interpretation, and [2] the associated need of positing a theory of motivation. These theoretical challenges coupled with the more obvious institutional pressures of maintaining some measure of scientific credibility have ensured that, despite sometimes more radical intentions, relational thinking has not strayed too far from the positivist worldview from which psychoanalytic practice has ostensibly sought to free itself. In this fashion relational analysis has, for all of its significant advances, perhaps fallen short of its pluralistic ideals. In seeking to offer a more nuanced response to these challenges than has been provided by the important contributions of relational thinkers, I argue that Jung's work might play a significant role. Before pursing this argument, however, I will first consider how the tension between founding truth and clinical pluralism has also found expression in Jungian discourse.

Parallels in analytical psychology

Historically, analytical psychology has been influenced by collective pressures in a manner somewhat distinct from the psychoanalytic mainstream. While psychoanalysis in the mid-twentieth century managed to secure a considerable degree of institutional authority by way of the field's association with medicine, analytical psychology has never enjoyed this kind of widespread acceptance.[9] For Jungians there has always been both more to prove and, conversely, less to lose. This state of affairs leads to a conundrum as to whether the field is best served in pursuing legitimation, or in more radically questioning the ground upon which such legitimation is commonly thought to rest. In contrast to the challenges faced by the Jungian community, within the English-speaking psychoanalytic world questioning the basic assumptions of the wider clinical paradigm has in considerable extent started at home – that is, owing to the extent that the psychoanalytic world infiltrated medical psychiatry, the early relational questioning of psychoanalytic dogma partly reflected a wider recognition of the problems raised by critical theory in respect of institutional assumptions about mental illness. However, it was precisely as the relational movement began to emerge in the early 1980s that the American psychoanalytic orthodoxy had started to lose its influence in the medical community. Publication of the DSM-III in 1980 heralded the shift away from a psychodynamic diagnostic paradigm, with Greenberg and Mitchell's trailblazing text appearing three years after. Much has changed since; while early relational analysts might be construed as nonconformists seeking to critique a psychoanalytic discourse that was still relatively ensconced in the societal mainstream, contemporary relationalists now reflect the majority sensibility in a field that has been largely sidelined. This leaves the psychoanalytic community at present struggling with questions not dissimilar to those that have historically troubled Jungians – whether to align with the mainstream sensibility, or critique it.

Contemporary relational analysts seek to negotiate between the needs of societal recognition and a commitment to underlying ideals. Likewise, while some Jungians seek to make Jung's psychology more palatable to the wider scientific community, others in the field continue to emphasize those aspects of Jung's work that are liable to be considered all but inadmissible by conventional academic standards. As indicated earlier, one way of thinking about this dual tendency is in terms of the distinction between developmental and archetypal strands of discourse. While the former has sometimes been criticized for moving too far in the direction of deterministic science,[10] the latter has seemingly waned as a distinct clinical approach owing to the absence of a firm theoretical grounding. This dynamic is reflected in debates concerning whether psychoanalysis should be conceived as an empirically based science or a relationally constituted hermeneutic. Apposite to dichotomous thinking of this kind, Saban (2013) has argued for the need of retaining the inherent ambiguity of Jung's work. Surely a similar case can be made in reading Freud. The question remains, however, as to how this tension is to be held more effectively in carrying the work forward.

Perhaps the most significant element of Freudian thinking that would seek to preserve this theme of ambiguity is expressed in Freud's (1915) insistence that the notion of drive be considered a liminal concept existing, as he puts it, "on the frontier between the mental and the somatic" (pp. 121–122). Yet the instability of this approach has made it difficult to retain. While Greenberg (1991) seeks to argue that drives should be explicitly conceptualized as endogenous forces of the mind and not endo-somatic impulses drawn from biology, for want of a philosophical justification his approach comes to seem arbitrary. It is the inclusion of biology in Freud's drive concept that implicitly holds the promise of a comfortable grounding in the metaphysics of Western science. By excluding the biological from a definition of the drive, the need for a different form of justification becomes apparent – one that is liable to be very much out of step with the assumptions of the mainstream clinical world. Alternatively, the biological aspect of the drive can be retained with an explicit recognition that it is upon this discourse that Freud's psychology will ultimately ground its truth claims. In this light, Freud's outlook can be interpreted to reflect an appropriate scientific caution in refusing to claim an exact equivalency between the claims of his psychology and the assumedly objective truth of biology.[11]

In a Jungian context, the ambiguity of the Freudian drive concept is paralleled in the notion of the archetype. This is given most obvious expression when Jung (1947) adopts the spectrum of light as a metaphor expressing the two poles of the archetype as matter and spirit. Samuels (1985) writes:

> The student of archetypes can follow the downward path and explore the worlds of ethology and biology in the hope of constructing a scientific picture of what it is to be human. Or the upward path may be followed, leading to the world of spirit. Or a dual path can be taken which emphasises the bifurcated nature of the archetype. Jung developed all three paths but, in his later work, followed the "upward" direction.
>
> (p. 28)

Should this pursuit of the upward direction be interpreted merely as a failure on Jung's part to maintain the tension reflected elsewhere in his psychology between the biological and spiritual? When Jung sought to engage the downward path it was in order to establish a scientifically defensible basis for his archetypal thinking. As Hogenson (2010) observes, however, Jung's interest in grounding his Kantian approach to archetypes in evolutionary theory expresses a confused effort to resolve epistemological arguments with recourse to the incompatible domain of biology. But while the secular outlook of Freudian thinking seemingly necessitates the biological as a ground, Jung's spiritually oriented approach does not. Jung might yet rely on his notion of the archetype as a spiritual a priori to provide authorization for meaning. Yet a recurrent theme of Jung's work is the assertion of his supposed empiricism and the invocation of Kant in seeking to ward off metaphysical claims. For Jung, Kant's philosophy confirms that all knowledge is restricted to the phenomenological experience of the subject:

> The fact that I am content with what can be experienced psychically, and reject the metaphysical, does not amount, as any intelligent person can see, to a gesture of scepticism or agnosticism aimed at faith or trust in higher power, but means approximately what Kant meant when he called the thing-in-itself a "merely negative borderline concept." Every statement about the transcendental is to be avoided because it is only a laughable presumption on the part of a human mind unconscious of its limitations.
>
> (Jung, 1954, para. 82)

It is this phenomenological Jung that has been emphasized by Hillman and the archetypal school. The fate of this approach, however, has arguably come to suggest the limits of a phenomenological stance for clinical practice. While Hillman's psychology had originally emphasized *via negativa* and "not knowing," in the latter phases of his career he explicitly came to recognize the limits of this (Hillman, 1989).

The archetypal school's refusal of metaphysics serves to illustrate the insufficiency of Jung's interpretation of Kant as the basis for a clinically applicable psychology. Just as psychoanalysts like Greenberg (1991) have emphasized the necessity of a theory of motivation, this has recently been expressed in a Jungian context with Kime's (2013) observation that the reification of the noumenal is essential in applying the concept of the archetype to the clinical practice of analytical psychology:

> In phenomenology, the noumenal is disguised and disappears into a current, which exists in the practices of amplification and interpretation. It appears in the open again when we ask "what guides you in your choice of material to use in amplifications?" or "why do you make a particular interpretation or connection to some particular instance

of patient behaviour?" An answer to such a question minimally must have it that there was some relevance, some connection, something in common between that which triggers the analysts' response and the response. This much is difficult to dispute. My contention is that even such a basic requirement for an answer to such questions is already a disguised reification of the noumenal, regulative force, which gives meaning to the concept of "similar" in the psyche. One cannot have a concept of "similar" psychic shape without having an ontology that includes the (reified) notion of "shape."

(p. 59)

This seems to imply either the need of a return to biology and a rejection of the spiritual path as a possible means to grounding, or else a revised approach to the theme of metaphysics. It might be stressed again, however, that the former outlook does not actually circumvent metaphysical assumptions – rather, owing to the extent that Western science has conducted itself under the false pretense of not having enlisted foundational truth claims, biological discourse merely provides a convenient cover such as to avoid making the clinician's underlying assumptions more explicit. If practice is to proceed on a more pluralistic basis these claims cannot afford to go unchallenged. In seeking to mount such a challenge, however, clinical applicability appears threatened – this has been expressed within the psychoanalytic mainstream in terms of the effort to integrate constructivist thinking, and within analytical psychology in terms of the archetypal school's emphasis on phenomenology. Yet the pluralistic striving of these two strands of discourse cannot afford to be discarded. Besides seeking to establish a respectful approach to practice reflecting the contemporary needs of multiculturalism, the theme of pluralism is at bottom another way of talking about the problems raised in seeking to promote receptivity towards the radically unfamiliar. Any question of enabling the unconscious to emerge in relationship thus seems contingent on retaining as much space for alterity as is clinically sustainable. This being so, we might seek to establish a reading of Jung's psychology that promotes a maximal feeling for difference yet without foregoing a clinically necessary grounding in truth. I will now argue that a reading of this nature is available via the upward trajectory reflected in Jung's late work, and with support from the "participatory" approach recently emphasized in transpersonal psychology.

The participatory approach

Can Jung be considered a participatory thinker? Certainly his innumerable Kantian protestations would give us to suppose otherwise. In other moments, however – particularly when Jung's theological sensibility comes to the fore – a different picture emerges. Consider the following passage from *Liber Novus* which occurs in the second of the *Seven Sermons*:

> God is not dead. He is alive as ever. God is creation, for he is something definite, and therefore differentiated from the Pleroma. God is a quality of the Pleroma, and everything I have said about creation also applies to him.
> But he is distinct from creation in that he is much more indefinite and indeterminable. He is less differentiated than creation, since the ground of his essence is effective fullness. Only insofar as he is definite and differentiated is he creation, and as such he is the manifestation of the effective fullness of the Pleroma.
>
> (Jung, 2009, p. 348)

These statements express a participatory attitude towards the immanence/transcendence distinction – an approach that, it might be added, surely has radical implications for Jung's thinking about the archetypes. We might recall Otto's (1928) definition of the numinous experience as a revelation of the divine that is at once objectively present, yet absolutely unapproachable. Far from positing God's transcendence as the stable bedrock of meaning, it is precisely in the extent that God transcends creation that divinity's essential nature becomes less defined. Jung takes up the question of humanity's relationship to God most explicitly in *Answer to Job*, stating: "Whoever knows God has an effect on him" (Jung, 1952a, para. 617) and "The encounter with the creature changes the creator" (para. 686). These sentiments are paralleled in a different light in *Memories, Dreams, Reflections* – Jung offers the following account of his experience on the Athi Plains:

> There the cosmic meaning of consciousness became overwhelmingly clear to me: "What nature leaves imperfect, the art perfects," say the alchemists. Man, I, in an invisible act of creation put the stamp of perfection on the world by giving it objective existence. . . . Now I knew

what it was, and knew even more: that man is indispensable for the completion of creation; that, in fact, he himself is the second creator of the world, who alone has given the world its objective existence – without which, unheard, unseen, silently eating, giving birth, dying, heads nodding through hundreds of millions of years, it would have gone on in the profoundest night of non-being down to its unknown end. Human consciousness created objective existence and meaning, and man found his indispensable place in the great process of being.

(Jung, 1963, pp. 255–256)

How might a lofty passage of this nature be shown to have direct relevance for contemporary clinical practice? The participatory paradigm has been adopted by transpersonal theorist Jorge Ferrer to significantly challenge assumptions often attending a spiritually oriented psychology. Within the field of transpersonal psychology, the theme of pluralism has come to reflect a leading theoretical concern. Transpersonalists have often sought to endorse the spiritual claims of divergent wisdom traditions by attempting to reconcile them within an overarching intellectual framework drawn from the philosophy of religion. So-called *perennialism* offers a grand narrative approach to spirituality effectively holding that while there are many legitimate paths to truth, truth itself is singular. A kind of perennialism is in fact apparent in certain aspects of Jung's work. Consider, for example, the following statement: "I prefer the term 'the unconscious,' knowing that I might equally well speak of 'God' or 'daimon.' [. . .] When I do use such mythic language, I am aware that 'mana,' 'daimon' and 'God' are synonyms for the unconscious" (Jung, 1963, pp. 336–337). This approach is reflected most strongly by the classical school, which, in its propensity for translating mythological material into Jungian terminology, can sometimes lead to a sense that Jung's psychology should be considered a skeleton key with which the Jungian analyst might unlock the world's wisdom traditions. As Edinger (1977) puts it: "By seeing all functioning religions as living expressions of individuation symbolism [. . .] an authentic basis is laid for a true ecumenical attitude" (p. 37). And even more explicitly: "These dreams [. . .] express a common viewpoint, a kind of perennial philosophy of the unconscious which seems to have more or less universal validity" (Edinger, 1972, p. 199). It is this kind of thinking that might elicit considerable skepticism from theorists of a more postmodern bent as to the viability of Jung's psychology for a pluralistic practice. Likewise, the perennialism conventionally adopted within transpersonal circles suggests that the world's religious traditions offer different interpretations of the same spiritual reality. In seeking to reconcile divergent approaches to spirituality with an underlying conception of truth, the perennialist sensibility threatens to impose restrictive limits on the tremendous diversity of religious experience.

By contrast, the approach endorsed by Ferrer (2002) holds that spiritual events arise out of participation in the emergent dynamics of a fundamental mystery.[12] Such an outlook allows for the ways in which spirituality is shaped by social and linguistic factors, yet not to the exclusion of the transpersonal. This notion of the transpersonal cannot be interpreted as final, because the spiritual dimensions of experience are understood to be enacted co-creatively in the encounter between the individual and the cosmos; any question of transcendence is always to be taken as a particularized expression of the emergent mystery.[13] Ferrer (2017) states: "The key point is that *there is no need to conflate Kosmic and universal if the Kosmos is considered a plural cornucopia creatively advancing in multiple ontological directions*" (p. 208, emphasis in original).

Despite the extent to which Jung's ideas have sometimes been adopted to serve a perennialist agenda, Jung's archetypal thinking nevertheless offers a significant means of translating into clinical practice the pluralistic sensibility expressed in the participatory approach adopted by Ferrer. Such an approach entails emphasizing the role of the personal myth[14] coupled with a recognition of the archetypes as world-constituting. I have sought to show (Brown, 2013, 2017b) how Jung's (1948) notion that "*wherever we meet with uniform and regularly recurring modes of apprehension we are dealing with an archetype, no matter whether its mythological character is recognized or not*" (para. 280, emphasis in original) can be read as a participatory claim that by definition precludes a final biological grounding for archetypes.

Jung (1951) writes:

A kind of fluid interpenetration belongs to the very nature of all archetypes. They can only be roughly circumscribed at best. Their living meaning comes out more from their presentation as a whole than from a single formulation. Every attempt to focus them more sharply is immediately punished by the intangible core of meaning losing its luminosity. No archetype can be reduced to a simple formula. It is a vessel which we can never empty, and never fill. It has a potential existence only, and when it takes shape in matter it is no longer what it was. It persists throughout the ages and requires interpreting ever anew. The archetypes are the imperishable elements of the unconscious, but they change their shape continually.

(Jung, 1951, para. 301)

Citing this passage, Tarnas (2006) emphasizes that Jung is portraying the archetypes as universal forms that are nevertheless shaped by human participation (p. 86). Expanding upon this notion, Tarnas (2012) argues that the archetypes can be considered both in terms of the immanence of Aristotle's universals *and* the transcendence of Platonic forms. In his response to Martin Buber, Jung (1952b) makes this point categorically when he states: "These powers are numinous 'types' [. . .] and such types are, if one may so express it, immanent-transcendent" (para. 1505).[15] Honoring both sides of this distinction emphasizes the core role of gnosis in Jung's psychology – a theme that Jung himself tended to undermine by virtue of his efforts to retain scientific respectability by insisting on his status as a Kantian. It is as a direct consequence of such claims that, speaking from a Freudian perspective, Mills (2013) is able to legitimately question whether the archetype need even be postulated when the drive serves the same purpose. Mills takes the following position:

What I believe Jung wants to secure is an empirical basis for a justified psychoanalytic metaphysics grounded through phenomenological psychology. [. . .] By focusing on the phenomenology of experience, he attempts to sidestep the pitfalls associated with speculative metaphysics; yet no matter how phenomenology is positioned, one can never escape the implicit ontological assumptions that underlie our experience of experience.

(Mills, 2013, p. 36)

While the extent to which Jung was consciously and consistently pursuing a psychoanalytic metaphysics is certainly questionable, I believe that Mills is nevertheless correct in suggesting that this is an underlying thrust of his thinking.[16] In fact, it is precisely for this reason that Jung's archetypal thinking goes further than Freud's conception of drive as a basis for contemporary clinical work. The notion of the archetype as a spiritual a priori, when considered from a participatory perspective, offers an anchor for practice that nevertheless retains a fundamental recognition of its own status as an expression of the clinician's subjectivity. While Jung's phenomenological side-stepping is prone to undermine the experiential basis upon which the archetype's numinosity is justified, a participatory outlook has the great merit of enabling us to acknowledge the role of gnosis in Jung's thinking without his psychology being reduced to dogma. This reflects Jung's (1963) emphasis on undergoing the original experience without neglecting his (1946) core relational assumption that the clinical encounter will entail a transformation in both parties. As he states in *Aion*: "Just as these concepts arose out of an experience of reality, so they can be elucidated only by further experience" (Jung, 1951, para. 63).

Re-grounding practice

Insofar as spiritual concerns have to do with the living experience of meaning, secularly minded clinicians are liable to perceive spiritually informed approaches to practice as a possible threat to clinical receptivity. As Pargament (2013) puts it, however, "When it comes to religion and spirituality, no one is neutral. This general rule of thumb applies to atheists and agnostics as well as theists, and it applies to psychologists as well as their clients." Because spiritual commitments are always reflected in our definitions of reality, to define spirituality will always in itself reflect a commitment of spirit. This is readily forgotten in context of the clinical situation which, in its tendency to isolate, assess, and diagnose, often assumes a great deal from the outset. Thus the endeavor to include spirituality within the clinical domain is deeply important yet very much problematic. It is important because such a move promises to challenge the biases of the Western psychiatric paradigm. It is problematic because it threatens to destabilize our clinical assumptions in ways that can be disturbing and difficult to accommodate.

The legacy of religious dogmatism engenders an understandable suspicion that endorsing a spiritually informed approach to practice must inevitably clash with pluralistic ambitions. From a participatory outlook, however, engaging the theme of spirituality in fact provides a much more effective stance from which to theorize difference. This outlook can also be expected to foster an increased clinical respect for spiritual experiences and the essential quality of "knowing" often associated with them.

Relational epistemologies often struggle to account for such experiences without reducing them. Postulating a basis for the experience of meaning that can be considered in some sense transcendent, relational discourse might adopt the notion of a spiritual ground so as to provide a more open-ended approach to meaning. A participatory outlook problematizes the immanence/transcendence distinction such that this ground is itself considered paradoxical and evolving. Such an approach offers a means by which to uphold a contextual ethos without reducing subjective experience by measuring it against a unitary conception of reality, or in conceiving meaning as merely an effect of language.

Earlier in this chapter I suggested that if clinicians are to embrace a pluralistic approach to practice by refusing to endorse biology as the final ground of meaning, two needs emerge: [1] the need of establishing a pluralistic philosophical basis that will nevertheless authorize interpretation, and [2] the associated need of positing a theory of motivation. I am suggesting that the participatory paradigm offers a framework by means of which to conceptualize the former challenge, while Jung's archetypal thinking offers a complementary approach to the latter. If the relational nature of this outlook is to be adequately recognized, then the clinician's motivational framework must be conceptualized as an expression of their own truth (see Colman, 2013) and not assumed universally binding. At the same time, this truth is taken to be grounded in the spiritual referents of the personal myth and not merely a socially determined product of the clinician's relationship to language. I have argued elsewhere (Brown, 2017b) that this position can only be sustained on an ethical basis, and that the analytic situation must be regarded fundamentally as a trial of faith conducted in fallibilistic orientation to the Other. This position seeks to reflect an analytic tension between the striving to understand and a willingness to be challenged and surprised.

The value of the "participatory" label lies in its non-systematic nature. This paradigm offers a way of talking about a general orientation towards life that, owing to its countercultural nature, has been insufficiently formulated as a distinct trajectory in the history of Western ideas. Given that most clinicians do not work from exactingly elaborated philosophical models, the participatory designation can serve as a useful basis by means of which to speak in a generalized sense about a readily available reading of Jung's work that has, I feel, been insufficiently recognized. This reading emerges as a possible means of mediating between the claims of classical, developmental, and archetypal lines of thinking – it ameliorates the classical danger of treating Jung's work as a fixed framework for interpretation, it non-dismissively challenges the developmental approach's tendency to privilege biology as an interpretive ground,[17] and it supplements the archetypal approach with a metaphysical sensibility such as to support clinical practice. Finally, a participatory reading of Jung's archetypal thinking also offers a powerful means of demonstrating the value of Jung's psychology for relational psychoanalysis. Against expectations, therefore, emphasizing those aspects of Jung's work usually regarded as most speculative might in fact suggest a particularly rich opportunity for locating Jung's thinking in contemporary debate.

While the practice of analysis certainly needn't entail committing oneself to a particular school of thinking, Jung's emphasis on the irreducible role of the personal factor suggests that the effort to avoid giving voice to underlying commitments can only be expected to render them more unconscious – in fact, it is precisely such an approach that typically betrays a commitment to dominant narratives. Despite Jung's efforts to portray himself as a Kantian empiricist, in light of the present intellectual climate a central value of his work may run quite contrary to this. In keeping with this suggestion, McGrath (2012) has recently argued for the importance of an explicitly speculative approach to psychology which refuses to accept empirical psychology's pretensions of metaphysical neutrality. Clinical "facts" do not precede our understanding of them. Although it might be argued that there is no speculation without experience, it is equally the case that there is no experience without speculative concepts. The emphasis in mainstream psychology on the former attitude is one-sided and, remaining unchecked, leads to a conservatism with implications that are as much clinical as they are political.

Notes

1 An earlier version of this chapter was published as a paper in the *Journal of Analytical Psychology* (Brown, 2017a).
2 In taking this approach, Hillman appears centrally influenced by Christou's (1963) expansion upon the ways in which this distinction is made by Jung.
3 Needless to say that the developmental school is by no means exclusively aligned with such an outlook.

4 Samuels (1998, 2008) has since argued that the archetypal approach can no longer be considered a distinct clinical school.

5 The notion of the numinous comes from Rudolf Otto. While Otto (1928) asserts that the numinous cannot be strictly defined, he speaks of it as a "non-rational, non-sensory experience or feeling whose primary and immediate object is outside the self" (p. 8). For Otto, the numinous is intended to signify an emotional experience of the presence of that which is "entirely other." In touching upon the nonrational, such an experience cannot be translated into language. It is a directly apprehended experience of a truth unmediated by theoretical concepts. Similarly, William James defines mystical experience as both noetic and ineffable. James, however, stops short of asserting the existence of the numinous as corresponding with an *a priori* notion of the holy. Otto's post-Kantian approach is centrally influenced by the figures of Friedrich Schleiermacher (1768–1834) and Jakob Friedrich Fries (1773–1843) [see Otto (1931)]. Schleiermacher relates religious experience to a mode of feeling that cannot be reduced to the ethical or rational. Fries, meanwhile, introduces the intuitive notion of *Ahndung*, or intimations of the transcendent. These intimations are of a nonconceptual aesthetic-religious nature. Referencing this notion and drawing from Schleiermacher's emphasis on universal contemplation, Otto speaks of an "overplus of meaning" that extends beyond the empirically given reality:

> This overplus, while it cannot be apprehended by mere theoretic cognition of the world and the cosmic system in the form it assumes for science, can nevertheless be really and truly grasped and experienced in intuition, and is given form in single intuitions. And these, in turn, assume shape in definite statements and propositions, capable of a certain groping formulation, which are not without analogy with theoretic propositions, but are to be clearly distinguished from them by their free and merely felt, not reasoned, character. In themselves they are groping intimations of meanings figuratively apprehended. They cannot be employed as statements of doctrine in the strict sense, and can neither be built into a system nor used as premises for theoretical conclusions. But, though these intuitions are limited and inadequate, they are none the less indisputably true, i.e. true as far as they go; and for all Schleiermacher's aversion to the word in this connection they must certainly be termed cognitions, modes of knowing, though, of course, not the product of reflection, but the intuitive outcome of feeling. Their import is the glimpse of an Eternal, in and beyond the temporal and penetrating it, the apprehension of a ground and meaning of things in and beyond the empirical and transcending it. They are surmises or inklings of a Reality fraught with mystery and momentousness.
>
> (pp. 146–147)

Otto's conception of the Holy (a domain of experience which is posited in distinction from reason, ethics, and aesthetics) places an emphasis on the nonrational, but not to the complete exclusion of the rational. To exclude the rational entirely would lead to an uncritical mysticism – an outlook that would be incompatible with Otto's desire to justify Christianity as the highest form of religion. Jung's work further complexifies the relationship between the empirical and the religious – his insistence on the primacy of the psyche establishes a position of tension between the two.

6 By "clinical pluralism" I intend to signify an approach to practice that would, in recognition of Levinas's philosophy of the Other, seek to acknowledge the extent to which the patient must inevitably elude our efforts to grasp him or her. Although some clinicians may feel that this commitment to pluralism should be considered only a side concern and not by definition central to the practice of analysis, this would constitute a major ethical claim that seems to imply an underlying assumption of the analyst's sociocultural authority. Furthermore, it seems clear that the philosophy of the Other, in concerning itself with the fashion in which we tend to occlude the unfamiliar by imposing the familiar, is by definition intimately related to that of the unconscious, and that to dismiss the former as being only of minor significance implies an underestimation of the latter.

7 While some psychoanalytically informed infancy researchers have sought to conceptualize the findings of empirical science as a challenge to conventional theorizing, the nature of this challenge is assumed to be in negotiating with science rather than in questioning foundational assumptions. It is ironic, for example, that Lachmann (2001) should portray infant research as having "challenged our tendency to seek the familiar" (p. 184), where in support of the five models approach put forward by Lichtenstein, Fosshage, and himself, he relies upon the notion of inborn behaviors that he considers "clearly observable" (p. 181). Empirical science positively *exalts* in the familiar, for it is only in replicability that a question of fact is considered to have been established.

8 Similarly, in considering Jungian engagement with ideas from science, what seems critical for an approach to practice that would seek to orient itself towards the unconscious is whether such engagement tends to reinforce entrenched conceptions of reality or destabilize them. The former outlook is typified where Jung's work is positioned as in need of scientific grounding, while the latter is reflected in a more tricksterish and playful approach to ideas – this kind of playfulness is typified for example when, following an extended reflection on the notion of emergence, Hogenson (2004) makes wry allusion to "the emergence of emergence" (p. 44) and thus implicitly draws attention to the limits of his own metaphor.

9 Ironically, Freud's initial attraction to forging a professional relationship with Jung had much to do with Jung's status within the medical community.

10 Adams (2004) refers to the developmental school as the "causal" school (p. 64).

11 It is this kind of reading that has caused many contemporary Freudians to endorse the idea that Freud's approach was merely a stop-gap measure, and that his hope was ultimately to see his failed *Project for a Scientific Psychology* taken up once more in context of the findings of modern neuroscience. This tendency underscores the ethical significance of maintaining the drive's ambiguity not only in terms of upholding a pluralistic approach to practice but also because the deterministic character of Western science tends to suggest that mind (if it is to be given credence at all) is an epiphenomenon of matter. Such an outlook tends to refute the basic character of analytic practice in which context it seems necessary to assume that individuals have some capacity for creative autonomy (see Brown, 2017b).

12 The potential compatibility of this outlook with a relational approach to clinical work is reflected clearly where Hartelius (2016) states: "In participatory thought [. . .] existence is not self-existent, but relational: The object is not primary, but something that arises, as it were, out of a network of relationships, a sort of intersubjective field" (p. v).

13 As Gargiulo (2007) puts it, "An everyday transcendence appreciates the open-endedness that the world presents, an open-endedness that humans likewise exemplify" (p. 106).

14 Jung's notion of the personal myth bears comparison with Gadamer's notion of prejudice. On this note, the following reflection of Stern's (2015) seems particularly fitting: "While it is true that we do sacrifice the original form of our prejudices in the course of new understanding, we do not actually move or see *beyond* them; we see *with* them, or *through* them, or by *means* of them" (p. 199). An archetypal perspective also offers a different way of thinking about Gadamer's "fusion of horizons"; an idea that Kulkarni (1997) links with Jung's notion of the transcendent function.

15 Emphasizing this distinction in terms of "radical immanence," Dourley (2015) cites this passage and suggests that Jung in effect reverses the usual weighting between transcendence and immanence by undermining Western assumptions concerning the self-sufficiency of God. This interpretation finds clear confirmation in the passage from the *Seven Sermons* previously cited.

16 Roderick Main (2013) argues for the importance of recognizing in Jung's work the co-existence of secular and religious perspectives: "His psychology can be understood coherently both empirically, without reference to transcendent reality, and metaphysically, with reference to transcendent reality" (p. 367). In Main's perspective, far from betraying mere intellectual clumsiness, this dualism has significant value in articulating the possible importance of Jung's thinking for contemporary social theory. Main cites the recent work of Jürgen Habermas and Charles Taylor, both of whom have identified the dangerous political consequences attendant to the Western intellectual hegemony of secularism. In response to this tendency, Habermas and Taylor have each sought to find a way of including the religious within

contemporary debate. For Habermas, this intention is articulated in terms of an approach that would encourage religious citizens to translate their beliefs into a language that is more accessible to the nonbeliever, while secular citizens are responsible to help facilitate this process. Main observes that, despite an apparent intent of including the religious within debate, Habermas's "postmetaphysical thinking" continues to privilege the secular. This is apparent not only in the most obvious sense of professing to be "postmetaphysical" in the first place but also in emphasizing the one-sidedly cognitive notion of "translation" (a process that essentially requires the religious citizen to ameliorate their position for the sake of broader intelligibility). Main considers Charles Taylor's outlook to be more compelling. Taylor challenges the notion that secular discourse is any less a construction than the religious, and hence the idea that secularity can be understood as a state of affairs that emerges naturally in the absence of positive religious beliefs. Consequently, he does not hold religious citizens accountable to an expectation that they should translate their concerns into a more "neutral" language. Taylor advocates inhabiting an open space between immanence and transcendence. Main perceives that Jung's dual secular-religious approach is very much complementary to this notion.

17 It remains open to question how far a participatory approach to practice should entail suspending the application of scientific truth claims – insofar as these claims reflect the spontaneous participatory commitments of the clinician then they would appear valid, but only with the proviso that their coincidence with accepted thinking not mislead the clinician into believing that they are dealing in objectively proven facts. The question of proof seems directly opposed to the sensibility of the analytic situation, in which context the emergence of meaning is surely the central concern rather than the preservation of past assumptions (see Brown 2017b).

References

Adams, M. V. (2004). *The fantasy principle: Psychoanalysis of the imagination.* Hove & New York: Brunner & Routledge.

Beebe, B., & Lachmann, F. M. (2003). The relational turn in psychoanalysis: A dyadic systems view from infant research. *Contemporary Psychoanalysis, 39*(3), 379–409.

Brown, R. S. (2013). Beyond the evolutionary paradigm in consciousness studies. *The Journal of Transpersonal Psychology, 45*(2), 159.

Brown, R. S. (2017a). Bridging worlds: Participatory thinking in Jungian context. *Journal of Analytical Psychology, 62*(2), 284–304.

Brown, R. S. (2017b). *Psychoanalysis beyond the end of metaphysics: Thinking towards the post-relational.* Abingdon, UK & New York: Routledge.

Brown, R. S. (2018). *Re-encountering Jung: Analytical psychology and contemporary psychoanalysis.* Abingdon, UK & New York: Routledge.

Buechler, S. (1997). Attachment theory as a secure base for psychoanalytic exploration. *Contemporary Psychoanalysis, 33*, 157–161.

Christou, E. (1963). *The logos of the soul.* Vienna: Dunquin Press.

Colman, W. (2013). Bringing it all back home: How I became a relational analyst. *Journal of Analytical Psychology, 58*, 470–490.

Dourley, J. (2015). Conspiracies of immanence: Paul Tillich, Pierre Teilhard de Chardin and C. G. Jung. *Journal of Analytical Psychology, 60*(1), 75–93. doi:10.1111/1468-5922.12114

Edinger, E. F. (1972). *Ego and archetype.* New York: C. G. Jung Foundation for Analytical Psychology.

Edinger, E. F. (1977). The new myth of meaning. *Quadrant: Journal of the C.G. Jung Foundation for Analytical Psychology, 10*(1), 23–38.

Fajardo, B. (1993). Conditions for the relevance of infant research to clinical psychoanalysis. *International Journal of Psychoanalysis, 74*, 975–991.

Ferrer, J. N. (2002). *Revisioning transpersonal theory: A participatory vision of human spirituality.* Albany, NY: State University of New York Press.

Ferrer, J. N. (2017). *Participation and the mystery: Transpersonal essays in psychology, education, and religion.* Albany, NY: State University of New York Press.

Fonagy, P., & Target, M. (2007). The rooting of the mind in the body: New links between attachment theory and psychoanalytic thought. *Journal of the American Psychoanalytic Association, 55*(2), 411–456.

Freud, S. (1915). Instincts and their vicissitudes. In J. Strachey (Ed.), *The standard edition of the complete psychological works of Sigmund Freud* (Vol. 14, pp. 109–140). London: The Hogarth Press.

Gargiulo, G. J. (2007). Transcending religion: Reflections on spirituality and psychoanalysis. *Annual of Psychoanalysis, 35*, 97–108.

Greenberg, J. R. (1991). *Oedipus and beyond: A clinical theory.* Cambridge, MA: Harvard University Press.

Hartelius, G. (2016). Participatory transpersonalism: Transformative relational process, not the structure of ultimate reality [editor's introduction]. *International Journal of Transpersonal Studies, 35*(1), iii–ix.

Hillman, J. (1989). Back to beyond: On cosmology. In D. R. Griffin (Ed.), *Archetypal process: Self and the divine in whitehead, Jung, and Hillman* (pp. 213–232). Evanston, IL: North Western University Press.

Hogenson, G. B. (2004). Archetypes: Emergence and the psyche's deep structure. In J. Cambray & L. Carter (Eds.), *Analytical psychology: Contemporary perspectives in Jungian analysis* (pp. 32–55). New York: Routledge.

Hogenson, G. B. (2010). Responses to Erik Goodwyn's "approaching archetypes: Reconsidering innateness". *Journal of Analytical Psychology, 50*, 543–549.

Jung, C. G. (1946). The psychology of the transference. In *Collected works* (Vol. 16, pp. 353–537). Princeton, NJ: Princeton University Press.

Jung, C. G. (1947). On the nature of the psyche. In *Collected works* (Vol. 8, pp. 159–236). Princeton, NJ: Princeton University Press.

Jung, C. G. (1948). Instinct and the unconscious. In *Collected works* (Vol. 8, pp. 129–138). Princeton, NJ: Princeton University Press.

Jung, C. G. (1951). The psychology of the child archetype. In *Collected works* (Vol. 9i, pp. 151–181). Princeton, NJ: Princeton University Press.

Jung, C. G. (1952a). Answer to job. In *Collected works* (pp. 355–470). Princeton, NJ: Princeton University Press.

Jung, C. G. (1952b). Religion and psychology: A reply to Martin Buber. In *Collected works* (Vol. 18, pp. 663–670). Princeton, NJ: Princeton University Press.

Jung, C. G. (1952c). Synchronicity: An acausal connecting principle. In *Collected works* (Vol. 8, pp. 417–531). Princeton, NJ: Princeton University Press.

Jung, C. G. (1954). The visions of Zosimos. In *Collected works* (Vol. 13, pp. 57–108). Princeton, NJ: Princeton University Press.

Jung, C. G. (1963). *Memories, dreams, reflections* (R. Winston & C. Winston, Trans. A. Jaffe, Ed.). New York: Pantheon Books.

Jung, C. G. (2009). *The red book: Liber novus* (M. Kyburz & J. Peck, Trans. S. Shamdasani, Ed.). New York & London: Norton.

Kime, P. (2013). Regulating the psyche: The essential contribution of Kant. *International Journal of Jungian Studies*, *5*(1), 44–63.

Kulkarni, C. (1997). *Lesbians and lesbianisms: A post-Jungian perspective*. London & New York: Routledge.

Lachmann, F. M. (2001). Some contributions of empirical infant research to adult psychoanalysis: What have we learned? How can we apply it? *Psychoanalytic Dialogues*, *11*(2), 167–185.

Main, R. (2013). Secular and religious: The intrinsic doubleness of analytical psychology and the hegemony of naturalism in the social sciences. *Journal of Analytical Psychology*, *58*, 366–386.

McGrath, S. J. (2012). *The dark ground of spirit: Schelling and the unconscious*. Hove & New York: Routledge.

Mills, J. (2012). *Conundrums: A critique of contemporary psychoanalysis*. New York: Routledge.

Mills, J. (2013). Jung's metaphysics. *International Journal of Jungian Studies*, *5*(1), 19–43.

Otto, R. (1928). *The idea of the Holy: An inquiry into the non-rational factor in the idea of the divine and its relation to the rational*. London: Oxford University Press.

Otto, R. (1931). *The philosophy of religion: Based on Kant and Fries*. London: Williams & Norgate.

Pargament, K. I. (2013). *What role do religion and spirituality play in mental health?* Retrieved from www.apa.org/news/press/releases/2013/03/religion-spirituality.aspx

Saban, M. (2013). Ambiguating Jung. In J. Kirsch & M. Stein (Eds.), *How and why we still read Jung: Personal and professional reflections* (pp. 6–25). London & New York: Routledge.

Samuels, A. (1985). *Jung and the post-Jungians*. London & Boston: Routledge & Kegan Paul.

Samuels, A. (1998). Will the post-Jungians survive? In A. Casement (Ed.), *Post-Jungians today: Key papers in contemporary analytical psychology* (pp. 15–32). London: Routledge.

Samuels, A. (2008). New developments in the post-Jungian field. In P. Young-Eisendrath & T. Dawson (Eds.), *The Cambridge companion to Jung* (2nd ed., pp. 1–18). Cambridge, UK: Cambridge University Press.

Stern, D. B. (2008). "One never knows, do one?" Commentary on paper by the Boston change process study group. *Psychoanalytic Dialogues, 18,* 168–196.

Stern, D. B. (2015). *Relational freedom: Emergent properties of the interpersonal field.* Hove, UK & New York: Routledge.

Strenger, C. (1991). *Between hermeneutics and science: An essay on the epistemology of psychoanalysis.* Madison, CT: International Universities Press.

Tarnas, R. (2006). *Cosmos and psyche: Intimations of a new world view.* New York: Viking.

Tarnas, R. (2012). Notes on archetypal dynamics and complex causality in astrology. *Archai: The Journal of Archetypal Cosmology, 4*(39–60).

Teicholz, J. G. (2009). A strange convergence: Postmodern theory, infant research, and psychoanalysis. In R. Frie & D. Orange (Eds.), *Beyond postmodernism: New dimensions in clinical theory and practice* (pp. 69–91). London: Routledge.

Teicholz, J. G. (2010). The Achilles heel of psychoanalysis: Meditations on motivation: Commentary on paper by Robert P. Drozek. *Psychoanalytic Dialogues, 20,* 569–581.

Afterword

Modern psychology was born of disenchantment. Annexing the soul to the pineal gland, Descartes gave voice to a style of consciousness that enabled material reality to be studied as if independently of the mind. With the dawning scientific age, the emergent quest for equality sought to "measure-out" the material world so that it might be commodified and shared. In breaking with religious dogma, the search for equality thus came to rely upon the authority of science; the stability of the emerging order was dependent upon adopting a system of values thought to rest upon an objective and consensually verifiable reality. Attendant to this new ideology came a tendency to dismiss as valueless that which resists direct scientific comprehension.

As a clinical practice, the discipline of psychology functions in a distinctly ambiguous fashion. In attending to the soul's rumblings as they manifest as "psychopathology," clinical work can be understood as an attempt to address the soul's state of confinement. However, this vocational ideal can often seem to be in conflict with the needs of societal adaptation. In the extent that the culture in which we live opposes systemic change, the creative function of the clinical situation is impeded. Patients may seem as though restricted in the availability of societal forms that would enable them to realize the difference that they might embody, and clinicians are seemingly limited by the expectation of upholding an "evidence-based" approach to practice. While indigenous cultures have considered that the suffering individual (as an outlier) poses an urgent question for the present structure of the community, psychology when conceived purely as an empirical science is founded on strict adherence to norms and accepted truths. The medical model has weaponized a materialist conception of reality such as to enforce a notion of mental health founded in acceptance of the system. Fundamental to this outlook is the reduction of the human subject in order to preserve the objective validity of empirical science's truth claims. The individual comes to be understood as a mere byproduct of matter. As foot soldiers for scientific consensus, clinicians are thus enlisted to police the border between self and world – this being reflected in a clinical sensibility that focuses on the "impractical" fashion in which patients are understood to ascribe past experience to present circumstances.

To re-ensoul the world is to decolonize reality. In adopting "the unconscious" as its foundational principle, psychoanalysis has been uniquely placed to uphold a position that would seek to give expression to the soul's telos. However, this possibility was significantly stifled by the field's early attempts to model itself along positivistic lines. The "one-person" orientation of classical analysis reflected a claim of having been able to decisively separate oneself from the world – freeing oneself from paranoia so as to achieve psychological objectivity. In seeking to challenge this emphasis on objectivity and the sovereign individual, the relational turn reflects a significant step towards the re-enchantment of psychoanalysis. However, this possibility has been significantly limited as a consequence of the relational movement's reliance on the explanatory value of a secular approach to social causes. Although this sensibility has clear merit, leaning too heavily on it reduces "the unconscious" to a mere synonym for habit. The idea of "relationship" comes to be foregrounded to the extent that the creative autonomy of the individual is outright denied. Thus, rather than directly fostering re-enchantment, this movement can, on occasion, seem merely to shift psychoanalytic practice from Freudian paternalism to the more insidious authoritarianism of *mother knows best*. Emphasizing the determinative role of social relations is itself liable to result in an occlusion of difference. This is a possible danger wherever practice is conceptualized pragmatically in terms of challenging habitual organizing patterns. While cultivating reflection on our personal assumptions is no doubt worthwhile, this approach is liable to grow reductive if emphasis comes to rest on adaptation at the expense of self-expression.

In seeking to extend psychoanalytic thinking so as to engage more thoughtfully with "non-ordinary" states of consciousness, it is necessary to acknowledge the extent to which such experiences can appear to dissolve the barrier between knower and known. Within psychodynamic discourse, it is a common intellectual refuge to assert that fundamental reality is unknowable. I have drawn attention to the fashion in which spiritual experiences often suggest a sense of disclosed truth. The assertion that fundamental reality is unknowable is, without due care, prone to do a disservice to experience.[1] Given that such an assertion in itself constitutes a fundamental claim about the nature of reality (i.e. that it has the quality of being unknowable), such a position only underscores the unavoidable nature of the problem. I have argued that the implicit philosophical sensibilities of relational thinking are secular. Even when contemporary psychoanalysis engages the question of spirituality with ostensible open-mindedness, the basic assumptions of contemporary discourse have often already dictated to the conversation. Furthermore, while a classical Freudian approach would be more likely to ascribe to a frank rejection of spirituality, in seeking to appear neutral on this issue relational thinking runs the risk of failing to acknowledge its own underlying commitments.

More positively, I have emphasized the ways in which relational thinking points towards the possible emergence of an explicitly transpersonal psychoanalysis. Reflecting on the nature of a two-person psychology if we allow more explicitly for a teleology of the unconscious, I have sought to show how evolving relational conceptions of recognition, enactment, and pluralism point to the need of a more direct concern for spirituality. In approaching this question I have found extensive value in engagement with Jungian psychology and the transpersonal movement. Any undertaking to approach psychoanalytic thinking from a spiritual standpoint cannot afford to neglect the enormous contributions offered by both these fields. Jungian psychology underscores that spiritual and religious concerns cannot be considered distinct from psychological ones. Although it is certainly of note that Jung's thinking is in many respects complementary to relational theorizing, I have suggested that the greater significance of Jung's work for relational psychoanalysis is as a means to pushing the field forward. At the same time, Jungian psychology might benefit from an examination of the ways in which the more esoteric aspects of Jung's work may in fact suggest the possibility of a further reconciliation with the psychoanalytic mainstream. As an institution, analytical psychology has not sufficiently integrated the implications of the synchronistic worldview with clinical practice. If Jung's psychology is to reflect more than a reaction to the extraversion of Western society, then it is necessary that the claims of his late work be further integrated into practice. Jung's introvert bias is naturally reinforced by many Jungians, the majority of whom share his introversion and, like Jung, find themselves living in an extraverted society. Thus, there is perhaps a general tendency within the field to first receive Jung as a validator of the inner life, and to sometimes lose sight of the more challenging dimensions of his psychology. Ironically, via the theorizing of intersubjectivity and enactment, it is the psychoanalytic mainstream that now offers the possibility of more thoroughly explicating and integrating the implicit *clinical* importance of Jung's ideas about synchronicity. It seems to me that this project also has relevance for transpersonal studies. In the extent to which transpersonal thinking has sought to explore questions of clinical practice, emphasis has often been placed on the value of alternative treatment modalities such as mindfulness meditation, art therapy, psychedelics, breathwork, hypnosis, and body-based approaches. Significantly, in its 50-year history the field of transpersonal psychology has failed to generate a noteworthy theory of clinical interaction.[2] Meanwhile, conceptions of psychoanalysis within transpersonal circles often remain mired in the past, and direct engagement with the contemporary Jungian movement is markedly absent. In the present text I hope to have demonstrated that all three fields might find value in mutual engagement.

Notes

1 This can be related to the question of interpretation in the clinical situation. In emphasizing the constructed nature of truth and the seeming limits of our formulations in capturing something of the unformulated experience, it still remains to be acknowledged that there are moments within the therapeutic situation wherein an interpretation's sense of "fit" is such that the experience of a "truth" having been touched upon, if only momentarily, seems undeniable.

2 Some possible reasons include [1] a wish to distance from the field of talk therapy which was already dominated by psychoanalytic and behavioral approaches, [2] a corrective emphasis on human potential to the possible neglect of the practical demands of a more conventional form of clinical practice, and [3] the historical emphasis Ferrer (2002) has identified on private (i.e. "one-person") conceptions of spirituality.

References

Ferrer, J. N. (2002). *Revisioning transpersonal theory: A participatory vision of human spirituality*. Albany, NY: State University of New York Press.

Mitchell, S. A. (2000). *Relationality: From attachment to intersubjectivity*. New York: Routledge.

Index

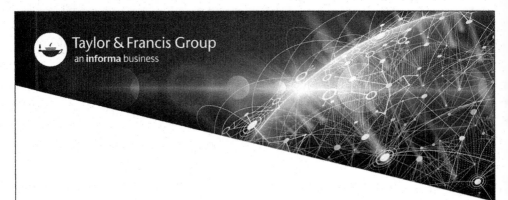